LIGHT ON A GRAY AREA

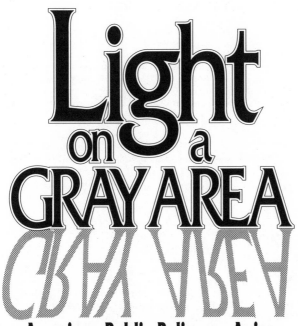

Light on a GRAY AREA

American Public Policy on Aging

Stephen Sapp

ABINGDON PRESS
Nashville
in cooperation with
THE CHURCHES' CENTER FOR THEOLOGY
AND PUBLIC POLICY
Washington, D.C.

LIGHT ON A GRAY AREA:
American Public Policy on Aging

Copyright © 1992 by Abingdon Press

This book is printed on recycled, acid-free paper.

Library of Congress Cataloging-in-Publication Data

Sapp, Stephen.
    Light on a gray area: American public policy on aging/Stephen
Sapp in cooperation with the Churches' Center for Theology
and Public Policy, Washington, D.C.
      p. cm.
    Includes bibliographical references and index.
    ISBN 0-687-38310-2 (pbk.: alk. paper)
    1. Aged—Government policy—United States. 2. Aging—
Religious aspects—Christianity. I. Churches' Center for Theology
and Public Policy (Washington, D.C.) II. Title.
HQ1064.U5S27   1992
261.8'3426—dc20
                                      92-20501
                                          CIP

Scripture quotations, unless otherwise noted, are from the New
Revised Standard Version of the Bible, copyright 1989 by the
Division of Christian Education of the National Council of the
Churches of Christ in the USA. Used by permission.

Scripture quotations marked KJV are from the King James Version
of the Bible.

92 93 94 95 96 98 99 00 01 — 10 9 8 7 6 5 4 3 2 1

MANUFACTURED IN THE UNITED STATES OF AMERICA

For Mary

with whom I look forward
to growing old

CONTENTS

AAA	Area Agency on Aging
AARP	American Association of Retired Persons
AoA	Administration on Aging
AGE	Americans for Generational Equity
COLA	cost-of-living adjustment
DI	Disability Insurance
DRG	Diagnosis Related Group
FICA	Federal Insurance Contributions Act
HCFA	Health Care Financing Administration
HI	Hospital Insurance
LTC	long-term care
NARFE	National Association of Retired Federal Employees
NCOA	National Council on the Aging
NCSC	National Council of Senior Citizens
NRTA	National Retired Teachers Association
OAA	Older Americans Act; *also* Old Age Assistance
OASI	Old Age and Survivors Insurance
PIA	Principal Insurance Amount
SSI	Supplemental Security Income
TFR	Total Fertility Rate

PREFACE

I n an "Alumni College" session at the University of Miami in April 1991, twenty honors undergraduates in my Religion and Bioethics class met with about twice as many alumni—most of whom were over sixty years old—to discuss various bioethical issues, particularly questions of termination of treatment. The first question asked of the college students by an alumnus was, "Do you see us older people as a burden on society, and especially on you younger folks?"

The concern expressed in that question may be seen as the primary impetus for this book. Certainly many people today, both old and young, are asking precisely that question or some variation of it, and nothing approaching a consensus has emerged with regard to the answer. In fact, the answers proposed so far may portend greater social unrest than this nation has seen since the Vietnam War era. There can be little doubt that the demographic situation that underlies the question holds far greater significance for the nation than did the factors that prompted the opposition to that war, the last great mobilization of the public on a matter of public policy.

Given the significant aging of its population that the United States faces during the next half-century, the question is critical for public policy makers to acknowledge openly and to address straightforwardly. Unfortunately, as Harry R. Moody has aptly observed, "Attempts to promote a wide-ranging debate about the future of

11

aging policy in America have not been notably successful. Instead, public discussion has been dominated by appeals to sentiment and fear of antagonizing interest groups. Stereotypes have abounded, opinion has been polarized, and policy initiatives have been made only through crisis management."[1]

Those who stand in the Christian tradition—public servants and private citizens alike—and who feel an obligation to improve the quality of life for all the members of the society in which they live have a serious responsibility in this situation. Not only must they strive to further the debate on aging policy, but they must also ensure that it takes seriously the ethical teachings of their faith, values that in fact were formative for the morality of our society at large. The Churches' Center for Theology and Public Policy is to be commended for fostering this undertaking through its stated purpose of "interpret[ing] the implications of Christian theology and ethics for public policies, in order to enhance the political witness of the churches and the public vocations of Christians." The charge given to me when I was asked to write this book was "to challenge current conceptions of public policy concerning aging, to call attention to the theological/ethical dimensions of it, and to suggest ways in which the debate should be recouched." I hope I have done so.

Light on a Gray Area has been written while I serve as master of Eaton Residential College at the University of Miami. Living with 394 undergraduate students may not at first appear to be the ideal setting for writing about aging, but they are the ones who, along with the baby boomers, will be most directly affected by the demographic changes described and discussed in this book. Thus I found considerable inspiration and motivation in my living situation, and conversations with the residents of Eaton both challenged some of my assumptions and gave me valuable (and generally encouraging) insights into the future as seen by those who must live it. My students over the course of several semesters in Religion and Bioethics and Religious Issues in Death and Dying also stimulated and helped refine my thinking on many issues addressed in this book as we enjoyed lively discussions in my living room.

My special gratitude goes to Angela Abrahamson, the best Residence Coordinator/Assistant Master one could hope to have, whose willingness to take on most of the administrative responsibility and many other tasks for the college while I was writing afforded me much needed time and energy. Angie is truly one in a million. Norm Parsons, Linda McDonald, and Linda Farmer, Eaton's Associate Masters, also continued their diligent service that allowed the extensive program of the college to continue unabated during my "preoccupation." Eaton's Resident Assistants, outstanding undergraduates whose service "in the trenches" really makes the whole system work, deserve mention here as well. I also appreciate the support and encouragement of Robert Redick, Director of Residence Halls, and Patricia Whitely, Associate Director of Residence Halls for Residence Life and Staff Development.

Many other people, of course, have contributed in various ways to this project, including all those unnamed souls whose frequent question "How's the book going?" motivated me to strive to have something positive with which to respond. Some individuals, however, merit special recognition. It is safe to say that without the initiative and encouragement of two people this book would not have been written. Rex Matthews, Senior Editor of Academic Books at Abingdon Press, recalled a conversation he and I had at the Society of Christian Ethics annual meeting in January 1990 and pursued an idea I had mentioned to him then. He continued to encourage and support me throughout the project. James A. Nash, Executive Director of the Churches' Center for Theology and Public Policy, responded enthusiastically to the proposal and handled all the details for the Center. Further, Abingdon's Ulrike Guthrie was a gracious, efficient editor who was a pleasure to work with and made the book better. Don Baker did a fine job of copyediting that readers will appreciate as much as I do. I am grateful to have worked with such fine practitioners of their craft and am honored to join Alan Geyer, Pam Couture, and Jim Nash as part of the Abingdon/Churches' Center's outstanding series on ethics and public policy.

13

The members of the Department of Religious Studies at the University of Miami have been friends, colleagues, and critics; and I am grateful to them for playing all those roles. Daniel Pals, whose performance as chair of the department is a model for all holders of such office, read every chapter (usually at times when he had many other things to do), made extremely helpful suggestions, and encouraged constantly. Steven G. Ullman—Vice Provost, in the Departments of Management, Economics, and Family Medicine and Community Health, Director of Health Administration Programs, and fellow residential college master—read the first four chapters and offered professional insight into a number of issues. The fact that I did not incorporate all of their suggestions does not mean that they were not good ones.

My parents, L. J. and Lottie Sapp, and my mother-in-law, Mary C. Manley, provided ceaseless support, encouragement, understanding, and editorial input, without which my task would have been much more difficult. They remain outstanding examples of those who are the subject of this whole enterprise.

My sons Eric and David also understood my commitment and consequent inability to share their lives as fully as they had come to expect. I am eagerly looking forward to making good on all the promises of the past year that began, "I'm sorry, I can't right now, but when I'm through with the book . . ."!

Finally, the place of preeminence in these acknowledgments, as in my life, goes to Mary. She has been instrumental in my accomplishment of earlier projects, but she is the primary reason that this book has come to be. From the Lotus 1-2-3 spreadsheet she devised to help me track my progress to the suggestions she offered regularly to improve content and style, from her unwillingness to let me get away with less than the best I could do to constant encouragement and assumption of a greater share of family responsibilities, as always she has been there. She knows how much of this effort is hers, and it is safe to say that chapter 7 owes its existence to her expert input and guidance. Dedicating the book to her seems an inadequate expression of gratitude for all she has done and all she is, but it is a heartfelt and loving dedication nonetheless.

SOME THOUGHTS ON THE ROLE OF THE CHURCHES IN PUBLIC POLICY

Here is Edward Bear, coming downstairs now, bump, bump, bump, on the back of his head, behind Christopher Robin. It is, as far as he knows, the only way of coming downstairs, but sometimes he feels that there really is another way, if only he could stop bumping for a moment and think of it. And then he feels that perhaps there isn't. —Winnie-the-Pooh[1]

When it comes to public policy concerning aging, many people in the United States feel very much like Winnie-the-Pooh, and they wish longingly for that "other way" that Pooh could only imagine. At times it is easy even to join Pooh in feeling that "perhaps there isn't" another way. Such confusion is hardly surprising given that public policy is a complex entity that evolves over time with many different forces and factors at work, usually without any real plan, philosophy, or method. Indeed, aging policy in this country has been and remains largely an *ad hoc* enterprise, with new policy—which is more likely to be merely revision of old policy—often prompted by an impending crisis (e.g., bankruptcy of the Social Security trust funds). Thus it usually reflects political expediencies of the moment, with virtually no regard for long-term consequences and thus, arguably, for truly ethical considerations. Little wonder that skeptics might come to share Marshall McLuhan's view that the best politics has to offer is yesterday's answers to today's problems.

I prefer, however, the more positive and useful admonition of the late Senator Sam J. Ervin of North Carolina, renowned for his role in the Watergate hearings: "If men and women of capacity refuse to take part in politics and government, they condemn themselves, as well as the people, to the punishment of living under bad government."[2] Christians are certainly "men and women of capacity," and I will argue that what they have to contribute is of great value in guiding public policy in this particularly difficult area. The pressing need is to determine the way in which this contribution can best be made in an increasingly pluralistic society.

THE IMPORTANCE OF PUBLIC
POLICY CONCERNING AGING

But why is public policy concerning aging so critical? Many social commentators claim that in the aging of the United States over the next half-century, we face a crisis of heretofore unimagined (and perhaps currently unimaginable) magnitude. This crisis, however (if indeed it exists), needs to be seen in terms of the Chinese understanding of that word. In Chinese the word for "crisis" consists of the two characters that mean "danger" and "opportunity," and that is the way I view the current situation in this country. How we respond to the predicted crisis—as individuals and as a nation—will determine which aspect of the crisis proves dominant: Will it be yet another *danger* threatening the very social fabric of the United States? Or will it turn out to be a tremendous *opportunity* to recapture the vision of a country in which all people are valued as members of a community that assures a decent quality of life to *all* its citizens?

Demographers project that by the year 2040, one out of every four Americans may be 65[3] or older (compared to one out of eight today), and as much as 65 percent of the federal budget (compared to around 30 percent today) will be required to support current programs for the elderly, assuming *no increase* in benefits. In 1987, Phillip Longman was the first research director of Americans for Generational Equity (AGE), a group formed to combat what its founders perceived to be inequitable treatment of the young for the benefit of the old. He published a widely cited book titled *Born to Pay*, a reference to the plight in which he sees today's younger generations. Among numerous similar remarks, Longman asserts, "So long as the wealthy

16

elderly demand, in addition to return on their capital, to be provided with across-the-board old age subsidies, the resentment of the young in general can only increase."[4] Janet Otwell and Janet Costello of the Illinois Department on Aging more neutrally report:

> Above all, the '80s have brought a changed perception of the elderly from "needy" to "greedy." This perception, with its accompanying theme that the elderly now have too much and the kids not enough, may be strong enough to adversely affect public policy during the '90s to meet the crucial, demonstrable needs of the rapidly growing older population, particularly the "old-old."[5]

So much for the "danger" side of the aging crisis. What about the "opportunity" it might afford us? Over a decade ago, pioneer gerontologist Carroll Estes offered an insightful and significant observation:

> The major problems faced by the elderly in the United States are, in large measure, ones that are socially constructed as a result of our conceptions of aging and the aged. What is done for and about the elderly, as well as what we know about them, including knowledge gained from research, are products of our conceptions of aging. In an important sense, then, the major problems faced by the elderly are the ones we create for them.[6]

By focusing our attention on aging, the elderly, and their proper place in a postmodern society, the demographic situation we face may thereby enable us (or force us) to rethink our ideas about this inevitable—assuming nothing untoward happens earlier—stage of life. As Ken Dychtwald, an entrepreneurial gerontologist/futurist of some note, has observed, "America is having an identity crisis, one that can be resolved only through the adoption of a dramatically new image of aging."[7] I will argue that in addition to rethinking aging, we also need to reconceptualize the relationships among the generations. If this reconceptualization is guided by values that Christians can affirm, the apparent crisis can turn out to be a great opportunity.

17

Much more needs to be said about these assessments, but wherever that discussion leads, the United States faces a situation that demands wide-ranging public discussion of the ethical implications of the aging of our society. Unfortunately, despite signs of a growing awareness of the impact of this monumental demographic change, too little serious discussion is yet taking place. Dychtwald and Flower again aptly comment, "How strange that while we have spent the past 10,000 years trying to live long and grow old, now that we are having some success we don't know what to make of it. Our nation has yet to figure out a positive and hopeful way to think about itself growing up" (p. xix). Cynics might well echo the sentiment of Theodore Marmor and his collaborators when they point out that the United States is hardly likely to change from a nation of sports fans into one of policy analysts overnight.[8] Nonetheless, in a democratic society public discourse on matters of such gravity is essential and must be encouraged.

THE VALUE DIMENSION OF PUBLIC POLICY

The subject matter of this book is both *ethics* and *public policy,* and when we begin to talk of either, we enter the realm of values. This statement probably causes little surprise with regard to the first subject, ethics. After all, what is ethics if not a systematic analysis of questions of value? Regarding public policy, however, the claim that values are of major concern might at first appear curious in a society that likes important decisions to be made on a factual basis, believing *factual* to mean "neutral" and "value-free." Nonetheless, public policy does reflect our basic values, what we as a society consider important and not important, or at least more important and less important. Willard Gaylin has put it bluntly: "The translation of values into public policy is what politics is all about."[9]

Unfortunately, as gerontologist Elias S. Cohen has affirmed, "Too few gerontologists, public administrators, economists and sociologists have concerned themselves with the relationships between legal and moral obligations. We need to examine how they interface, what affects them, and what we need to understand about how and why societies raise or lower their expectations."[10] Phillip Longman also recognizes that the real issue goes far beyond the technical: "Our problem is as much cultural as it is economic. . . . Behind the abstract and bloodless debate over fiscal policy, trade, and general national decline lurk the terrifying ethical and societal issues that have created our deficit state."[11] Despite our fascination with numbers and our desire to be "scientific" and "rational," policymaking remains an inherently subjective and thus emotionally weighted activity. One thing is certain: Whatever we might like the process to be, public policy is never determined by purely technical studies or totally objective calculation.

What all of this means is that one must be wary of anyone who claims to be looking at the issues "objectively," to be presenting "facts" that lead to unavoidable conclusions about what one (or one's country) should or should not do. Indeed, as William Temple, the great wartime Archbishop of Canterbury, so aptly put it, "There is no such thing as an uninterpreted fact," which is much the same point that that great compendium of Jewish wisdom, the Talmud, made some fifteen centuries earlier by affirming, "We do not see things as *they* are; we see things as *we* are." More recently, Marmor and his coauthors observe with regard specifically to aging policy that "all analysis is interpretive and that the same events or facts will always have multiple meanings or implications for social welfare policy."[12] In short, anyone who claims to be presenting "obvious," incontestable facts that argue conclusively and unquestionably for a particular position on any ethical *or* public policy issue is being either incredibly naive or downright duplicitous (Reinhold Niebuhr's sage observation that the powers of human self-deception are virtually limitless comes to mind in this context!).

This reminder of the subjective, value dimension of public policy on aging has a more personal aspect as well, which merits stating at this point. We need to remember that our basic view of aging, and thus of people who are elderly, is not a scientific, factual matter at all, even though obviously certain facts are relevant. The question of attitudes toward aging—what it *means* to grow older and how one should treat older people—is a theological/philosophical question, that is, a question of value and ultimately of faith. Modern medicine can describe better and better the biological processes that bring about the aging of the human organism, and the social sciences can study the impact it has on individuals and societies, but the question of what aging means and how one should respond to it—both in oneself and in others—goes beyond any factual discussion to a fundamental understanding of the nature and the purpose of human life itself. Thus the discovery of what constitutes "a good old age" lies ultimately in the realm of a person's values and understanding of human existence.

In this realm, religion serves for many people as the source of their values and of their answers to life's "big questions," even if unconsciously. Certainly several of the "biggest" of these questions relate to the meaning of growing older, one's responsibilities to the elderly, and impending death. The aging process and the approach of death focus one's attention on ultimate concerns, and these are precisely the issues that religion addresses. Even those who are not overtly or self-consciously "religious" absorb the attitudes and the beliefs, the *Weltanschauung,* of the cultural environment in which they grow up; and culture tends to reflect dominant religious beliefs, which in this country are primarily those of Judaism and Christianity.

THE ROLE OF THE CHURCHES IN PUBLIC POLICY

Thus an important issue demands our attention before we can move on. It is perhaps easy to imagine counseling someone on a personal level about the religious dimensions of aging and one's responsibilities toward the elderly, but what exactly is the appropriate role of religious individuals and institutions with

regard to public policy (if indeed such a role exists at all)?
Exploration of this question could itself constitute an entire
book, and many have been written that address it.[13] Here I
merely want to offer a few of my thoughts on the matter and
thereby make explicit some of the presuppositions from which I
will be operating.

I see several benefits to having the churches[14] play a role in
public policy debate. First, as suggested above, acknowledging
and accepting the religious dimension in the discussion forces
the value question to the fore. At a minimum, religious
participants in policy considerations should see that they fulfill
this role. Values are central to any policymaking process, though
all too often they are implicit and unarticulated. Identification
and articulation of the relevant values, however, may help to
underscore commonalities among the different sides, thus
making appropriate compromise more likely, or at least may
help to make explicit what the real differences are so that the
debate can take place on more rational and therefore productive
grounds.

As a corollary, by insisting on the importance of the value
question for public policy debate, Christians can contribute to
identifying and setting the priorities for that policy. That is,
values are simply judgments that one option is better than
another for some specified reason. By encouraging open
discussion about values, the churches can guide policy formulation toward an explicit expression of exactly what the
policymaking process is trying to achieve, not just in technical
terms but in terms of the underlying judgments about what is
more important and what is less important. Through this
process, priorities more in keeping with the real wishes of the
populace should arise.

In addition to assisting those involved in making public policy
to understand and to respect the different positions being put
forth and to be more aware of priorities, consideration of the
religious dimension will benefit the policymaking process itself.
Any discussion of important issues can only be enriched by the
inclusion of as many perspectives as possible. To *ex*clude the

21

perspective of the churches, with their long tradition and rich literature concerning ethical issues, will impoverish any discussion. That truly represents a great loss for public policy debate. Marmor and his collaborators recognize this fact when they write, "We would thus do well to attend to several points of view before imagining that we know what has happened, or will happen, as a result of any particular social welfare policy or proposal."[15] Philosopher Daniel Callahan agrees: "A wise pluralistic society, I should think, would be one that recognized not only the limits and boundaries of particular religious viewpoints but also the value of appropriating for its common purposes those religious values that could safely and profitably be used."[16]

Furthermore, insistence upon a prominent place for questions of value in public policy discussions raises the level of discussion above the petty partisan politics of *ad hoc* expediency to a level of more enduring, universal values. By keeping constantly before us theological values and ethical norms, religious input into policy discussions refuses to let us settle always for what will "work," for what is realistic, but instead forces us to ask what is right, what is good. In this way it helps us to fulfill what James A. Nash, Executive Director of the Churches' Center for Theology and Public Policy, has called a "prime moral duty" of Christians—namely, "to seek the expansion of the parameters of the politically possible."[17] Ethicist Duncan B. Forrester amplifies the point:

> The powerful can speak for themselves. They do not need the church to do the job for them, although they warmly welcome churchly and theological support and are vigorous in recruiting it. The powerful usually lay down what is accepted as "possible," and present the defence of their interests as "realism." A part, and a central part, of the theological task is to redefine possibilities, to open things out, to increase the number of options, to restore hope to those who are condemned by "realism" to a perpetuation of oppression. As Charles Elliott has effectively argued, we do not know what is possible until we have tried it.[18]

In fact, theologian Jürgen Moltmann argues that Christians have a unique contribution to make in this regard. The resurrection of the crucified Christ always kindles anew hope for the saving future of God, a future of "righteousness and the passing of evil," of "freedom and the passing of humiliation," of "men's true humanity and the passing of inhumanity." Because of this future, Christian hope is "not only, as Kierkegaard thought, the 'passion for the possible.' Hope reaches out further over against historical possibilities and can even be characterized as a 'passion for the impossible,' the *not yet* possible" (emphasis added).[19]

Thus the participation of the churches in the policy process heightens the possibility of making policy that will endure, at least in the sense of serving the needs of all the people (including future generations) better than current policy appears to. In short, if one is committed to making decisions on the basis of values, it is important to understand fully the basis and the implication of those values. Public policy, especially in this area, is too important just to parrot platitudes; it needs to be based on a serious examination of values. And some values have stood the tests of both time and rigorous examination. Among these values are the ones of Jewish-Christian tradition that argue, for example, for concern for others, especially those less fortunate. Christians do not have a monopoly on these values, but they do have a basis for following them, a reason to adhere to them that demands obedience—namely, the life, death, and resurrection of Jesus Christ. This provides the motivation to persevere and to refuse to give in to the fads of the times, regardless of how unpopular or sentimental Christian values may seem at a given moment in history. From the Christian perspective, these values survive and have an inner dynamic precisely because they represent God's will for humanity.

Several considerations arise beyond this more personal perspective, however. To be effective, any public policy must be implemented and accepted by people who understand themselves in some way to be "religious." In response to a question about how the churches can speak to a "largely secular, agnostic world," noted sociologist of religion Robert Bellah refers to studies that show that "sixty to seventy percent of Americans belong to a religious organization, forty percent go to church every week, [and] ninety percent say they believe in God."[20] In fact, religion appears still to be in some way a source of values for most people in America, despite various indications to the contrary.[21] A recent Gallup poll, for example, reported that 88 percent of those polled responded affirmatively to the question, "Do you ever pray to God?" In terms of the content of the prayers, 96 percent said they pray to "thank God for his blessings," 91 percent to "ask God to forgive your sins," and, perhaps most significantly, nine out of ten prayed to "ask God to provide guidance in making decisions." Although some of the respondents may have asked for guidance about which stock to buy or which lottery numbers to pick, many more surely meant that they pray for divine guidance in making decisions of the kind with which aging policy ideally ought to deal. Thus, if such policies are to have the impact their proponents hope they will, it only makes sense to consider in their formulation and development the religiously based values of the populace upon whose acceptance their ultimate success or failure depends.[22]

Similarly, although Mark Twain claimed a century ago that Congress is the only native criminal class in America, public opinion of politicians seems to have reached an all-time low recently, with some polls ranking only used-car salesmen lower in trustworthiness. In the wake of the congressional check-bouncing scandal, *Newsweek* magazine reported a Gallup poll in which 78 percent of those surveyed disapproved of the way Congress is handling its job and 75 percent answered no to the question, "Do members of Congress understand the problems and concerns of people like you?" (March 23, 1992, p. 28). Part of the reason for this low estimation is that politicians are perceived to act only out of partisan political concern and self-interest, with little concern for higher values. Policies proposed by such public officials might be seen in a better light and thus find greater acceptance if they are the result of a process in which value questions such as those prompted by religious considerations play a more explicit role.

For example, Robert Bellah believes that the churches possess "some of the most important resources for how we think about what is a good human being and what is a good society." He then points out that in the "entire tradition" of the United States "from the revolution of colonial times to the present . . . separation of church and state means we have no established church; it doesn't mean the church is not a public institution that speaks to public issues, again, with many voices." Acknowledging the great religious diversity in this country, he nonetheless affirms that a "vigorous dialogue, even a conflict of views contributes to helping us think about things." His conclusion is that "a vigorous religious input into the public discussion is very healthy."[23] In *The Good Society,* Bellah and his coauthors further contend that "religious bodies are very much part" of the "public," understood as "the citizenry who reflect on matters of common concern, engage in deliberation together, and choose their representatives to constitute the government." This participation comes about "not because they are governmentally 'established' religions with legal privileges but because they enter into the common discussion about the public good."[24]

In a similar but more explicit vein, Duncan B. Forrester notes that "today we have to consider a widespread uncertainty about the grounding of social values and goals." In such a situation, he continues, Christians must set forth the Christian faith as a legitimate path to reality and a way to answer the query of Pilate to Jesus, "What is truth?" He concludes, "In short, theology may claim to provide a basis, perhaps the most adequate basis for wise and humane policy formulation. In the public realm, as in the church, its task is to bear witness to the truth."[25]

Clearly, I am writing as a Christian who is concerned about the issues this book addresses. My interpretations, analyses, and suggestions are necessarily based upon my Christian convictions. I see nothing in that statement, however, that disqualifies my views from taking their place in the marketplace of ideas, to be evaluated and accepted or rejected on their merits. Anyone commenting on any subject is doing so from the perspective of a certain value system. Mine happens to be Christian and to have been stated explicitly as such. One can find one's values unabashedly and explicitly within one's religious tradition and should feel no awkwardness whatsoever in that. At least such a person has an acknowledged source for his or her values. One cannot expect others merely to accept such values if they do not share that particular faith commitment, and so one must be prepared to make one's case on grounds that will be compelling to anyone. But both the source of one's values and the motivation to see them embodied in public policy can come legitimately from one's faith. Thus Christians should not apologize for taking a particular stance on a matter of public policy but must learn to argue for their position on the basis of what constitutes a truly healthy and just human community.

It is true that Christians cannot hope for a "Christian society" in which the beliefs of the faith serve as the foundation for the civil order. Given human nature as demonstrated in virtually all communities that have claimed to be based explicitly on a particular religion—so-called theocracies—it is a lack of hope to be little lamented. Nonetheless, what Christians, both as private citizens and as public servants, can and should hope for is a society that *reflects* the beliefs and the values on which they have chosen (or been called) to base their lives. This, after all, is only what anyone with an interest in his or her society does. The only difference is the content (and, some would argue, the source or origin) of those beliefs and values.

My basic thesis therefore is a simple one: Christians should advocate and support public policy that is in line with values that are Christian. This is not at all the same as "imposing" Christian values on society or attempting to "Christianize" the state or anything of the kind. It hardly seems reasonable to ask Republicans to advocate policy that is not in keeping with Republican values, or Kantians to endorse a proposal that is clearly based on utilitarian reasoning. Indeed, for Christians to do otherwise than to work for policy in accordance with the basic values by which they order their lives and in which they find answers to life's ultimate questions would leave them open to the charge of hypocrisy. My purpose here is not to say that a certain policy must be adopted by the United States because it is the "Christian" thing to do. I am suggesting only that those who identify themselves as Christians ought to take very seriously the values that will be delineated in this book (and other values that they may identify in their tradition) as they deliberate about the direction in which policy on aging should go and as they advocate for policy based upon that deliberation.

In an excellent volume on Christian faith and medicine, Hessel Bouma III and his coauthors make a statement that summarizes quite well what I have said and thus can serve as a fitting conclusion to this section:

> There are good reasons for not appealing to one's Christian convictions in certain contexts, but it is lamentable if Christians never speak candidly *as Christians*. . . . It is lamentable both for the pluralistic society in which we live and especially for the Christian communities with which we identify. A genuinely pluralistic society nurtures and profits from the candid articulation and vigorous defense of particular points of view. Faithful members of the Christian community want most of all to live (and die and suffer and give birth [and, we might add, grow older]) with Christian integrity, not just with impartial rationality.[26]

THE PLAN OF THE BOOK

Before concluding with a look at what this book will do, let me say a word about what it will not do. It is not another treatment of the health care crisis in the United States brought on by the aging of our population, nor is it an attempt to diagnose and prescribe for what ails health care in this country. This book has a different focus—namely, the ethical implications of public policy on aging. Health care is an important—some would claim the most important—element in this topic, and it is arguable that the aging of our population will have a greater impact on the health care system than any other phenomenon we have yet encountered (including AIDS). Public policy on aging, however, includes much more than health care. Indeed, the analyses in this book suggest that the best hope we have of dealing with the health care implications of our aging society is to consider the issue in a much broader perspective than one that concerns health care alone.

I also do not intend to get into the "micro" issues that tend to occupy more technical works on this topic. The purpose of this book is not to present a detailed plan to solve the problems of an aging population. In fact, I agree with Paul Tillich's acknowl-edgment that "Christianity cannot offer technical advice for economic planning." He goes on to point out, however, that the question of an economic system able to provide "certainty of decent livelihood for all is much more largely in the realms of political and moral decisions," realms where religious values are "decisive."[27] Thus my goal is not to offer technical economic solutions to the problems this country faces as it grows older. Rather I want to delineate the most significant of those problems, present some basic Christian theological/ethical concepts that are helpful in addressing them, and offer some directions in which those who stand in the Christian tradition may look for guidance in resolving these issues.

In order to do this, I shall propose in chapter 7 an approach I call "value congruence analysis." As I stated above, values play a crucial role in the formulation and the evaluation of any public policy, though usually such values are poorly articulated, if acknowledged at all. If we are to devise coherent public policy regarding aging, these covert values that underlie policy must be made overt. Before doing this, however, it is essential to understand the overall situation that prompts the need for the policy in the first place. The first step in the analysis, therefore, is to describe the problem or dilemma. Next comes an examination of various responses to the dilemma that are already in place, followed by the third step, an explication of the values relevant to the situation. With this background, strategies to deal with the dilemma can be proposed, leading finally to the actual value congruence analysis, in which the proposals are evaluated in light of the identified values.

As just noted, however critical it may be to acknowledge the centrality of values for good policymaking, it is also essential to bear in mind that an ethical analysis of public policy on aging requires more than sound values. Karl Barth, the preeminent Protestant theologian of this century, once suggested that to do Christian theology responsibly, one must have the Bible in one hand and the newspaper in the other. One of my seminary professors adapted Barth's statement to assert that Christian ethical reflection requires two elements, facts and faith. A significant component of the value congruence model, and a major part of this book, must therefore be an attempt to ascertain the facts that constitute the context for examining the ethical implications of aging policy. Chapter 1 presents the basic demographic data that make this area one of such pressing concern. Chapter 2 explores some of the implications of these numbers and of several social trends that make them even more significant.

The next two chapters offer an analysis of various responses to the aging of America, embodying the model's second step. Chapter 3 presents an overview of current public policy, focusing especially on Social Security, the program with the greatest impact on the elderly. Chapter 4 surveys briefly some of the organizations that have been founded both to represent the interests and the needs of older persons and to counter the "inequity" some younger people perceive in current aging policy.

After these four chapters of "exposition" of the dilemma and some of the responses to it, chapter 5 represents the third step in the congruence model, the explication of values relevant to the dilemma, and begins the more interpretive portion of the book. This chapter is my attempt to articulate the major theological/ ethical values of the Christian faith that should most directly affect public policy on aging and that will be important in what comes later.

Next, chapter 6 continues the consideration of values by assessing the controversy that has arisen over the issue of "generational equity," followed by an analysis of the attitude underlying the claim that competition for resources will lead to warfare between young and old. The stage will then be set for the constructive work of the last two chapters, the presentation of the value congruence model in chapter 7 and a discussion of its implications for the churches' role in public policy and aging in chapter 8.

Finally, Christians are not the only citizens of the United States whose religion provides a source of values to bring to public policy discussions. Because such discussions benefit considerably from the articulation of different points of view, and because policymakers need to become familiar with the religious/cultural backgrounds of increasing numbers of older people in this country who do not come from the Jewish/Christian tradition, this book contains an appendix that presents an overview of the most significant "minority religions" in the U.S. and describes major concepts in each relevant to aging and the elderly.

Before getting on to the task at hand, let me reiterate that the goal of a work such as this book cannot be to propose a complete revision of current public policy on aging. That is not within my competence as a Christian ethicist. My goal rather is twofold: first, to define the context within which any informed discussion of aging policy must take place; and second, to explore the values of the Christian tradition most relevant to that discussion. My hope is that individuals who are interested in public policy issues and also are committed to their faith can then be guided better by these values in whatever role such people play in the policy process. The thesis of this book is that Christians should apply the central values of their religious tradition to public policy discussions, and I offer one way that this might be done. I do not intend, however, to undertake a detailed application in this volume. Presumably different people will apply the values in different ways (and perhaps identify different values as central). They would then likely advocate different strategies for public policy on aging. This is as it should be in a pluralistic, open society.

An exercise such as that proposed in this book is no simple undertaking. I have found my own assumptions and preconceived positions challenged and modified on more than one occasion, and I hope to do the same for others. As Mark Twain so bluntly put it, "Loyalty to petrified opinion never yet broke a chain or freed a human soul." Perhaps through this process of challenge and modification, however, we can begin to discover that "other way" Christopher Robin's "silly old bear" was looking for and thus turn the danger posed by the looming demographic crisis into the opportunity it holds for us to reassert the values Christians have always affirmed.[28]

CHAPTER 1

THE DILEMMA:
THE NUMBERS GAME

Benjamin Disraeli once said, "There are three kinds of lies: lies, damned lies, and statistics." Disraeli's warning should be heard, especially with regard to the topic of this book, because the way in which one chooses to present and interpret the voluminous statistics available definitely affects the impression conveyed of the future of the aging United States. Still, any serious discussion of the ethical implications of public policy on aging must rely on a rather large serving of numbers, because the numbers both demand attention in their own right and are crucial to reaching informed decisions in this arena.

As we embark on the quest to make sense of what is happening to the United States demographically, it will be wise to keep in mind also that "projections are not forecasts," and "to the extent that they are tales of future dread or future delight, they probably say more about the personality of the forecaster than about the likely state of the world."[1] Thus when anyone claims that "based on the current rate of x, by the year 2030 [or even 2000!], y will inevitably be the case," it is time to raise a very large question mark about the validity of such a forecast. Required by law to project 75 years into the future, for example, the Social Security trustees make three sets of projections—optimistic, pessimistic, and intermediate—based on different assumptions about relevant variables. Most analysts use the intermediate projections as the most reasonable because there is no particular reason to be either optimistic or pessimistic. Thus the accepted "reasonable" prediction of the future health of Social Security becomes merely the middle ground between two extremes, neither of which anybody really thinks is likely! As Marmor and his coauthors observe, "Mathematically there is no better strategy, but that does not make the prediction a good one."[2]

Although this caveat is doubtless appropriate when applied to projections of such things as economic and social trends, it is hard to imagine what event short of some tragic cataclysm could significantly affect the direction and magnitude of the shift in age of our population over the next half-century. People of good will can disagree about the exact numbers involved in this change, its precise impact, and proper responses to it (as we shall see in subsequent chapters!). It is impossible to argue that it will not take place or will not have a profound effect on our nation.

With this preamble, then, we can move on to the numbers.[3]

FACTORS CONTRIBUTING TO POPULATION AGING

Several factors contribute to the age of a society's population, three of which are most important: fertility, mortality, and immigration.[4] Not surprisingly, *fertility* makes the biggest difference. If many babies are being born, the age of the population is lower because there are proportionately more children; if few babies are being born, the population on average grows older.

Mortality plays a more complicated role in population aging, depending largely on which subpopulation's mortality is the major factor. In less developed countries where mortality rates are high, improvement in public health and nutrition almost always leads to a decrease in infant and child mortality first. Thus more children survive, coupled for some time with continued high fertility, because parents are accustomed to having a large number of children in order to ensure that at least some survive into adulthood. The result is a population that as a whole tends to be younger. In developed countries, however

34

(where the improvement just described has already happened), decreases in mortality occur at the other end of life through various life-extending medical advances, thus increasing the proportion of older people. In such countries, birthrates also tend to be low because greatly reduced infant and child mortality reduces the need for having many children. The lower birthrate causes further aging of the population.

Finally, *immigration* from other countries may reduce the overall age of the country receiving the immigrants, because immigrants are, for the most part, young and often continue for at least the first generation the higher fertility patterns they tend to bring with them. We must now look at the ways in which these factors have influenced the aging of the population of the United States.

Fertility

World War II ended in late 1945, and American servicemen returned to their wives and sweethearts eager to catch up on what they had been missing and perhaps to try to erase in a loving spouse's embrace memories of the horrors they had experienced. Many of the women were forced out of their factory jobs when returning servicemen reclaimed them, and one can speculate that other women were happy to give up jobs and return to the traditional roles to which they had been socialized. The economy was booming with the aftereffects of the war effort and pent-up demand, and thus the stage was set for what must have appeared to be a most desirable activity—"starting a family." Indeed, as exhibit 1.1 shows, that is what Americans did, in numbers unprecedented in the history of the nation.

As many of the children who would have been born over a four- to five-year period came "all at once," so to speak, immediately after the war, a "culture" of childbearing and large families was thus created. Short-term surges in birthrate had occurred before in similar circumstances, but such increases had been relatively brief (as they were in virtually every other country after World War II). In the United States, however, the exceptionally high number of births continued unabated for

EXHIBIT 1.1

BIRTHRATE IN THE UNITED STATES BETWEEN 1910 AND 1988

(Births per 1,000 Women Aged 15-44)

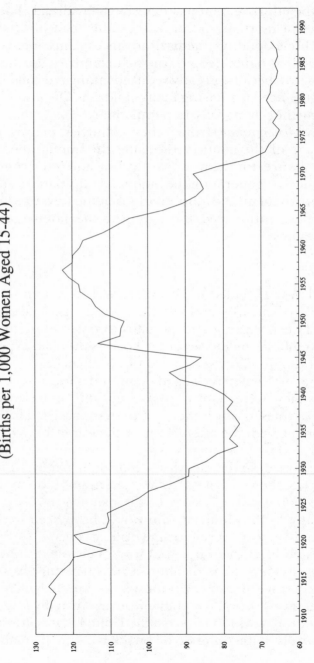

Source: National Center for Health Statistics, *Vital Statistics of the United States, 1988*, vol. 1, Natality. Department of Health and Human Services Publication No. (PHS) 90-1100 (Washington, D.C.: U.S. Government Printing Office, 1990), pp. 1-2.

almost two decades. During this period, approximately one-third of the current population of the United States was born (some 75 million people). Beginning in 1946 (the first year of the famous "baby boom"), the total fertility rate (TFR)—the average number of children born to women during their childbearing years—started to rise. The result was the birth of over 3,400,000 babies that year (contrasted to only 2,300,000 in 1933). The TFR continued its climb throughout the 1950s, peaked at about 3.8 in 1957 (4,300,000 births), dropped to 3.17 in 1964 (the last year of the baby boom), and fell precipitously to 1.74 in 1976. Since then it has remained around 1.8 (interestingly, developed countries need a TFR of about 2.1, the so-called replacement level, to maintain a stable population).

Although the numbers just cited demonstrate the volatility of fertility rates, there is little reason to assume that the foreseeable future holds the prospect of any significant rise in birthrates. Ecological concerns, the necessity for both parents to work to maintain the desired standard of living, the current problems in the economy, the sheer cost of rearing and educating children, and changes in personal values toward greater emphasis on self-fulfillment all coalesce to suggest that large numbers of children are not in the plans of most young people today (one factor that might change this assessment—immigration—will be discussed below). In fact, it has been estimated that one-quarter of baby boomers will have only one child and another one-fifth will not have even one. The extremely high fertility rates of the baby-boom years are thus being followed by what is often called the "birth dearth," which is likely to continue. This phenomenon will further propel the age distribution of our population upward, because there are and will be fewer young people to balance the older cohorts (and, not incidentally, to have children of their own as they get older).

Mortality

It appears that fertility rates—both the very high ones of the baby boom and the very low ones of the birth dearth—will play a major role in the projected "graying of America" that has

EXHIBIT 1.2
LIFE EXPECTANCY AT BIRTH IN THE UNITED STATES
BETWEEN 1900 AND 2000

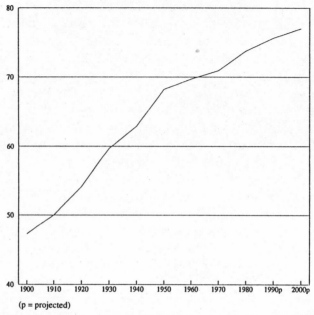

(p = projected)

Sources: U.S. Bureau of the Census, *Historical Statistics of the United States, Colonial Times to 1970,* Bicentennial Edition, Part 1 (Washington D.C.: U.S. Government Printing Office, 1975), p. 55; U.S. Bureau of the Census, *Statistical Abstract of the United States, 1991: The National Data Book,* 111th ed. (Washington, D.C.: U.S. Government Printing Office, 1991), p. 73.

attracted so much attention recently. Undeniably compounding the effect of fertility, however, is a second important element, the reduction in mortality rates, which already has made its impact felt. The most obvious effect of this change is in life expectancy at birth, which, as exhibit 1.2 shows, has seen dramatic improvement in this century. For example, an American born in 1988 can expect to live to be almost 75, some 28 years longer than someone born in 1900. During the decade of the 1980s alone, men added three-fifths of a year and women one-fifth of a year to their life-spans. Though the major reason for the increase in life expectancy at birth is reduced death rates

38

for children and young adults, life expectancy at 65 has increased by 2.6 years since 1960 (after gaining only 2.4 years from 1900 to 1960). In fact, a person reaching 65 in 1988 could have expected to live another 16.9 years (14.8 for males and 18.6 for females). Currently, over 80 percent of Americans live from birth to age 70, up from 20 percent in 1900.

The reduction in mortality and the consequent increase in life expectancy already have had a significant impact on the number of older persons in this country. For example, the first federal census in 1790 found that those 65 and older accounted for less than 2 percent of the total population of the young nation; by 1900 the proportion had grown to only 4 percent, or approximately three million persons. Today the comparable figures are approximately 12.5 percent 65 and over, or thirty-one million (see exhibit 1.3). This means that the number of those over 65 in the United States now outnumbers the *entire* population of Canada.

Each day in 1989, 5,960 people in this country marked their sixty-fifth birthday while fewer than 4,300 who were 65 and older died. The net gain represents a *daily* increase of nearly 1,670 elderly Americans.[5] Not surprisingly, over the past two decades the number of those 65 and older has increased more than twice as fast as the rest of the population.

As should be clear by now, this growth in the number of older people is expected to continue. In fact, those over 55 are the *only* age group likely to show significant growth during the twenty-first century. The growth rate will taper off during the next decade or so, but when the baby-boom cohort reaches 65, between 2011 and 2030, a rapid increase will occur. As acknowledged earlier, projections are risky and vary according to assumed fertility and immigration rates. Still, a reasonable expectation is that by the year 2030, 66 million Americans will be 65 or older. This number is two-and-one-half times greater than the elderly population in 1980 and roughly 22 percent of the projected total population (and possibly more than the number of those under 25 at that time). In fact, by mid-1983 Americans over 65 already had become more numerous than teenagers for

EXHIBIT 1.3

NUMBER OF PERSONS 65 YEARS OF AGE AND OLDER IN THE UNITED STATES BETWEEN 1900 AND 2050

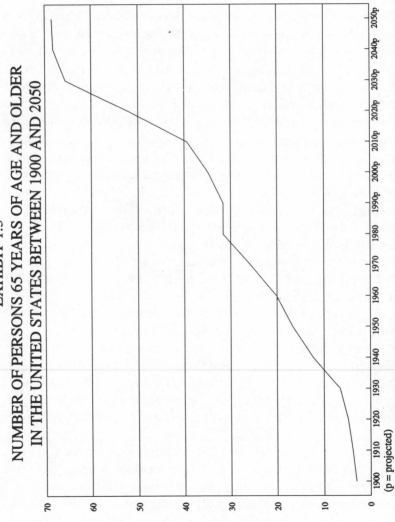

(p = projected)

Sources: U.S. Bureau of the Census, *Historical Statistics of the United States, Colonial Times to 1970,* Bicentennial Edition, Part 1 (Washington D. C.: U.S. Government Printing Office, 1975), p. 15; U.S. Bureau of the Census, Current Population Reports, Series P-25, No. 1018, *Projections of the Population of the United States, by Age, Sex, and Race;* by Gregory Spencer (Washington D.C.; U.S. Government Printing Office, 1989), p. 7.

the first time in the history of the United States and are predicted to outnumber them by more than two to one by 2025 (in contrast, at the founding of the United States, about half the population was *under* 16). The 65-plus population is expected to peak at around 69 million in 2050 (see exhibit 1.3).

In addition, the older segment of the population is itself becoming older. Between 1900 and 1989, those aged 65-74 (18.2 million) increased by a factor of eight, but those 75-84 (9.8 million) increased by a factor of thirteen and those 85 and older (3.3 million) by a factor of twenty-four. Even more strikingly, the last group, termed by demographers the "oldest old," has grown from a few hundred thousand in 1900 to over 3 million today and is projected to number between 15 and 20 million by 2050. Those 85 and over, who are 10 percent of the older population today, will make up as much as 30 percent of the elderly by the middle of the next century. By that same time, persons 75 and over will constitute more than half of the 65-plus population. Currently, only 6 percent of those 70 and older are 90 or more; by 2060, 15 percent will be in that age group. Not surprisingly, the number of people over 100 will rise significantly as well, from about 3,000 thirty years ago to 50,000 today, and to well over 100,000 by the turn of the new century.

These last numbers are especially noteworthy because they contain major implications for provision of care. Carl Eisdorfer, an internationally recognized geriatric psychiatrist and one of the founders of the organization now known as the Alzheimer's Association, estimates that the need for care doubles with every five years of age over 65. More specifically, a graph in the American Association of Retired Person's *Profile of Older Americans: 1990* (p. 13) shows that 23 percent of the entire noninstitutionalized population 65 and over have difficulty with "personal care activities" such as eating, dressing, and bathing. Of those 65-74, only 17 percent have such difficulties, whereas 28 percent aged 75-84 do; of people 85 and over, however, almost one-half (49 percent) experience these problems.

The numbers describing the aging of the elderly segment of

the population are also significant because they can serve to remind us of something often overlooked (or perhaps simply not recognized by many younger people)—namely, that "the elderly" or "those over 65" are far from being homogeneous. In fact, this group consists of several different cohorts that vary rather markedly in a number of ways, as we shall see later.[6] As we think about public policy concerning aging, it would be good to keep in mind the comment of Robert Butler, founding director of the National Institute on Aging, that as they age, individuals grow less and less similar—children of 7 months are much more alike than are older people of 70.

Actually, this aging of our country has been occurring for some time, and the emphasis on youth brought about by the baby boom is merely an aberration in a long-term trend. In 1820, the median age[7] of the population of the United States was a mere 16.7. Each decade thereafter saw an increase until 1950, when the median age reached 30.2. The baby boomers caused a small decrease over the next two decades (to 28.1 in 1970), followed again by an inexorable climb to the current median age of 33, with a rise to 42 expected by 2050 before leveling off.

Despite the rather breath-taking increase in both numbers and proportion of the elderly during this century and projections of much greater increases to come in the next, as mentioned above the growth rate will actually slow over the next fifteen or so years because of the relatively low number of births during the Depression and World War II. Noting this fact, Barbara Rieman Herzog has observed that "we have a breather—time to establish the policies which will have such an impact when the retiree bulge finally occurs between 2010 and 2040."[8]

It is apparent that wide-ranging public discussion of the issues addressed by this book is essential in order not to waste the opportunity afforded by this lull. We do not want to reach the year 2010 and have to apply to our society the inscription found carved on an old tombstone: "I told you I was sick." Concerned citizens (and churches) will have to insist that our political leaders enter into this discussion because, as Marc Levinson has observed, "long-term problems barely register on Washington's political monitors." He goes on to quote a congressional pension expert who says, "You can't do anything here unless there's a crisis."[9] In this case, *now* is the time to seek answers to problems that will not go away because by the time this crisis is upon us, it may well be too late to do much about it.

Immigration

It may seem odd that a rather detailed presentation of the numbers concerning the aging of the United States has preceded discussion of the third major factor suggested earlier as affecting such numbers. In fact, this sequence reflects the conventional wisdom among demographers about the role that immigration has played in the process, namely that it is not a very important factor. James H. Schulz and his coauthors, however, have challenged this conventional wisdom. They make a strong case that immigration during the early part of this century did contribute to the phenomenon we have been examining.[10] From 1905 to 1914, an average of over one million official immigrants entered this country each year (many of them single Chinese men who were forbidden by U.S. policy to bring wives with them). Because these immigrants tended to be young, at first they lowered the overall age of the population. As they married and had children, they also had a significant indirect effect upon the coming baby boom: Their children (and grandchildren) became parents of some of the baby boomers. Official immigration since the 1920s has seldom been more than 400,000 a year, leading many to assume the impact on population age to be minimal. Schulz and his collaborators argue, however, that the combination of large numbers of "undocumented" immigrants and recent increases in official immigration (e.g., more immigrants entered the U.S. in 1987 than in any year since the 1920s, and immigration from Cuba since 1960 and from southeast Asia during and after the Vietnam War has been high) has led to a more significant effect on U.S. population age than is generally granted.

The problem is that it is difficult to determine what that effect

43

is without an accurate breakdown of the age structure of the immigrants, and such data are not readily available. It is obvious that any survivors of the heavy immigration early in the century are now quite old, contributing to the aging of the population. Also, many of the Cuban and southeastern Asian immigrant families of the 1960s and 1970s included elderly members. On the other hand, more recent immigrants from Latin America tend to be in their prime childbearing years and may well be producing more children than people who have lived in the U.S. all their lives.[11] Added to this uncertainty is the impossibility of predicting future immigration policy and patterns. The best conclusion may be that though Schulz and his coauthors are probably correct that immigration has played a greater role than is usually granted, fertility and mortality have been and will remain the truly significant factors in determining the course of population aging in this country.

CONCLUSION

Over the next half-century the United States faces something of a "demographic revolution" (or perhaps better, the playing out of a revolution that has been taking place for some time). A complex interplay of changing rates of fertility, mortality, and immigration has resulted in a situation unlike any previously experienced in this country. A nation that has been virtually obsessed with youth and interests of the young for over forty years now faces an unprecedented aging that cannot help having profound effects on every facet of society.

Thus, as impressive as the numbers presented in this chapter are in their own right, what they *mean* is even more significant, especially for our interest in the ethical aspects of public policy on aging. We now turn our attention to an attempt to begin to understand this meaning.

CHAPTER 2

THE DILEMMA: BEYOND THE NUMBERS GAME

U nderstandably, one might feel a little overwhelmed at this point, in part because of the sheer mass of information presented in the preceding chapter but also because of the current and especially potential significance of those numbers. As noted gerontologists Donna Cohen and Carl Eisdorfer observe,

> The aging of our society is perhaps the great bittersweet success of the century. That people are living longer is a tribute to science, medicine, better economic conditions, improved sanitation, and other public health measures. However, we face many challenges in dealing with some of the problems of an aging population.[1]

It is time to begin to interpret the numbers now before us and to point to some of the issues they raise for the public policy that must respond to these challenges. It will also be helpful to consider some other changes taking place in this country that may interact in critical ways with the aging of our population. Not surprisingly, in order to present as complete a picture of the current situation as possible, it will be necessary to introduce some new numbers throughout this chapter as well.

THE IMPACT OF THE BABY BOOMERS

I recall vividly the thrill my classmates and I received around the time of our graduation from high school when we saw ourselves (that is, the "Class of 1964") on the cover of *Time* magazine. That honor seemed extremely impressive to an almost eighteen year old, and in the years since then *Time*'s recognition has proved to be well deserved. Indeed, it is hard to overstate the effect that the baby boomers—that huge group of children born between 1946 and 1964—have had and will continue to have on virtually every facet of American society. A group of over 75 million, moving through the course of a nation's history like the now familiar image of the "pig in a python," cannot help having a major influence, even if unintentionally and often unknowingly. What the members of a smaller age group could do without creating more than a breeze over the social landscape, when multiplied by 75 million becomes a hurricane that literally can rechart that topography. As Ken Dychtwald and Joe Flower aptly observe, "At each stage of their lives, the needs and desires of the baby boomers have become the dominant concerns of American business and popular culture."[2] A brief survey of the past four decades will corroborate this judgment.

In the 1950s children set the tone for the nation's activities and interests, with surges in infant- and child-related businesses and elementary education (America's school enrollment increased 52 percent in that decade). The 1960s saw a comparable rise in high school enrollment (with more high schools built in 1967 than in any year before or since) and in marketing aimed at teenagers. The most noteworthy phenomenon of this period—the campus unrest and social upheavals from the mid-1960s into the 1970s—is more easily understood when one realizes that a whole generation was passing through adolescence at the same time in numbers that made the "rebellion" and rejection of tradition that is normal to that period in life a national happening.

As the 1970s unrolled, the baby boomers for the most part left rebellion behind and concentrated on finding out what it meant to be an adult in the world they had a major role in creating. Movements arose that offered various avenues to personal growth and to meaning in interpersonal relationships, and attention turned from a concern about the state of the world to a more inward focus on the self. The decade of the 1980s saw the baby boomers establishing themselves in the work world in large numbers, and not surprisingly career and financial concerns came to the fore. The inward focus of the 1970s continued, only now directed not so much toward self-awareness as toward financial success. The "yuppies" were born, and the most important thing in America seemed to be making a killing on the stock market. The boomers were aging, however, and considerable interest in health, exercise, and diet also arose. As the 1980s wound down and the last decade of this century began, some disaffection with the materialistic values of the 1980s and a revival of the other-directed concerns of the 1960s began to appear, with a rise, for example, in efforts to preserve the environment and a general increase in volunteerism.

From this four-decade synopsis of the movement of the baby boom generation through American society, we can conclude that "America should have learned a potent lesson about the aging of the boomers . . . : when they arrive at any stage of life, the issues for them at that stage—whether these are driven by financial, interpersonal, or even hormonal forces—will become the dominant social, political, and marketplace themes of the time."[3] As the passage of the baby boomers' parents into old age, coupled with their own arrival into mid-life, forces this extraordinary generation to confront the multifaceted issues of aging, new "dominant themes" are sure to emerge that will have a profound impact on the United States as the "baby boomers" become the "elder boomers."

OTHER FACTORS IMPORTANT FOR POLICY CONSIDERATION

Some of these new themes are not so new after all. Although it is true that the baby boomers will continue to have a profound effect upon the United States as they grow older, the groundwork for their aging has already been laid by their

EXHIBIT 2.1
LIFE EXPECTANCY AT BIRTH
BY SEX AND RACE
IN THE UNITED STATES
BETWEEN 1900 AND 1990

	1900	1945	1990
White			
Female	48.7	69.5	79.6
Male	46.6	64.5	72.7
Black			
Female	33.5	59.6	75.0
Male	32.5	56.1	67.7

Sources: U.S. Bureau of the Census, *Historical Statistics of the United States, Colonial Times to 1970,* Bicentennial Edition, Part 1 (Washington, D.C.: United States Government Printing Office, 1975), p. 55; U.S. Bureau of the Census, Current Population Reports, Series P-25, No. 1018, *Projections of the Population of the United States, by Age, Sex, and Race: 1988 to 2080,* by Gregory Spencer (Washington, D.C.: United States Government Printing Office, 1989), p. 7.

parents, whose experience of old age is considerably different from that of *their* parents in a number of ways.

Older Women and the Gender Imbalance

The impressive increase in life expectancy that has occurred this century was discussed earlier. In that discussion, one important fact with major significance for public policy on aging was not mentioned, namely, that gains in life expectancy vary according to several variables, most notably race and sex.[4] The "average" life expectancy of around 75 is actually a weighted average of several different values (see exhibit 2.1). Although the reasons for all these differences are interesting and not without policy implications, the aspect of the matter with the greatest potential import results from the sex differences. Put simply, the longer life expectancy of women means that there are many more women than men among the elderly. The larger proportion of women at all adult ages becomes even more marked once the older years are reached: In the 65-69 age group, for every 100 women there are about 85 men; for those 80-84, only 54 men are still alive for every 100 women; and once the century mark is attained, there are more than three women for every man.

The major reason that this demographic reality warrants notice from a public policy perspective is that all of the traits that tend to describe the aged *poor*—widowed, living alone, very old—are much more characteristic of older women than of older men. Indeed, women are almost twice as likely as men to experience poverty during their later years. For example, in 1988 only 8 percent of American men over 65 were below the official poverty line, but 14.9 percent of women that age were (around 20 percent of widows). The median income for white married couples was around $21,000, but for a woman living alone only $8000 (a little more if she were white, but only $5000 if she were African-American). In fact, the annual income of four out of five elderly American women is less than $13,000. Not surprisingly, between two-thirds and three-quarters of the elderly poor are women, and of those who are female, elderly, from a racial minority, and living alone (the "multiple-jeopardy" group), 55 percent are poor (59 percent of those aged 85 and over).[5] Exhibit 2.2 provides a more detailed breakdown of rates of poverty by sex and race.

The fact that more women today are engaging in careers and thus becoming eligible for private pensions and larger Social Security benefits of their own may mean greater retirement income security in the future, but the more traditional employment histories of women who are elderly now or approaching old age will continue current disparities for some time to come. Social Security benefits are based upon the recipient's average lifetime earnings, and women have typically worked fewer years and for lower pay than have men (the same can be said for both female and male minority elders). Compounding the problem of lower benefits, women are twice

EXHIBIT 2.2
RATES OF POVERTY BY SEX AND RACE
1988

| | All persons 65 + | | Persons Living Apart from Relatives* | |
		All 65 +	Blacks	Hispanics
Percent in Poverty				
Women	14.9	25.5	56.5	53.6
Men	8.0	19.6	35.6	32.9
Total	12.0	24.1	50.0	46.1
Number of Poor (in thousands)				
Women	2,518	1,854	348	80
Men	965	425	100	28
Total	3,482	2,279	448	108

*Likely to be living alone

Source: U.S. Bureau of the Census, Current Population Reports, Series P-60, No. 166, *Money Income and Poverty Status in the United States: 1988 (Advance Data)* (Washington, D.C.: U.S. Government Printing Office, 1989).

as likely as men to rely totally on Social Security in their old age (though the average monthly benefit for a retired female worker is less than three-quarters that of a male) and therefore not surprisingly are also twice as likely to receive Supplemental Security Income (or SSI, the means-tested public "welfare" administered through the Social Security Administration; see chapter 3 for a further description). In fact, three-quarters of all the elderly who receive SSI are women living alone.

A brief look at marital status and living arrangements among the elderly illustrates further implications of this gender imbalance. Currently, women 65 and over are only about half as likely to be married as similarly aged men (42 percent versus 77 percent), and they are almost four times as likely to be widowed.

Thus older women are much more likely to live alone (among all elderly people living alone, two out of three are widows) or in the home of a relative. This difference is even greater than the percentages seem to indicate because of the much larger number of older women than men: Slightly under 2 million elderly men live alone whereas some 6.9 million women do (16 percent of all men 65-plus and 41 percent of women); by 2020 these figures are expected to climb to slightly over 2.5 million men and almost 11 million women. Living alone also puts a woman at much higher risk of institutionalization: Three-quarters of all nursing home residents are female, with a like percentage of these women over 80; 84 percent are unmarried, and 93 percent are white, indicating a racial factor at work here as well.[6]

Beth B. Hess's conclusion is an apt one: "For the near future . . . the fact that most older people are women has enormous consequences for quality-of-life variables such as income adequacy, housing, health care, transportation, and the probability of eventual institutionalization."[7] U.S. Commissioner on Aging Joyce T. Berry agrees. In her keynote address to the American Society on Aging annual meeting in March 1991, Berry commented that of the 9 million older persons who live alone in the United States, some 7 million are women. Thus "with regard to special needs, aging is indeed an older women's issue." Stephen Crystal's succinct assessment is still valid ten years after he offered it: "Severe need in old age has now become and will continue to be largely a woman's problem."[8]

Lack of Income Security

This discussion suggests another factor that policymakers need to consider: the question of income security. One of the greatest changes of the past three decades for the elderly concerns their financial status. In 1960 more than one-third of older persons were poor; five years later this number had dropped to 28.5 percent. Over the past 25 years the downward trend has continued, until today the poverty rate among the elderly (over 12 percent) is a little below the national average

51

of about 13 percent. One would think that this laudable improvement would be a cause for rejoicing by everyone. Interestingly, however, at the same time that the elderly poverty rate has decreased, serious criticism has arisen that the amelioration of the plight of the elderly has been won at the expense of younger people, especially children (whose poverty rate is over 20 percent). These claims are supported by data such as the median net worth of those 65 and over (slightly more than $60,000, almost twice the average for all Americans) and the elderly's rate of home ownership and average equity (73 percent and over $54,500 in 1984). Chapter 8 contains a more detailed consideration of this charge, but at this point a few details about the current financial situation of the elderly will be instructive.

Older people *as a whole* are unquestionably in better shape financially today than ever before. In fact, today's elderly are the first people in history as a group to reach old age basically healthy, financially secure, and retired. In 1988, for instance, the overall median income for households in the U.S. was $26,000; for households headed by a person 65 or older the median was $19,000, reasonably comparable given that the latter are more likely to own the home, not support children, and have fewer, if any, job-related expenses.

Taking all those 65 and over together on virtually any economic measure, however, suffers from the basic shortcoming of any "average" (and calls to mind the old quip about the man who drowned trying to cross the stream with an "average depth of six inches"—although the stream was only inches deep most of the way across, unfortunately he stepped in the one hole six *feet* deep!). An average often disguises some very wide variations within that age group. During the 1980s, for example, the wealth of upper-income elders rose "by very, very much," but income for the bottom one-fifth of older persons declined, especially for minorities. The average annual income for female householders also declined, from $11,000 to $10,000 between 1985 and 1990.[9] Indeed, to no one's surprise, in 1989 the poverty rate for elderly whites was about 10 percent, but for older Hispanics the rate climbed to 21 percent and for African Americans up to 31 percent. Furthermore, the elderly, who are only 12 percent of the total population of the United States, make up 28 percent of the poor.

The problem is clearly reflected in a consideration of what has been called "contingency assets"—that is, resources readily available to supplement income in the event of a financial crisis (excluding home equity and interest in a family business). Although it is frequently asserted that the elderly of this country are income-poor but asset-rich (see the median net worth and home equity figures cited above), this claim does not apply to a sizable segment of older Americans. Concentration of wealth in the hands of a small number of those over 65 seriously skews the figures, with regard to home equity also because even if the poorer elderly own their homes, those homes are of modest value, older, and more likely to need repair.[10] These poor people also have few liquid resources at their disposal to use to respond to a financial trauma in their lives. Indeed, almost two-thirds of the elderly below the poverty line have contingency assets of under $500, and it is only those whose incomes are more than twice the poverty threshold who have over $5000 in such assets.[11] It is true that this widening gap between the elderly haves and have-nots merely reflects a more general trend in our country.[12] It is not, however, a trend to be celebrated when it applies to any age group.

In addition to these inequities, the widely applauded decrease in the number of the elderly poor overlooks a very fundamental problem, the rather questionable federal definition of *poverty*.[13] The official "poverty line," the amount deemed adequate by the government for survival, is determined by taking an estimate of the amount a low-income family spends each year for food and then tripling it, on the assumption that such a family must spend one-third of its income for food.[14] It should be noted that the food budget used was originally described in 1964 by the U.S. Department of Agriculture as "designed for temporary or emergency use when funds are low." Furthermore, the calculation assumes that the elderly need less money than

53

younger age groups because they eat less, an unfair assumption according to many nutritionists, at least as far as nutrients if not calories are concerned. Indeed, it could as easily be argued that because of the physical changes brought about by aging, the elderly need a *higher* quality diet than younger people.

Whatever the basis of the federal poverty threshold, its effect is that in 1992 someone over 64 who lived alone and had an income of $6810 (a little over $567 a month) was not "poor"; for an elderly couple, the amount was $9190 ($765 a month).[15] Of some significance is the estimate that merely applying to those 65 and over the same income standard used for those under 65 would result in a four-point jump in the poverty rate for the elderly, from just under 12 percent to between 15 and 16 percent, several points higher than the national average.[16]

Based on the slightly lower 1989 official poverty line ($5947 for an elderly individual living alone and $7501 for an older couple), about 3.5 million older people that year were below the poverty threshold (over 11 percent). Still using the official standard, another 2.3 million qualified as "near-poor"—that is, with incomes no higher than 125 percent of the poverty line.[17] Thus over 18 percent of the elderly were poor or near-poor. And as many as five million more are extremely vulnerable to a major economic setback—such as death of spouse, major illness, even a serious burglary—because their income does not exceed twice the poverty level. So when we consider the poor, the near-poor, and the very vulnerable (keeping in mind also the low official poverty line), we discover that despite the great gains of recent decades, some 35 percent of all the elderly in the U.S. are hardly living lives of luxury, and in fact not even of comfort. As already discussed, and of no surprise, most of these are precisely the persons who are already the least able to do anything about it.

This analysis suggests yet another problem with some of the more traditional measures of poverty among the elderly. Financial security consists of more than the mere ability of current income to meet immediate economic needs, of whatever nature. To be truly secure, one must have "insurance" (however defined) against unforeseen occurrences that might demand resources beyond those readily at hand. Given this more complete understanding of financial security, the prevailing assessment of the economic status of the elderly based on current income and assets can be seen to be less than adequate. A somewhat personal example will help to make the point and will add several new dimensions to the earlier discussion of "contingency assets."

For several of the years that my wife and I were in graduate school, our combined income was below that which necessitated filing a federal income tax return—around $5,000 at the time, as I recall. Yet never did we feel "poor" or even financially insecure because of several factors: We were in good health with little prospect of any kind of catastrophic illness in the near future, and we had very inexpensive yet quite adequate student health insurance through our respective universities; we both had parents who were financially secure and would have come to our aid if something terrible had happened (and did so less dramatically by co-signing for a small loan, thus enabling us to establish credit and later borrow on our own); and perhaps most important, our future earning power was certain to jump significantly when we completed our degrees and was limited only by the vagaries of the job market and other such factors that most members of our society face constantly. In fact, our situation was secure and promising enough that at one point my wife was urged by her physician to accept free medicine from the county health department because we were below the poverty line. She declined, arguing that we could afford to pay.

By the current income and assets test usually used today to determine the financial well-being of the elderly, however (we owned only a $2,100 car and a $4,000 mobile home), we would have appeared considerably worse off than the 80-year-old widow who lived by herself on an income of $7,500 and had assets of $25,000. Yet I would submit that the widow's situation was much more precarious than ours, for the opposite of many of the same factors mentioned above: Her health, though perhaps still good, could be expected with some certainty to begin to deteriorate fairly soon, and chances are that her only insurance coverage would be Medicare, which as we shall see is far from complete; the resources available to her from family members might very well be limited (and, as will be shown shortly, are likely to be even more so in the future); she would not generally be considered a good prospect for a loan to see her through a catastrophe of any sort; and her earning power, if it still existed at all, would be extremely limited. Any serious assault on her financial position, then, would quickly deplete her seemingly more adequate resources, rendering her dependent on various forms of public assistance such as Medicaid and Supplemental Security Income, with virtually no prospect of escape. The current claims that the elderly are no longer at risk economically and are much better off than other segments of society thus must be scrutinized more carefully than is often the case in public debate.

Concerning the relative financial status of the elderly, Stephen Crystal summarizes the situation well when he says, "To paraphrase a familiar quotation, our nation is moving toward two worlds of aging, one poor, one comfortable—separate and unequal."[18] The conclusion of noted gerontologist Robert H. Binstock, writing in 1983 when the concerns of the "generational equity" movement were just beginning to be heard, is still worthy of note: "The challenges of maintaining or improving the economic status of the elderly in the years ahead are primarily political, not economic."[19]

Implications of Age for Work, Retirement, and Leisure

Influencing the above matters in a number of ways is a complex of issues concerning work, retirement, and leisure. Although today retirement is taken for granted, it is worth noting that until quite recently most people worked until they simply could work no longer.[20] A century ago, three-quarters of American males 65 and older were still in the work force; even in 1950, just under one-half still worked. Today only about 15 percent do (and eight percent of women 65 and over). The nearly universal coverage of Social Security and its rising benefits, the rapid expansion after World War II of private pension plans (which increased threefold between 1945 and 1955 and covered more than half the work force by the mid-1980s), and the influx of baby boomers into the work force combined to encourage more and more workers to begin to enjoy the leisure they had worked long and hard to ensure, and to do so earlier and earlier. Indeed, today more people receive their first Social Security check at 62 than at 65, and the average age of retirement is 55 for blue-collar workers and under 61 for all men (down from 65 in 1970).

Despite recent shifts in federal policy toward discouraging early retirement (as reflected in legislation that abolishes mandatory retirement at any age and gradually raises to 67 by 2022 the age at which one can receive full Social Security benefits), the trend toward retiring early is continuing, especially for men.[21] Whereas in 1980 sixty percent of men 60-64 years old worked, the 1990 census reveals only 55 percent still employed. Taeuber points out that as more people retire earlier (as well as live longer), Social Security and private pension benefits must be spread over a greater period of time.

On the other hand, there is likely to be a countervailing trend toward an increasing number of older people reentering the work force, often in jobs different from the ones in which they spent their younger years. As the National Council on the Aging's 1991 Annual Report puts it, "A rapidly changing economy will almost certainly cause a growing need for retraining in job skills—not once, but three or four or more times—during a 'career' or, as is more likely, 'careers.' "[22] Indeed, a number of surveys in recent years have indicated that as many as two out of five currently retired people would prefer to be working and that as people get closer to retirement, their desire to keep working increases (only about one in four wants to retire totally, and more than three in five anticipate either part- or full-time employment after retirement age). Just under half of workers 55-64 would be interested in learning new skills to enable them to assume different responsibilities.

The demographics discussed earlier suggest several reasons

why these desires may come to be satisfied. First, most consumers prefer to deal with people similar to themselves, especially in service-related jobs, which are expected to increase over 27 percent by the end of the century (goods-producing jobs will show virtually no change). As the population itself ages, more older people will therefore be needed for such work. Second, the current low fertility rates will mean that there are fewer young people to fill jobs. The Bureau of Labor Statistics projects that the turn of the century will see a million fewer sixteen to twenty-four year olds than today while as many as five million workers reach retirement age, creating a labor shortage over the next several decades that older workers may have to make up. Their own need also may encourage more older people to work longer: Pressures on Social Security and private pensions may push even later the age at which one receives benefits (which themselves may possibly be reduced). At the same time, there may be increased incentives to continue working, such as allowing older workers to retain full Social Security benefits despite higher earnings.

An interesting finding of the 1990 census related to this area is a marked increase in the number of older people who have graduated from high school. In 1980 fewer than 50 percent of those 75 or older held high school diplomas; in 1990 73 percent did. This change reflects the commitment to universal public education made in the United States earlier in this century. The implications for the future are great in terms of increased demands for continuing education of all kinds and the prospect for a better informed, more capable, and more affluent group of older persons. Already the proportion of students over 25 on college campuses has increased from a little over one in five in 1970 to almost one in two today. On the other hand, the current state of education in this country leaves much to be desired, and, as Elias S. Cohen rightly points out, looking beyond the baby boomers' old age, "If 25% of America's youth drop out of high school, the cohorts of elders reaching 65 or 70 in 2035 and beyond will have a hard time in a society that is increasingly urban, tech-oriented and even more dependent on literacy at all ages."[23]

Family Issues

Another area in which the imbalance between men and women, as well as a number of other factors, will have an increasingly significant impact is a whole complex of what we might call family issues. Several important changes have occurred already in the American family structure, with more almost certain to come. Because many of these changes affect the traditionally central role of the family in caring for its older members, they are of special concern in the realm of public policy.

Greater Life Expectancy After Childrearing

Increased life expectancy has contributed to a particularly important change, one that often does not receive the attention it deserves. Until quite recently, work occupied almost all of a man's life (with perhaps some secondary family responsibilities). For a woman, childrearing was her life's work. Today the situation is vastly different, as we have seen already with regard to work. The impact on the family has been equally profound, especially for women (and particularly when coupled with another change to be discussed shortly, the increased number of women who work).

For the first two centuries of European settlement on this continent, the common situation was for one or both parents to be dead before the youngest child was completely grown. As recently as the middle of the last century, a mother lived an average of only two years (to age 61) after her youngest child married. By 1950, however, the average mother was only 48 at the marriage of her youngest child, and she could expect to live some thirty more years.[24] Today most parents will live more years after completing their childrearing responsibilities than they spent carrying out those duties. Indeed, a frequently cited projection is that the typical American woman will spend more years providing some kind of care to her (and/or her husband's) *parents* than she did taking care of her children (or, increasingly, child). Clearly a major reorientation in our thinking about the nature and purpose of the family is in order as it evolves from the locus for rearing children to increasingly complex web of relationships among adults of several generations.

Later Marriage, Later Childbearing, and Fewer Children

Contributing to this evolution of the family are several more interrelated changes with special relevance to our concerns. Both men and women are marrying later, with the median age at marriage for women (over 23) the highest ever in this country and for men (about 26) close to the record set around the turn of the century. Not surprisingly, as people marry later, they tend to have children later. This trend is probably reinforced by the concern many women have to establish themselves in their careers before starting a family. Whatever the reasons, births to women 35 and older increased 71 percent between 1975 and 1985 relative to the decade 1965-1975. Women also are waiting longer between marriage and first childbirth and between births of children. A final factor in this area is the already noted reduction in fertility rates, resulting in fewer children per couple. In fact, the drop in overall birthrate in this country is attributable not so much to a reduction in the number of women who are having children as to a reduction in the number of children each woman has. In particular, the number of families with four or more children has declined precipitously in recent years.

The trends mentioned in the preceding paragraph all contribute to a diminution of the family-support system that traditionally has provided the bulk of care for the elderly in our society. For example, whereas at the beginning of this century the ratio of adults between the ages of 18 and 64 to those 65 or older was almost fourteen to one, currently for every person 65 or older there are fewer than five people between 18 and 64. Logically, the fewer children one has, the fewer adult offspring will be available to provide care (either directly or through financial support) in one's old age. Census data bear out this conclusion. The chance of being institutionalized in old age is over twice as high for those with the smallest families compared to those with the largest.

A related concern results from the increased longevity discussed previously. By the time adult children become caregivers, many of them are themselves old. As we saw, the "old old" are the fastest-growing segment of the elderly population, and the longer parents live, the older their children will be during the time the parents need care. A major study by the National Center for Health Services Research found that in 1982 1.2 million infirm persons 65 and over were cared for by 2.2 million people. More than half of those being cared for were 75 and older. The caregivers' average age was 57, and one-third were 65 and older.[25]

Thus in many instances the "old old" are being cared for by the "young old," and the situation is only going to get worse in the decades ahead. For example, in 1920 there were 21 people 80 or older for every 100 who were between 60 and 64; six decades later the ratio was 53 to 100. Current projections suggest that by 2030, for every 100 persons 60-64, there will be as many as 80 still alive in their ninth decade! These numbers have profound public policy implications, especially given our nation's unwillingness so far to address seriously the problem of long-term care.

Increased Number of Women in the Work Force

Another widely noted trend is the increased number of women in the work force, a change that affects many of the others discussed here as well. Traditionally the American family has been seen as consisting of a father who works to support his family and a mother who stays at home rearing the children and "keeping the house." Today, however, fewer than one in five American homes follow this pattern, and over the past two decades the number of married women who have school-age children and work outside the home has increased from 30 percent to around 60 percent (with some estimates even higher). In fact, according to the Bureau of Labor Statistics, in 1990 the 56.5 million women who worked made up 45.4 percent of the total labor force and represented 57.4 percent of all women of working age (projections for 2000 put the respective figures at 65.6 million, 47.3 percent, and 61.5 percent).[26]

The trend toward more working women is especially interesting among middle-aged and older people. Between 1964 and 1988, the proportion of women 45 to 54 years old in the labor force rose sharply from 50.8 to 70.3 percent while participation by men of the same age *decreased* slightly from 95.6 to 90.6 percent. During the same period the number of working women 55 to 64 increased from 40.6 to 45.3 percent, while men of that age range experienced a major decline from 85.4 to 67.0 percent.[27]

Considered solely from the point of view of aging policy, the impact of this trend appears to be mixed. On the one hand, as noted above, women typically have suffered financial insecurity in later life because our system bases old age benefits on income-producing opportunities earlier in life, in which fewer women have participated. As more women engage in employment patterns similar to those of men, the benefits they earn in their own right should increase (including eligibility for private pension plans, an important supplement to Social Security for many males). These benefits will lead to greater security for women when they retire, a positive development and one to be encouraged by public policy.

On the other hand, the rise in the number of women who work, both younger and older, has some potentially negative implications for care of the elderly (leaving aside the still-debated impact on childrearing). Research shows that spouses of frail elderly are their primary caregivers. In most cases this means the wife rather than the husband is the caregiver, because women not only outlive men but men usually marry younger women as well. As more older women work, either fewer are available to care for their infirm husbands, or to do so they must give up work that may be both personally satisfying and financially necessary.

The real problem arises, however, as more and more middle-age women participate in the work force. Traditionally the nonworking "housewife," usually a daughter or daughter-in-law, has been the primary source of care for the elderly once the spouse no longer can serve that function. In fact, as many as eight or even nine out of ten adult-children caregivers are female. Little wonder that gerontologist Elaine Brody has observed that the widely heralded "family support system" for the elderly is only a euphemism for "adult daughters (and daughters-in-law), who are the true alternatives" to institutionalization.[28] Thus those who typically have been looked to for the care of many of the elderly in our society (even today it is estimated that 80 percent of all home care for older people is provided by their families) and who have been able to do so must make a difficult choice: either take on a very stressful and perhaps impossible dual responsibility (counting only worker and caregiver and ignoring for the moment mother, wife, and perhaps other roles), or refuse to assume the care of the elderly parent. Whatever the decision, considerable stress and pain are likely to be caused for both the younger and older generations.

Furthermore, caring for an elderly parent has become arguably more difficult in recent years for a number of reasons beyond the dilemma just mentioned. Both generations are more committed to their independence, a major measure of which necessarily must be relinquished by all parties in a typical caregiving relationship. It seems safe to say also that there is less support from society than in the past for giving up one's own freedom and ambition to care for an elderly parent. In addition, our highly mobile society and its consequent geographic separation have led to greater emotional distance between the generations in many cases. Finally, because of improved health care today, responsibility for an elder tends to last longer and to entail dealing with more chronic and especially difficult illnesses such as Alzheimer's disease and cancer. Seldom anymore does an elderly relative "go quickly" from pneumonia or the other killers of the past.

The "Sandwich Generation"

The demographic and life-style trends discussed thus far have contributed to the rise of another new phenomenon directly related to the family, the so-called "sandwich generation." This apt phrase refers to those who still have parental responsibilities for their children when they have to become caregivers for their parents. Given the traditional responsibilities for both child-rearing and elder care, this is again primarily a problem for women. Not surprisingly, such individuals often describe themselves as being "squeezed" unmercifully between the two obligations.

This unpleasant position has several components: *emotional,* as the pressures of rearing children in today's turbulent world collide with those of assuming more and more of the parental role for one's own parents; *physical,* as the demands of being both parent and adult caregiver vie with work and other obligations for a limited amount of energy and number of hours; and *financial,* as the ever escalating costs of higher education for one's offspring compete with the largely family-borne expenses of long-term care.

Available data suggest that the actual number of people who have primary responsibility for the care of both children and elderly relatives is considerably smaller than popular media reports might lead one to believe (e.g., slightly fewer than one million women with a disabled parent both work full-time and have a child under fifteen).[29] Nonetheless, it is worth noting that 3.6 million American men and women are members of the sandwich generation—that is, they have both one or more children under fifteen and an elderly parent needing personal care. It is reasonable to assume that were some form of comprehensive long-term care program (as well as a child-care program) in place, their decisions about both child care and elder care might be quite different. This seems especially the case for women, who are still expected to (and in fact do) provide the great bulk of care and are much more likely than men to rearrange work schedules, reduce the hours they work, or quit their jobs altogether in order to carry out their elder-care responsibilities.

Increased Incidence of Divorce

Complicating the situation even further is yet another phenomenon distinctive to contemporary society: the greatly increased rate of divorce of the past several decades. The changes already considered would be confusing and complicated enough if they affected only one man and one woman joined together until "death do them part" (even if that parting were many years later than previously imaginable). The situation becomes considerably more complex, however, when one notes that more than 50 percent of marriages currently end in divorce, a 43 percent increase since 1970.

Of course, the ever more common divorces among their children and grandchildren can cause great pain for older people, especially if they depend on those younger people for care and support in any significant sense.[30] Even without such dependence, though, just sorting out the new relationships can be problematic and confusing enough: Because of the high rates of divorce and remarriage among baby boomers, one-half of their parents will find themselves step-grandparents by the turn of the century (during the 1980s alone, over one million children experienced the divorce of their parents). Emotionally painful by itself, this situation is made even more difficult when one raises practical questions, such as inheritance particularly. Who should be the recipient of the older person's estate, not to mention earlier and probably less significant gifts?[31]

The well known divorce statistics also mean, however, that more people will enter old age divorced themselves (indeed, it is estimated that currently one-fourth of American women 45 to 64 have been divorced). Even though older people who are divorced constituted only 4 percent of all the elderly in 1989 (1.3 million), their ranks had increased over twice as fast since 1980 as had the older population as a whole (1.9 times for men, 2.9 times for women).[32] The 1989 figure represents about twice as many divorced elders as in the 1960s. Without a strong basis for and commitment to their union, especially considering the increasing years of life they must spend together beyond work and childrearing responsibilities, the possibility of their own divorce becomes more real for the elders themselves, and given the realities of aging, divorce can be especially traumatic. Added to the many kinds of losses associated with growing older, the sense of rejection, inadequacy, and failure often experienced in a divorce—especially if it is not desired—may be overwhelming for an older person. Certainly the chances of remarriage are lower for the elderly than for younger people, especially for women because of the gender imbalance noted above. And we have already seen that older single women have the highest poverty rates and are at greatest risk of institutionalization.

One comment in anticipation of the later portion of this book when some more specific suggestions will be offered: Perhaps one of the most effective policies that could be undertaken to address a number of the problems confronting our society with regard to the aging of our population would be to strive to strengthen and improve *all* marriages in order to avoid the difficulties just discussed, not to mention a number of others that have nothing to do directly with aging concerns.

Increasing Child-Care Responsibilities of the Elderly

Related to the last comment, one finding of the 1990 census that Cynthia Taeuber has labeled "disturbing" is that an increasing number of older people are assuming primary responsibility for rearing their grandchildren. During the 1980s the percentage of children under eighteen who lived with grandparents increased 25 percent, to 5 percent of all such children (3 million). Nearly half are African American, and 38 percent of these live with grandparents alone. Even more troubling is the fact that, according to Elbert Cole, founder of the Shepherd's Centers, 18 percent of all preschool children today are being reared by grandparents.[33] Although in one sense it may be encouraging that these children have such close contact with their grandparents (the lack of which interaction is a common lament among many families in our mobile society), one has to wonder about the reasons for it in many of these cases.

That this matter is important for public policy considerations is illustrated by a recent court challenge mounted by Grandparents Who Care, an organization of California grandparents who are rearing the children of their own crack-addicted children. They argue that simply because they are related to the children, they are denied benefits that non-related foster parents routinely receive (such as special medical care, respite, and counseling). The grandparents understandably want the same services for their grandchildren. Already the Ninth Circuit Court ruled in September 1989 that Oregon had to make foster care funding available to children who live with close relatives.[34] Once again we see that some long-held assumptions—such as the definition and nature of the family, the obligations it has to its various members, and the role that government can and should play in matters once considered "family affairs"—are being called increasingly into question by social changes at least tangentially related to the aging of our population.

Health Care

There can be little argument that health care is an area of great, if not the greatest, concern when it comes to public policy concerning the elderly in America (or any other age group, for that matter). U.S. Commissioner on Aging Joyce T. Berry, for example, after listing the critical needs of the elderly in this country today, asserted, "What is needed most is affordable and accessible quality health care."[35] Indeed, probably no other issue can generate as much heated debate across such a broad spectrum of society, perhaps because no other issue affects virtually everybody in the country so directly. This topic therefore must occupy our attention further in subsequent chapters; here some of the most relevant data will merely be highlighted.

The United States currently spends the most money ($738 billion in 1991) and the highest proportion of its Gross National Product (over 13 percent, up from 5.3 percent in 1960) on health care of any nation in the world (compared to about 9 percent in Canada, for example). If nothing is done to limit rising health-care costs, estimates range as high as 20 percent of GNP by the year 2000 and 37 percent by 2030. Health-care costs rose over 40 percent between 1985 and 1990, precisely during the time that significant cost-limiting policies were being implemented. Although we boast of having the best medical care in the world, we do not provide the best health. A 1990 survey of

10 leading industrialized nations found the people of this country to be the most dissatisfied with their health-care system.

Such findings are perhaps not surprising when one learns that, despite health-care spending of almost $2700 for every man, woman, and child in the country (171 percent more than Great Britain, 124 percent more than Japan, and 88 percent more than West Germany), the United States ranks twelfth in the world in life expectancy, twenty-first in deaths of children under five years of age, twenty-second in infant mortality, and twenty-fourth in percentage of babies born with adequate birthweight (trailing even Bulgaria and Hong Kong in the last category).[36] Furthermore, increasing numbers of our citizens are unable even to take advantage of health care because some 35 million Americans lack medical insurance that provides any meaningful coverage, and this number has been increasing by over one million annually since 1978.[37] During the 28-month period that ended in May 1987, 63 million Americans, over one-fourth of the population, went at least one month without health insurance, according to Census Bureau data.[38] Of all the industrialized countries, the United States and South Africa are the only ones that do not provide all their citizens with access to health care.

Indeed, most recent labor contract negotiations have turned more on health care benefits than on wages or working conditions, and some of the most anxious conversations in the work place other than about fears of being laid off concern possible cuts in medical benefits. Little wonder, either, given that the per-employee expenditure by American businesses for medical benefits rose $3161 from 1988 to 1990, an amazing 44 percent increase in two years.[39] Examples of a chaotic health-care system in crisis are all about: costs spiraling upward despite ever more draconian cost-containment measures, extravagant expenditures on exotic life-saving technology for the few in the face of cries of outrage at the lack of basic care for the many, and various proposals for rationing met with shocked outrage at the notion of putting an economic value on health or even on life itself. Where do the elderly fit into this picture?

It hardly comes as a revelation to anyone to hear the answer,

"Right in the middle of the foreground." As was noted in the last chapter, the need for medical care increases markedly with age, especially as people move into the ranks of the "old old."[40] In 1988 almost 30 percent of older people considered their health to be either fair or poor, compared to only 7 percent of those under 65. It is estimated that four out of every five older persons have at least one chronic health problem, and many have more than one. As many as one-quarter of the non-institutionalized elderly have problems with personal care activities like bathing and eating, and slightly more experience difficulty with home management tasks like shopping and preparing meals.

Though the elderly constitute only one in eight residents of the United States, in 1987 they used more than one in every three dollars spent on health care. This $162 billion expenditure averaged out to $5360 per older person, over four times the $1290 spent for younger people and almost four times the amount spent a decade earlier for the elderly. In 1988 the elderly averaged almost twice as many contacts with doctors as did younger people (nine versus five) and were responsible for one-third of all hospital admissions and 44 percent of all days of hospital care. Persons under 65 averaged 5.4 days per admission, in contrast to 8.9 days for older people. As would be expected, the length of hospitalization increases with age, and persons 85 and over, regardless of insurance or income, averaged 9.2 days per admission, compared to 8 days for those 65 to 74. In 1987 the largest portion of health-care expenses for the elderly went to hospitals (42 percent), followed by physicians (21 percent) and nursing homes (20 percent). Finally, it should be noted that a relatively small number of the elderly account for the major portion of these costs—namely, those in the last year of life. In any year about 6 percent of older persons die, but they generate almost 30 percent of Medicare expenditures.

Many people today assume that Medicare/Medicaid pays for these hefty expenses completely, and it is true that government programs—including Medicare ($72 billion), Medicaid ($20 billion), and others like veterans' benefits ($10 billion)—covered over three-fifths of the health-care costs of the elderly in 1987, compared to only one-fourth for those under 65. Nonetheless, the relative costs paid for by individuals themselves ("out-of-pocket" expenses) actually have increased since Medicare went into effect. In 1966, for example, the first year after its enactment, America's elderly paid 15 percent of their mean incomes for health care. That proportion dropped to 12.3 percent in 1977 but has climbed steadily since then to 18.2 percent in 1988.[41] In 1987 about $1500 or one-fourth of the average expenditure on health care per older person came from direct payments by or for the elderly. Because of the extensive cost-sharing provisions of Medicare (deductibles, coinsurance, and charges in excess of approved amounts), together with the well known "gaps" in its coverage (including lack of payment for many of the things older people most need), those elderly who find themselves in lower economic brackets cannot rest assured that their health needs will be met.

To illustrate this point vividly, consider that if income *after* paying medical expenses were used to compute poverty rates, the proportion of all older people who were poor in 1987 would have climbed by one-third, from 12 to 17 percent; the increase among those living alone would have been over two-fifths, from 19 to 27 percent. Note especially that the poor elderly, who are less likely to be able to afford private insurance to supplement Medicare and must negotiate a complex and often frustrating system to attain further public help, actually end up paying more of their income (16 percent) for health care than do those better off financially (only 2 percent for the richest one-fifth of the elderly). Finally, one out of eight elderly spends 20 percent or more of annual income on acute health care. Our current approach has hardly solved the problem of affordable health care for the elderly.

Further compounding the problems just mentioned is the fact that the poorer a person is, the more likely that person is to experience poor health as he/she ages. The poor elderly are twice as likely to consider their own health poor as are older people with moderate or high incomes. A group of researchers at the University of Michigan recently analyzed "two large

. . . and independent representative samples of the population of the contiguous 48 states" (total participants numbered almost 60,000). Their results "suggest that the vast bulk of what might be termed excess or preventable morbidity and functional limitation in the U.S. population—that is, morbidity and functional limitations prior to age 75 at least—is concentrated (both absolutely and relatively) in the lower socioeconomic strata of our society."[42]

Interestingly, health problems among the "older and oldest old" (over 75 or certainly 80) appear to be less dependent on socioeconomic status, suggesting that perhaps there are certain physiological limits beyond which even advantaged human beings must expect their bodies to begin wearing out. At any rate, acknowledging and addressing the socioeconomic roots of poorer health prior to age 75 could allow for significant improvements in health and thus reduce the cost of health care by "compressing" morbidity into the final years of life for everyone.

As is becoming apparent by now, gender differences appear in this area as in virtually all others. In the first place, the mere imbalance in the numbers of elderly women and men means that health care in one's later years concerns more women than men. Women on average outlive men by some seven years, and thus they are more susceptible to chronic illnesses and long-term disability, neither of which our health-care system is designed to handle. Because of their higher retirement incomes, men can better afford the "medigap" insurance that is increasingly necessary to cover the rising out-of-pocket costs of Medicare, though men spend fewer days in acute-care hospitals than do women and also much more often have spouses at home to care for them when they are discharged. Older women, though less likely to need hospitalization in any particular year, stay longer in acute-care facilities and are more likely to be discharged to another institution or to the care of a relative.[43]

Furthermore, we have seen that elderly women, especially minorities, suffer from disproportionately high poverty rates, and the strong correlation between poverty and health has just been described. Thus it is not surprising that elderly women

71

living in the community have higher mortality and morbidity rates, in particular suffering more from chronic illnesses like arthritis, hypertension, and diabetes, which lead to increased need for home health services or institutionalization. Because their incomes are inadequate to cover even the cost of basic necessities, the very people who need medical care the most are least able to afford it.

Long-Term Care

The good news on the health care front is that more Americans will live longer in the years ahead (i.e., mortality will continue to go down); the bad news is that we will have more impaired people as this happens (i.e., morbidity will go up). The increase in the number and the age of the elderly discussed in the preceding chapter raises yet another critical public policy issue—namely, an increased demand for long-term care (LTC). In 1989, the country was already spending an estimated $60 billion on LTC, and that figure can only go up. About 4.4 million elderly people in the United States today need some kind of LTC, and approximately 13.3 million more people are spouses and children who may at some time be their caregivers. Of these, 11.4 million are adult children, about equally divided between daughters and sons. Slightly over 4 million of the 13.3 million potential caregivers actually provide care to impaired elders. LTC policy therefore is of great concern not only to the 4.4 million disabled elderly but also to a considerably larger number of active and potential caregivers, many of whom are still at an age where they have significant child-care and/or work responsibilities. Thus "policy makers have begun to recognize the link between long-term care policies and family needs," because long-term care is, in short, "an issue that affects much of society, young and old."[44]

One of the problems that older people and their caregivers encounter, however, is that the American health insurance system (indeed, American health care in general) is geared toward acute care, that is, medical care for illnesses of relatively short duration and injuries that respond to intensive but short-term treatment. Chronic conditions requiring LTC are clearly distinguished from acute care. For example, Medicare will cover virtually all serious illnesses for those it insures but will not contribute toward their stay in a long-term care facility for a chronic debility (beyond 100 days of relatively acute care in a skilled nursing facility, and then only if admitted from a hospital, not from their home) or toward assistance that would allow a family caregiver to keep an elderly relative at home. Yet today the average cost of a year in a nursing home is around $30,000, with projections for the year 2010 reaching as high as $83,000.[45] To no one's surprise, the largest share of out-of-pocket health care costs for the elderly is attributable to LTC, especially nursing-home costs. Indeed, for those who paid over $2,000 out-of-pocket for medical care in 1986, more than 80 percent went for nursing-home care.[46] Yet over the next five decades, when the total population is expected to increase 40 percent, the number of nursing-home residents is expected to increase 350 percent, and the number of non-institutionalized elderly who require help in one or more activities of daily living (e.g., dressing, eating, toileting) will double, a number that will quadruple among non-institutionalized persons 75 or older.[47] These last figures are especially troublesome in light of the fact that, as Commissioner on Aging Joyce T. Berry pointed out in a 1991 speech to the American Society on Aging, "of the 9 million older people who live alone, almost a third say they have no one to provide care if they need it." A national survey conducted by Louis Harris and Associates in 1986 for the Commonwealth Fund suggested that that proportion is closer to between four and five out of ten.

The ill-fated Medicare Catastrophic Coverage Act of 1988 included several provisions intended to enhance the security of older persons in the face of large LTC costs, the primary cause of financial insecurity among those who are neither poor enough to qualify for Medicaid nor wealthy enough to buy the care they might need. Most of the bill (e.g., the provision of 150 days of nursing-home care without prior hospitalization) was repealed in 1989 under extreme pressure from elders' advocacy groups because of the bill's requirement that better-off elderly, in effect, pay for these services for those less well off. The spousal impoverishment provision and extension of Medicaid payment of Medicare premiums for poor elderly are all that remain of the bill.

Even the applauded improvement in the spousal impoverishment situation, however, appears to be a mixed blessing. The bill provided for a division of the assets of a couple (other than their home) so that at least $12,000 of those assets are allocated to the non-institutionalized spouse before any can be allocated to the institutionalized spouse. Though this new standard increases Medicaid eligibility of the institutionalized spouse, it helps the most financially insecure elderly little because they tend not to be married or, if married, not to have enough assets that protecting them makes any difference. In fact, by giving the non-institutionalized spouse more of the assets, his or her eligibility for Medicaid is reduced, probably increasing his or her financial insecurity.[48] It is apparent that the ad hoc, reactive approach to LTC policy thus far utilized by the federal government is inadequate to address the needs of the nation.

Given the lack of any significant public program to address LTC needs, a rapidly increasing number of insurance companies have jumped into this potentially lucrative market with a bewildering array of LTC policies, aggressively marketed as the "solution" to the problem. Indeed, the number of companies offering such coverage has grown from 75 in 1987 to 130 by mid-1991, and the number of policies sold has risen during the same period from 815,000 to 1.5 million. Among the most serious problems that *Consumer Reports* discovered in its examination of these policies are "tricky provisions in the way policies are written; the potential for unaffordably large rate increases; uncertainty about whether claims will be paid; and confounding policy language."[49] The cost of this insurance varies considerably depending on the company and the type of coverage, but it is all expensive. *Consumer Reports* concludes that "you have to be a bit of a gambler to buy a long-term-care policy" and estimates that a 65 year old who buys the second-rated policy would have to pay over 12 percent of the $17,000 mean annual income for someone that age. If one adds on the $1,000 a good

"Medigap" policy will cost, "decent protection comes to more than $3,000 a year, or $6,000 for a couple,"[50] over 18 percent of the individual's annual income. Unfortunately, the very people who most need such protection—the oldest, the poorest, those who live alone—are precisely the ones who have no hope of being able to afford it.[51]

This last point suggests that yet again gender differences are implicated in the discussion of LTC, in part because, as we have seen, women constitute the largest segment of poor elderly and also because women's greater longevity makes them more susceptible to the chronic illnesses that require such care. Of the 1.6 million severely impaired elderly still living in the community, more than two out of three are female (and almost seven out of 10 are poor or near-poor).[52] The chance of being institutionalized for more than two years of a 65 year old's remaining lifetime is about 14 percent today; but whereas the risk is only 7 percent for men, it is 20 percent for women.[53] It has been noted already that about three-fourths of the nation's 1.5 million nursing-home residents are women. Furthermore, we have seen that the vast majority of caregivers for the elderly are women (as many as three out of four, by most estimates), usually wives, daughters, and daughters-in-law. The wives—and increasing numbers of adult children caregivers—are themselves old or close to it (the Older Women's League estimates that 35 percent of those who care for the elderly are over 65 themselves). For younger women the assumption of the caregiver role also often means a painful decision between care and career. Indeed, women who work full-time are more than four times as likely to be primary caregivers as are men.[54]

Beth Hess's conclusion appears largely warranted: "Yet very few public resources are directed to caregivers of the frail elderly, in part because the mystique of 'woman as nurturer' allows policymakers to evade responsibility in the name of 'traditional family values.' " Indeed, she points out that some "political conservatives" have gone so far as to urge that public policy be directed not toward providing resources to foster community-based care but rather toward reversing the current low birthrate in order to ensure an adequate supply of caregivers (i.e., females) in the future.[55]

Two other researchers, Rhonda J. V. Montgomery and Mary McGlinn Datwyler, reach much the same conclusion as Hess: "The fact of the matter is, women will continue to bear a disproportionate amount of the responsibility for the care of older persons in our society until policymakers see this adaptation as a short-term, individual solution to what in reality is a societal problem requiring a long-term, public resolution." They contend, however, that the very primacy of women as caregivers may lock them into this role because as long as women are willing to give up their own interests—be they work, leisure, or others—to care for their elderly relatives, policymakers will feel no necessity to address the real issue—namely, how our society should provide quality care to *all* its older citizens.[56]

For public policy considerations, this discussion of long-term care of the elderly should not conclude without noting that not only will we have more old and older people in the decades ahead who need such care, we will also have more impaired children living longer than ever before because of improvements in neonatal medicine and probable continued strides in genetic medicine. Thus the costs incurred by society because of the vast increase in the sheer number of elderly who live longer will be compounded by the fact that impaired children (some of them seriously impaired), though significantly fewer in number, will have many more years of life to be cared for than will the elderly.

CONCLUSION

We now know quite a bit about the situation facing this country over the next half-century as we undergo an aging of our population unlike any we have experienced up to this point. As the "baby boomers" slowly metamorphose into the "elder boomers," the United States will experience a social upheaval that will demand the best its citizens have to offer in order to deal with the changes. Economic questions, of course, dominate most discussions of the situation, with serious questions being raised about issues such as the basic financial security of the elderly, especially in light of continuing concerns about the long-term solvency of Social Security and its ability to finance the retirement of so many people at once. Less quantitative issues are also important, ranging from devising new patterns of work and retirement through forging new understandings of the family to dealing with the aftermath of changes in traditional understandings of the family. Influencing virtually every one of these elements will be an underlying gender imbalance in which elderly women significantly outnumber men, not only in sheer numbers but also in their representation among almost all the disadvantaged, at-risk groups of older persons. This is especially the case with regard to income security and health-care and long-term-care needs.

One final observation is in order before we leave this broad overview of the situation facing the United States during the next half-century to look at the programs, policies, and organizations that have arisen to respond to these monumental changes. In the past, the needs of the elderly of this country (of virtually all countries, for that matter) have been met by family members, most of them adult children. With the rise of Social Security, however, this traditional responsibility began subtly to shift from the family to the government, although only in certain areas. Given this shift, it is not surprising that the sense of obligation of adult children to their elderly parents began to fade somewhat, accompanied to be sure by the older family members' appreciation of their increased independence. With Medicare another major step was taken in the transfer of elder-care from family to government. The problem we face today, though, is that some types of assistance traditionally provided by the family—especially long-term care, either low-level or intensive, plus emotional/psychological support— are not provided by the government, and the family is now less able and/or willing to continue to do so. It would appear, then, that the United States has failed to complete the process of shifting the provision of elder-care from the family to the state, resulting in a number of the difficulties outlined in this chapter.

CHAPTER 3

CURRENT RESPONSES:
PROGRAMS AND POLICIES

I n order to examine the ethical implications of public policy concerning aging in the United States, an obvious prerequisite is to determine what constitutes such policy. This may be a more difficult task than would at first seem likely. Stephen Crystal relates the response of a friend when Crystal mentioned that he was working on a book about public policy on aging: "I didn't think there was any."[1] Although this quip may accurately reflect a common assessment of the situation, as well as the experience of many older persons as they attempt to utilize public programs and services, our nation has addressed the issue of aging and the elderly for some time in a conscious if not always consistent way. This chapter examines the major results of this effort.

Before 1935 the federal budget contained almost no items designated especially for the elderly. By 1988, according to the U.S. Senate Special Committee on Aging, over one-fourth of the entire federal budget (almost $300 billion) was spent on benefits for the elderly. Projections based on the growing number of elderly in the U.S. have suggested that the portion of the federal budget devoted to older people may grow to 40 percent by the beginning of the new century and to 63 percent by 2025.[2] It is of course extremely unlikely that these projections will become reality, reflecting as they do the assumption of no changes in current policy; it has become clear that the country will have to devise new approaches to deal with the matter. If, however, we hope to address the ethical implications of U.S. aging policy, we must understand how that policy has evolved from the pre-1935 situation just noted to a set of circumstances that can prompt such mind-boggling projections for the next century.

SOCIAL SECURITY:
THE "MOTHER OF ALL AGING PROGRAMS"

Although there are other public programs that target the elderly, income security and health care dominate the expenditure, and Social Security, Supplemental Security Income (SSI), Medicare, and Medicaid are unquestionably the "big four." The Social Security Administration's budget request for fiscal year 1992 was $282 billion, and Social Security retirement pensions and Medicare alone make up about 60 percent of all social insurance payments to persons of all ages.[3] So when one speaks about policy concerning aging in the United States (and, not incidentally, about what many consider to be at the heart of some of the most vexing economic, political, and ethical questions it raises), the unchallenged starting-point must be Social Security, in language made familiar by the Gulf War of 1991, "the mother of all aging programs." It would be easy for any discussion of Social Security to consume an entire book on its own.[4] Indeed, former Commissioner of Social Security Dorcas Hardy once described the system that she oversaw as "the most complex program that God and the Congress ever made."[5] Therefore this treatment will be of a summary nature, so that we can move on to matters of more direct concern to us.

Interestingly, given its central place in U.S. public policy and the vast sums of their money it involves, an overwhelming majority of Americans know very little about Social Security, encountering it directly only when they notice the mysterious "FICA" (Federal Insurance Contributions Act) deduction on their paycheck stub.[6] Technically, what is commonly known as "Social Security" and is usually associated only with retirees'

79

monthly checks is actually a collection of different programs, more properly called Old Age, Survivors, Disability, and Hospital Insurance, or OASDHI for short. Each of these components deserves consideration, but first a brief interpretive history of the program is in order.

A Selective History of Social Security

Traditionally, Americans took care of themselves and their family members, and if for legitimate reasons this was impossible, the local community did so. Industrialization began to undermine this system, promoting greater urbanization, mobility, and poverty; and early in this century, the numbers of older people—many of them poor—began to increase. The Great Depression that began with the 1929 stock market crash changed things forever, forcing the federal government to take a role in many areas of its citizens' lives previously considered off limits to Washington. Separating economic want from moral failure for perhaps the first time in the country's history, Americans were forced to acknowledge that circumstances beyond someone's control could ruin that person financially. Out of this new understanding Social Security was born.

In fact, distinguished gerontologist Stanley J. Brody has suggested that over the past fifty years, avoiding what successive cohorts of the elderly have perceived as "economic catastrophes for the entire family" has been "the value that has shaped public policy" for the aged. And what has led to this emphasis? "The event that shaped their sensitivity was the Great Depression of the 1930s. It was a universal experience. It was the source of the felt necessity of the time: protection from economic catastrophe." This "felt necessity" was first translated into action through Titles I and II of the Social Security Act of 1935, which focused on "establishing an economic floor, providing what Franklin D. Roosevelt later described as one of the four freedoms, 'the freedom from want.' "[7] At first this "floor of protection" was very low, preventing only abject poverty.

Brody thus emphasizes the role of Social Security in the avoidance of economic catastrophe through the provision of a minimum level of subsistence, and rightly so, given that his interest is in identifying the motivating factor that led to Social Security. This emphasis, however, can lead to a misunderstanding of the philosophical (and political) underpinnings of Social Security. The value that Brody stresses is commonly called the principle of *adequacy* (or social adequacy). In the complex of principles and perspectives that went into the creation of this system, though, another value struggled with adequacy for priority, and in good American fashion, in the end both were incorporated into Social Security's basic philosophy. This second value is the principle of *equity* (or individual equity). Both are unarguably important and reflect deeply held American values. When put together in a single program, however, the two concepts possess a certain inner tension that has made Social Security a strange hybrid from the beginning and that continues to lead to confusion and uncertainty about its real goals.[8] As W. Andrew Achenbaum puts it, "The act was not simply a welfare package; it was not exclusively an insurance plan. It was intended to be both simultaneously."[9] We will encounter these principles again in later chapters, but some basic definitions are necessary here.

Americans have long prided themselves on their concern for the "underdog" and their willingness to "give somebody a hand" when needed (almost certainly a result of the underlying Jewish-Christian values of the country). This trait was embodied in Social Security in the principle of *social adequacy. Adequacy* refers to the attempt to assure that all persons have enough to live decently, in their later years especially. Our Social Security system does this by favoring those who have the greatest need for assistance. This policy in turn is accomplished in the basic pension program primarily by calculating benefits using a weighted formula that gives to lower-income workers proportionately higher benefits relative to their actual payments, in recognition that not everyone can be in a high-paying job that permits large contributions. In effect, some of the money put into the system by those better off is redistributed to those less well off in order to assure that every member of society has at

81

least an *adequate* level of income in later years. Benefits based on the principle of social adequacy tend to be needs-based in some way, either implicitly as in Old Age and Survivors Insurance (OASI) or explicitly as in Supplemental Security Income. Discussions of adequacy often involve matters like definition of what constitutes an "adequate" income and determination of who really needs the assistance available, how much they need, whether there should be conditions, and so forth. Such issues sometimes are avoided by making the benefits universal without a "means test," as in OASI and Medicare.

Deeply ingrained in the American psyche also, however, is the notion that one should be rewarded for working harder or longer and risking more, that what one receives should be fundamentally in proportion to what one has given, whatever the "currency" of the exchange. This concept was operationalized in Social Security through the principle of *individual equity*. *Equity* means that a relationship should exist between what a worker pays into the system and what the worker receives after retirement. This goal is accomplished in our system by tying benefits to contributions. Although the weighting in favor of lower-income workers described above exists, those who contribute more still receive higher absolute benefits in order to assure a fair or *equitable* arrangement. In terms of equity, the discussion tends to focus on who is getting how much relative to his or her own contributions and relative to what others are getting and whether the "return" is really fair. Interestingly, a concept of adequacy is also often interjected by questioning whether a recipient really "needs" a benefit, even if he or she has contributed a fair share.

Because of the initial emphasis on social adequacy, Title I, the needs-based program called Old Age Assistance (OAA), was originally the more important of the two basic programs, guaranteeing a minimum level of subsistence and thus avoidance of "economic catastrophe." As James Schulz and his coauthors point out, "Certainly in their formative years the first [public pension programs for elderly workers] in Europe and North America were not designed to provide a level of income sufficient to permit withdrawal from the labor force (that is, to permit retirement in advance of physiological decline)."[10] As time passed, however, OAA gradually began to yield place of priority to Title II, Old Age and Survivors Insurance, the program commonly known today as "Social Security," with benefits based loosely on contributions made by workers (note the difference in names: *assistance* versus *insurance*). This move led to a number of amendments and revisions, most of them aimed at extending coverage to more people and improving the benefits of all recipients, including the nonpoor elderly. By 1951, elderly people getting insurance benefits under Title II became for the first time more numerous than those getting public assistance under Title I.

In the late 1960s, however, a major change occurred in the goal of the income maintenance program: "The catastrophic orientation to minimum subsistence shifted to the goal of replacement of income on retirement from work."[11] The emphasis thus became the provision of a "retirement wage" that would allow people, if not induce them, to "retire" in the current sense of the word. Toward that end, the 1972 amendments to the Social Security Act instituted a number of changes: They raised OASI benefits 20 percent, producing a net gain from 1968 to 1972 of 72 percent (after an increase of 50 percent between 1965 and 1971); they provided for an annual cost-of-living adjustment (COLA) beginning in 1975; and they replaced the federal-state matching OAA program with a national minimum-income plan for the poor (Supplemental Security Income). Schulz and his coauthors observe that these changes demonstrate "a considerable expansion of the boundaries of public provision beyond the poorest members of society to incorporate the middle classes."[12] Significantly, they conclude that an approach "that relates the retirement income of the nonpoor aged to their income before retirement is clearly more oriented toward preserving the distribution of income than toward reshaping it."[13]

Still, in principle Social Security continues to serve the original purpose of adequacy. Indeed, in 1986 the "elderly poverty gap" (the total amount of money needed to lift all older persons in the country above the federal poverty line) was only $3.6 billion, a really rather small amount. Excluding Social Security benefits, however, increases the gap ten-fold, to $34 billion. Furthermore, without Social Security, instead of the roughly 12 percent of the elderly who are currently poor, the proportion would climb to half,[14] with a commensurate rise in the number of those who are near-poor. In late 1991, about 60 percent of those 65 and older received at least half of their income from Social Security, and 25 percent relied on it for 90 percent or more.[15] The contribution of Social Security to the alleviation of poverty and to the provision of basic adequacy of income among the elderly thus cannot be gainsaid.

Even so, the balance between adequacy and equity appears to have shifted in the direction of equity. Although the notion of equity was introduced to guarantee a *fair* return for higher income workers relative to their larger contributions, an analysis of benefits in proportion to payments shows that the "return" from Social Security is on average much higher for current retirees than the return one could have expected from personal investment. Furthermore, some critics argue that benefits for those least in need are disproportionately high relative to benefits for those most in need. Social Security appears to have served well the original plan that concentrated on avoiding catastrophe for those who were on the brink or already over it (adequacy), but the current manifestation of the equity principle has caused a drift, not toward providing too much support for those *most* in need, but rather toward being too generous to those *least* in need (see "Some Problems" below). The government's initial response to this situation, according to Brody, was to tax Social Security benefits for the first time, imposing the tax on one-half the benefits of those older people who had individual modified adjusted gross incomes over $25,000 (over $32,000 for couples). Brody thus concludes, "The societal commitment to only minimum economic support was reaffirmed,"[16] reflecting an effort to achieve once again a better balance between adequacy and equity.

84

It is important to note in this context, contrary to the understanding many people have, that Social Security is not an "investment" program into which one puts a certain amount in a safe place, leaves it there to earn interest till retirement, and then begins to withdraw the principal invested plus the interest earned. Social Security is what is called a "pay-as-you-go" system, in which the taxes of current workers pass almost immediately to nonworkers in the form of benefits (the variation in the fact of this arrangement—though not in its philosophy—caused by the large numbers of baby boomers will be considered below). It is, as Richard Margolis describes it, "less an annuity" than a "pact between generations," in which the current younger generation basically agrees to support the nonworkers of their day in anticipation of having the same done for them when they reach their later years.[17] That this would work well in a demographically stable population (or even better in one with a relatively high birthrate) is apparent. In 1935, for example, each retiree had more than 40 workers contributing payroll taxes toward his Social Security, and in 1950 there were still 17 workers per retiree. What will happen by the time the baby boomers clog the Social Security pipeline—when projections suggest that there may be as few as 1.78 workers per retiree in 2020—has caused a great deal of concern about the very solvency of the system and its ability to live up to its claim to be "a great deal for everybody!"[18]

Some of the pressure on Social Security today results also from the fact that its original intent was to provide a basic compulsory minimum of income support in retirement, with additional income envisioned from other sources such as personal savings and private pensions. Many people today, however, expect Social Security to provide, by itself, adequate benefits and types of coverage to assure a comfortable old age. For those who have jobs that provide private pensions or incomes high enough to purchase other investment instruments, Social Security can serve its original function. For many others, Social Security has become their sole source of income support in their later years. Of older people who live alone, for example, two out of five rely totally on Social Security for income. Among the poor and the near-poor in this group, *four* out of five do so. Conversely, of those in the moderate- to high-income range, only one in five is solely dependent on Social Security, with two-thirds of income coming from assets and earnings.[19]

The Structure of Social Security

With this brief look at some of the salient features of the birth and growth of Social Security as background, a more detailed consideration of its structure can be undertaken (see exhibit 3.1 for a summary table). As mentioned above, Social Security consists of several components, each of which serves a different function and, in some cases, a different constituency. With the exception of Supplemental Security Income and Medicaid, none of these programs is means-tested. That is, none requires the recipient to fall below a certain income/asset level in order to receive benefits.

Old Age and Survivors Insurance (OASI)

The heart of the Social Security program is Old Age Insurance, the first part to be enacted. As we saw above, the primary purpose of this part of the program has become "income replacement," that is, replacing the income (or some portion of it) lost when a worker retires. Originally only retired private-sector workers 65 and over were covered. Gradually compulsory participation has been extended until currently 130 million people (over 95 percent of the work force) are covered. Eligibility for benefits has consistently expanded also, from retired workers only to dependent children and spouses. Age of eligibility has decreased to 62 ("early retirement"), albeit with a reduction in benefits. Recognizing one of the major trends in American life, Social Security dependent and survivor coverage, originally limited to women who stayed married, has been extended in steps to women who divorce, until currently 10 years of marriage qualifies for benefits.

Today around 43 million people receive Social Security benefits that total $20 billion every month. Of these recipients

EXHIBIT 3.1
SOCIAL SECURITY AT A GLANCE

Program	Purpose	Eligibility
Old Age and Survivors Insurance (OASI)	Old age "insurance" (income replacement)	Retirees 62 and older, spouses, and other dependents
Disability Insurance (DI)	Income replacement	Disabled workers and disabled dependents, regardless of age
Hospital Insurance (HI) Medicare	Hospital insurance (Part A); outpatient coverage (Part B) optional at additional cost	Workers and dependents 65 and older who qualify for OASI, certain disabled persons, and persons with permanent kidney failure
Medicaid	Medical insurance for the needy	Persons of any age who meet eligibility requirements set by each state within federal guidelines
Supplemental Security Income (SSI)	Income supplementation for the needy	Persons who are 65 and older or blind or disabled who meet eligibility requirements set by each state within federal guidelines

some 28 million are retirees and dependents and over 4 million more are disabled. Survivors benefits go to almost 20 percent of those who receive Social Security, including around 5.5 million widows, widowers, and dependent parents and nearly 2 million children.[20] In 1992 the average monthly check is $629, with $1088 the maximum monthly benefit for a worker retiring at 65.

In a reversal of the trend since Social Security began, Congress in 1983 voted to raise the age at which a retired person can begin to receive full benefits (though ever so gradually in order to soften the blow for those who have been anticipating retirement at 65). From 2000 to 2005, the age will rise by two months a year to 66, and between 2017 and 2022, to 67. Furthermore, a person who delays his or her own retirement beyond 65 will benefit in two ways: First, for most people the added years are at a higher earnings level, resulting in higher benefits; and second, for each year worked between full retirement age and 70, benefits are increased by a set percentage, depending on year of birth (from 1 percent if born in 1916 or earlier, up to 8 percent if born in 1943 or later).[21] In addition, early retirement benefits will be reduced gradually, until those born in 1960 or later will receive 70 percent of their full retirement if they retire at 62 instead of the current 80 percent.

Social Security is financed by a special payroll tax, authorized by the Federal Insurance Contributions Act (FICA), that is levied on all wages earned up to a certain limit. The current maximum tax rate is 15.3 percent (split equally between employee and employer). The maximum amount of income subject to FICA stands at $55,500 in 1992, with the excess up to $130,200 taxed an additional 1.45 percent (the Medicare share of the Social Security tax rate). Thus a person who earns the maximum in 1992 would make $5328.90 in FICA contributions, an amount matched by his or her employer for a total of $10,657.80. It is interesting to note that when Social Security began in 1935, the payroll tax was one percent each from employer and employee on a maximum of $3000 of earnings (or $30 each). In 1951 the maximum tax paid by each was still only $30 a year, and in 1969 the rate had climbed to only 4.8 percent on a maximum of \$7,800 (or \$374 each per year).[22] Clearly recent inflation, improved benefits, and larger numbers of beneficiaries have required rapid increases in the taxes that support Social Security.

Social Security tax dollars are put into three trust funds for retirement and survivors benefits, Medicare, and disability insurance. Until fairly recently, the major portion of the money that came in was used in the same year for payments to nonworking beneficiaries (the "pay-as-you-go" aspect of the system). Whatever was left over—historically a relatively small amount—stayed in the trust funds to meet future needs. With the movement of the baby boomers through the work force, however, these surpluses are growing rapidly and will continue to do so into the next century. In fact, according to the Social Security Administration, each hour the agency takes in \$8 million more than it pays out,[23] over \$1.3 billion every week! The surplus is projected to reach more than \$1 trillion by the end of the century and as much as \$10 or even \$12 trillion by 2020 (under "optimistic" assumptions, assumptions that are seriously questioned by some critics of Social Security). The questions of what to do with this vast sum of money, whether it will really be there when needed by the baby boomers, and how it should be counted in federal budget calculations have generated some of the most heated recent debate in aging policy.

The calculation of a person's benefits is a complex and confusing process far beyond the scope of this book to relate.[24] Suffice it to say that several formulas are used based on the person's history of earnings. These formulas are manipulated in various ways to arrive at the Principal Insurance Amount (PIA), the full benefit one receives upon retirement at 65. In a particularly vivid example of the conflation of the adequacy and equity principles, the formulas used are weighted so that individuals with lower average earnings will receive a relatively larger rate of return than those who have earned more (adequacy). Still, the higher one's lifetime earnings, the higher the PIA; and years of no work or low-paid work will result in a lower PIA (equity). For example, a person who was 45 in 1991, earned $20,000 in 1990, had steady lifetime earnings, and retired at full retirement age (66) would receive approximately $863 a month in benefits; a person with identical characteristics except for earning $50,000 in 1990 would get $1392.[25] Thus, although the amount of one's benefits is not directly proportional to one's prior earnings, it is related to them.

The cost-of-living adjustment (COLA) mentioned earlier is based on the average Consumer Price Index (CPI). In 1991 the COLA was 5.4 percent and in 1992 was 3.7 percent. A favorite target of those who want to hold down spending, the COLA has resisted attack except for a six-month delay in implementation as part of the 1983 Social Security "bail-out." Interestingly, the COLA adjustment begins in the year a person becomes 62, even if he or she does not receive benefits until 65 or older.[26]

A retired person can work and still receive Social Security benefits, subject to an earnings limit in effect until age 70 (the "retirement test"). In 1992, the annual limit was $7440 for those under 65 and $10,200 for those 65-69. Earning more than this amount causes benefits to be offset by $1 for each $2 above the limit for those under 65 and by $1 for each $3 for those 65-69.

Disability Insurance (DI)

Disability coverage was added in 1956 for workers 50-64 and extended in 1960 to those under 50 (nonworkers qualify under the Social Security record of a covered spouse or parent). As with retirement benefits, the amount of disability benefits is tied to average lifetime earnings; in 1991 the average payment was $587 to a single person and $1022 to a disabled worker with a family. The definition of disability used is stringent: "You will be considered disabled if you are unable to do any kind of work for which you are suited, and if your inability to work is expected to last for at least a year or result in death."[27] The screening process is thorough and fairly lengthy; the Social Security Administration says that it usually takes sixty to ninety days, but in May 1991 the wait was as long as seven months because of staff shortages discussed below.

Supplemental Security Income (SSI)

One of the two means-tested portions of Social Security, Supplemental Security Income (SSI) represents the federalization in 1972 (implemented in 1974) of three federal-state programs that aid special groups of the poor: the elderly, the blind, and the disabled. SSI is administered by the Social Security Administration and is funded out of general revenues (not payroll taxes). It provides uniform eligibility requirements and minimum benefit levels nationwide and guarantees its recipients—the most needy among the elderly and the disabled—a basic level of income by supplementing whatever they receive from other sources. Thus SSI is the main mechanism in the public arena today for explicit implementation of the social adequacy principle (commonly known by the increasingly pejorative term *welfare*).

The basic SSI benefit in 1992 was $422 monthly for one person and $633 for a couple, subject to reduction depending on other income; some states increase this basic amount. In 1991, a nonworking single person qualified for SSI with an income less than $427 ($630 for a couple); some states allow more. For employed individuals the income limit was $899 a month, for couples $1305; the first $65 a month in wages is not counted, nor is half the amount over $65. In addition to the income eligibility test, an assets limit of $2000 per individual and $3000 per couple also applies, excluding home, car, some personal belongings, burial plot, and up to $1500 in burial funds.[28]

Although it was hoped at its inception that SSI would serve to bring all those below the poverty level at least up to it, such has not been the case for various reasons. The means test and its attendant "welfare" implications prevent some people from applying, and others who do apply are probably discouraged by the complexity of the process, the lengthy application, and the requirement to "requalify" every year. A major problem, however, seems to be that the people who most need the program do not know about it, whatever the reason; and the agencies that might be expected to inform them say they do not have the staff to do so. Estimates of those eligible for the program who do not apply because they are unaware of its existence run as high as one-half to two-thirds.

Adding to the problem is the fact that in a number of states, qualifying for SSI enables one to receive Medicaid, food stamps, and help with energy costs, none of which may be available unless one is receiving SSI. And if the recipient should happen to live "in the household of another," benefits are reduced by one-third regardless of the person's financial situation. As with Social Security, SSI seems to favor couples over those who live alone, especially unfortunate in this particular program because, as we have seen, the elderly who live alone (especially women) are the most financially vulnerable. In 1988, for example, couples received a guaranteed $532 a month from SSI, or 90 percent of the federal poverty standard; for a person living alone, the benefit was $354 a month, only 75 percent of the poverty threshold.[29] It should be noted also that though SSI does provide a measure of security to the elderly poor, many of the near-poor, should they suffer some financial crisis that consumes their "cushion," would remain ineligible under current standards on the basis of their OASI benefits alone.

Some Problems

Before looking at the last part of Social Security, Hospital Insurance (HI), some further problems with the parts just described need to be considered. A particularly vexing issue that is often pointed to as evidence of the inequity of Social Security concerns dependents' benefits, and particularly treatment of the working wife. This is an issue that will become even more important as the increasing number of women in the work force reach retirement age. The basic concern is that the current structure of Social Security benefits favors couples over singles and single-income couples over those who both work. The reason is that benefits are received by *families* but taxes are paid by *individuals*. Thus two workers with identical work histories will have paid the same amount into the system, but at

92

retirement, when the single worker receives only his or her benefits, the married worker will receive full benefits and his or her spouse will receive a dependent benefit, which is equal to half of the full benefits. Thus the married worker realizes a 50 percent greater return on his or her tax dollars than does the single worker. Furthermore, single persons must pay the portion of Social Security tax that supports dependent and survivors benefits even if they never have either.

When both spouses work, similar inequities arise. A working wife can receive benefits based on either her own work record or her husband's, but not both or any combination of the two. Generally, women's earnings are lower than men's; thus also are their FICA taxes and benefits, often even lower than the spouse's dependent benefit. In this case it is clearly to the woman's advantage to take the spouse's dependent benefit. Again, however, compare this couple to one with an identical earning history for the husband but no earning history for the wife. The two couples would receive exactly the same benefit though the first couple had paid significantly more in taxes (the wife's share) with no increase in benefits to show for it. And if the income earned by both husband and wife (assuming now roughly equal pay for them) is the same as that of another couple whose income was earned solely by the husband, the combined benefits of the working couple will be *less* than those of the second couple even though they paid in the same amount in taxes (because the dependent's benefit entitles the nonworking wife to half of her husband's primary benefit, which in this example is higher for the working husband than for the working couple). Furthermore, when these two women both become widows, the nonworking woman will be considerably better off because she will get 100 percent of her husband's benefit!

As troublesome as is the inequity between various types of beneficiaries *within* a generation, the greatest controversy revolves around the rather noticeable differences in benefits *between* generations. Because of a number of factors, workers who are retired already or will retire soon stand to receive much

93

higher benefits relative to their contributions than will those who retire farther into the future. Michael Boskin offers a concrete example: A member of the first group of retirees covered by Social Security left the work force at 65 in 1940. If he or she had had average earnings and had put into a private annuity at prevailing interest rates the total employee-employer contribution to Social Security, this retiree could have *expected* an annual annuity payment of $6.59. He or she actually *received* from Social Security $270.60, leaving $264.01 as a "transfer" from younger workers still paying Social Security taxes. If the comparison of benefits is extended over the expected life-span at the time, the retiree would have contributed only 2.3 percent of what he or she ended up receiving.[30]

This situation is most apparent in the first group of retirees because they did not work long enough for their contributions to amount to a very large sum of money and the system did not have enough time to become "fully funded," so to speak, before they retired. Boskin points out, however, that the same thing happens each time there is an increase in either the payroll tax or benefits.[31] If Social Security tax rates go up, the amount of money coming in from current workers rises, which often leads to an increase in benefits for those already retired with no further contribution from them. And because they did not pay the higher tax rate used to provide the increase in their benefits, they reap a "windfall." Boskin applies his analysis to current retirees and concludes that they and their employers have paid in only about one-fifth of what they receive in benefits, including interest.[32] Expressed differently, about four years after retiring, the average retiree in 1986 would have used up all the benefits expected from employee-employer contributions (again with interest). Clearly, Social Security retirement benefits have proved to be a very good deal for those who have retired up to now and who will retire in the near future.

Why is everyone not overjoyed at this exceptional situation? Primarily because, looked at from one point of view, Social Security retirement benefits represent an inequitable "intergenerational transfer." That is, the program appears to direct a substantial portion of the earnings of current workers—including those of low and middle income—to retirees, some of whom have far greater net worth (and perhaps actual income) than the workers, money the older persons did not really contribute to the system. In short, the poorer of the current generation are being compelled to transfer disproportionately large sums of money into a fund that supports, in addition to those who really need the support, the wealthier of the previous generation, hardly a fair arrangement in many people's eyes. Ken Dychtwald and Joe Flower, for example, cite estimates that 500,000 to 600,000 millionaires are recipients of Social Security benefits.[33] Certainly they paid into the system and deserve a *fair* return on that money. As we have seen, however, they are getting a return far in excess of any reasonable investment (particularly one with as little risk, at least for today's retirees, as Social Security), and the pay-as-you-go nature of the system means their payments actually are coming from today's workers, virtually all of whom are significantly poorer than are the retired millionaires. Recall also that Social Security taxes are paid on only the first $55,500 of income, and note further that only *wages* are subject to FICA. "Passive" income—that from investments—generates no money for Social Security, and the income of most wealthy people, at least after they accumulate enough to be considered "wealthy," comes largely from this source.

This last point suggests another problem, this one concerning the "retirement test" described earlier. In addition to paying no FICA tax on dividend and interest income, a retired person with such assets loses no Social Security benefits whatsoever because of that income. The less wealthy retiree between 65 and 70, however, who is willing to go on working in order to remain financially independent (or who has to work to survive), loses $1 in benefits for every $3 earned over the limit of $10,200. Considerable support exists for repealing the retirement test, because it appears to penalize those older people whose retirement income results from work rather than from investments. Some of these criticisms of Social Security, the major implement of public policy concerning the elderly, will

95

receive further consideration in subsequent chapters. Several other problems, though, can be mentioned here.

For instance, it should also be noted, as recent critics of Social Security are fond of doing, that the payroll tax is a "flat" tax, unlike the progressive income tax (which itself was significantly "flattened" in recent tax reform). That is, Social Security favors those who earn higher wages because workers pay the same percentage tax whether they earn $10,000 a year or $100,000. Individuals with higher incomes benefit further from the ceiling on taxable income because the more they earn, the lower their relative tax. The actual effect of the ceiling is basically to produce a progressively lower tax rate the higher one's earnings, perhaps the ultimate regressive tax.

Another problem with Social Security as currently structured is not often mentioned by those who raise the issues above, but it is one that should be of considerable concern to Christians. Illustrating the tension mentioned above between the fundamental principles underlying Social Security, Wilbur Cohen, one of its founders and for decades a major figure in social policy, is quoted as having said, "We need a system which creates no invidious distinctions based on income"—that is, a system of "universal entitlement," in which all persons are understood to be entitled to a certain level of benefits. This statement reflects the principle of social adequacy. Somewhat paradoxically, however, Cohen went on to add that it should also be a system "where an individual is entitled to receive benefits on the basis of his general contribution to society"—that is, a system in which those who produce more deserve more reward. This second assertion expresses the principle of individual equity.[34] Although Cohen's failure to use gender-neutral language can be excused because of the different era in which he spoke, it nonetheless reveals a basic flaw in his statement: By evaluating a person's "contribution to society" and thus claim upon benefits from Social Security strictly in terms of wages earned, Cohen failed to credit as a contribution the role women have traditionally played (and some still do) at home and as volunteers. Nor did he acknowledge that the amount of one's contribution (in purely financial terms) is often limited by factors beyond one's own efforts, as for example by the documented lower wages of females and people of color. Margolis rightly concludes, "Cohen mistakenly assumed an invariable connection between one's merit and one's salary,"[35] a common mistake in this society.

Social Security is not without its operational problems as well, partly the result of the current fiscal climate. Gwendolyn King, Commissioner of the Social Security Administration, speaking to the annual conference of the National Council on the Aging in May 1991 at Miami Beach, pointed out that 600,000 beneficiaries are added to the Social Security rolls per year, but the staff of her agency has been reduced 21 percent since 1981. A demand from another speaker that the Bush administration make funds available immediately to hire 6000 new employees led King to comment that she "salivates" at the thought of what she could do with that much new staff.

At the same meeting Charles Schottland, a *former* Social Security Commissioner, outlined the history of these reductions. Social Security was a favorite target of Ronald Reagan and his economic advisors, according to Schottland, and they initially attacked the program by changes in the law, such as elimination of the burial benefit and the survivors benefit for 18 to 21 year olds. When Congress said "no more" to this approach, the Reagan administration shifted to the budget reductions King had mentioned. According to Schottland, this has resulted in an "unethical, disgraceful, and illegal" situation in which, as noted above, people who unquestionably qualify for benefits (especially disability and SSI) do not get them for months because the agency does not have enough staff to handle claims and to disseminate information. A perceived lack of concern about "customer satisfaction" has prompted a wave of complaints from older people and their advocates, as well as a promise from the Social Security Administration to add telephone lines and to embark on more effective customer-relations training and monitoring.

All of these problems and others will play a role in the critiques

97

of current public policy to be examined in later chapters. Before leaving this section, however, an encouraging word is appropriate. Despite all the problems mentioned here and to be considered later, the vast majority of the American people are strongly behind the Social Security program, even though many also have serious reservations about its future. For example, the results of an extensive survey published in 1990[36] show overwhelming support among those interviewed for maintaining or increasing funding for the major Social Security programs, as well as for others such as Food Stamps and Aid to Families with Dependent Children. With regard to Medicare, 97.5 percent favored increasing or maintaining expenditures. The programs that are seen as assisting mainly older people— Medicare, Social Security retirement pensions, and SSI—all received majority support for *raising* expenditures. As for funding, over 80 percent said they were satisfied with Social Security taxes; almost 90 percent of those opposed any spending cuts; and 71 percent were willing to pay even higher taxes if necessary. Americans of all age groups, by a margin of almost nine to one, want Social Security to continue. Social Security in fact appears to have achieved what little else in this country has been able to gain—overwhelming support across race, age, class, gender, geographic, and party lines.

Hospital Insurance (HI)

Insurance against illness was a late addition to the Social Security package, coming into existence in 1965 as Titles XVIII and XIX of the Social Security Act, known today as Medicare and Medicaid. Hospital Insurance is now second only to old-age pensions in federal social insurance expenditures. Indeed, just as grave concern has been voiced with regard to the long-term solvency of Social Security, so numerous commentators from all political persuasions have expressed similar worries about Medicare. In 1989, Medicare paid more than $100 billion for the covered medical care of 32.5 million beneficiaries, an expenditure that is expected to approach $225 billion by 2005 (seven years *before* the baby boomers begin to be eligible). According to the "intermediate" projections of the Social Security Administration, Medicare may become a deficit operation as early as 1993, and its reserves will be used up by 1998.[37] Given the rapidly escalating medical costs in this country, it comes as no surprise that the health of a program of this magnitude should cause concern.

Medicare

The official name of this program is a good indication of its basic thrust. One might expect HI to stand for *Health* Insurance, not *Hospital* Insurance, but Medicare came into being in response to rapidly rising hospital costs and use by the elderly. Hospital benefits, or Part A, are available automatically at 65 to all those who qualify for Social Security. This part is "free" in that no extra charge is levied for the basic coverage. There are, however, significant "out-of-pocket" costs, such as (in 1992) a deductible of $652; a hospital copayment of $163 a day for the 61st to 90th days and $326 for the 91st to 150th (Medicare pays nothing after that); and a copayment for post-hospital care in a skilled nursing facility of $81.50 a day from the 21st to the 100th day (the patient pays everything after that).[38]

Outpatient ("routine") medical care, or Part B, on the other hand, must be purchased separately, though on a subsidized basis. In addition to a $100 annual deductible, the 1992 monthly premium for Part B of $31.80 will rise to $46.10 by 1995. Congress has mandated that premiums are to cover 25 percent of the costs of the program, and although Part B is voluntary, few elderly opt out of it (only about .003 of one percent at any given time).[39]

The health-care delivery system in the United States is geared toward the needs of a young to middle-aged population, in which acute health problems amenable to fairly quick treatment and cure are the norm.[40] Medicare developed out of such a system and, probably not incidentally, also was designed at a time when problems specific to the elderly were much less well known than today. Thus it is not surprising that its very structure and name ("Hospital Insurance") reflect a preoccupation with

99

short-term, acute, *curable* health problems. Such a reflection in late-twentieth-century America, however, is akin to that seen in antique mirrors: The source is recognizable, but the current image is not very helpful. As our population continues to age, long-term, chronic illnesses become more prevalent, and these are precisely the ones Medicare currently fails to cover.

In fact, the list of "expenses not covered by Medicare" in the Health Care Financing Administration's *1991 Guide to Health Insurance for People with Medicare* (p. 14) reads like a list of what one *would* expect to be provided by a program expressly for the elderly! In particular, Medicare does not pay for "custodial nursing home care, most outpatient prescription drugs, dental care or dentures [one-half of the elderly have no natural teeth, and a little more than two-fifths of these do not have well-fitting dentures], checkups and most routine immunizations, routine foot care, and examinations for and the cost of eyeglasses and hearing aids."

Furthermore, as the necessity for "cost containment" came to dominate policy considerations toward the end of the 1970s, Medicare instituted a "prospective payment" system, in which hospitals are reimbursed according to a standard schedule regardless of actual costs incurred. A schedule of 473 Diagnosis Related Groups (DRGs) tells hospitals how much they will be reimbursed for various procedures based on the relative complexity of the treatment and the average cost per patient for hospitals in a given geographic region. A hospital will get neither more nor less regardless of the actual cost of care (a formula provides some reimbursement for treatment that exceeds one-and-one-half times the DRG allowance).

This approach has led to shorter hospital stays and consequent savings, but not without negative results as well. For example, patients whose care may become expensive are increasingly refused admission, especially if their ability to pay is limited or absent. This practice has led to tremendous pressure on public hospitals, which usually end up with these patients. Also, because it has become financially advantageous (if not always actually necessary) for hospitals to discharge many

100

patients earlier than had been done before, the charge that patients are sent home "quicker and sicker" has often been made. Again, older people with more resources are able to purchase needed follow-up care of various kinds, but the less financially secure often have to fend for themselves, literally if they live alone. And because patients discharged so quickly require more follow-up outpatient care, the savings to Medicare under Part A may well be consumed by increases in Part B payments.

Medicare does provide almost "universal" coverage to the elderly, but as we have seen in other areas, so also here the poor elderly fare worse than those better off. People with more financial resources are better able to afford the items that Medicare does not cover, many of which are virtual necessities for any decent quality of life in old age. In addition, because of the other "out-of-pocket" expenses required—such as deductibles, coinsurance, and Part B premiums, all of which are fixed charges with no consideration given to ability to pay—the poor elderly are hit hardest, especially given the recent trend upward in all of these "cost-sharing" measures as a way to reduce the government's costs. Other less obvious and less quantifiable inequities exist as well. For example, the wealthier elderly in general know how to "use the system" better, can get to the doctor more easily, and usually live in areas with better medical service available.

Some of these problems are supposed to be addressed by Medicaid, the other component of the publicly funded health-care system of this country, and some of them are. But Medicaid is not without its own problems.

Medicaid

Medicaid is a means-tested program that teams the federal government with the states to provide health care for the poor. One way of thinking of the original intent of Medicaid is to see it as "Medicare for the poor." That is, just as Medicare was supposed to make the health-care system accessible to the elderly, so Medicaid was intended to open the door to quality

care for those of *any* age who could not afford it. Still, Medicaid
picks up health-care expenses not covered by Medicare for only
29 percent of the nation's poor elderly and 8 percent of the
near-poor elderly.[41] The ongoing problem of accessibility is well
illustrated by the 1989 law providing that elderly and disabled
persons eligible for Medicaid can have that program pay their
Medicare premiums, deductibles, and copayments, a potential
benefit of as much as $1,000 for a year in which a person is
hospitalized. Of the 4.2 million people estimated to be eligible
for the program, however, around 2.3 million have not applied,
many because they have not heard of the program and others
because the government officials whom they ask tell them they
know nothing about it. Furthermore, neither of the federal
agencies responsible for the program wants to spend the money
or has the staff to pursue those who have not applied, and the
states see the task of signing up eligible persons as the federal
government's responsibility.[42]

As mentioned above, the main purpose of Medicaid was to
provide medical care for the poor of all ages, and it still serves
that purpose to some extent (for the poor elderly, the payment
of Medicare premiums is a major means of doing this).
Medicaid, however, has come to be disproportionately the
provider of long-term care for the elderly. Medicare covers only
acute care, and private insurance for long-term care is far from
adequate in terms of affordability and coverage. Thus the
nursing-home benefit of Medicaid has taken on increasing
importance for the elderly. In fact, Medicaid pays about 55
percent of all nursing-home costs in the United States, with only
two percent paid by Medicare and one percent by private
insurance (families still pay around 42 percent of the costs of
long-term care).[43] In the decade of the 1980s, Medicaid
expenditures for nursing-home care more than doubled from
$9.7 billion in 1980 to $20.6 billion in 1989.[44]

Medicaid thus provides to the poor elderly a way of obtaining
long-term care for which they are unable to pay. But what of
older people who are not technically "poor" but still lack the
resources to pay $30,000 a year or more to a nursing home?

Because Medicaid is a program to provide medical care to the poor, one must be poor in order to receive such assistance. And the way people who do not start out poor become so is to "spend down" their assets until they reach a limit set by each state (within certain federal parameters, which in 1991 were a minimum of $13,296 and a maximum of $66,480, excluding the value of the home, its furnishings, and personal belongings). The amount of monthly income the non-institutionalized spouse can keep is also determined by the states, again within federal limits of $856 and $1,662.

If the institutionalized person is single with no dependents (the most likely scenario, as we have seen, because three-fourths of nursing home residents are women, and three-fourths of them are widows when admitted), the nursing home receives all of her income, Social Security included, except for a monthly allowance of $30 to $50 for personal items. A recent study suggests that as many as three-fourths of all elderly people 75 and over who live alone run the risk of spending down to impoverishment during their first year in a nursing home,[45] and the Special Committee on Aging of the U.S. Senate has estimated that paying for only 13 weeks of nursing-home care would impoverish one out of three elderly households.

This point recalls the discussion in chapter 2 concerning long-term care, seen by many as the next major battleground in the extension of benefits to the elderly (though many younger people as well would benefit directly from help in this particular area). For example, Stanley J. Brody calls long-term care "the third economic catastrophe" facing the elderly to which public policy must respond (the first two major needs of the elderly were basic subsistence, provided by Social Security, and acute medical care, provided by Medicare/Medicaid). According to Brody, "Repeatedly the need for continuity of care has been called a catastrophic need based on both the individual's and family's involvement in long-term care."[46] A first step in responding to this need was taken by Congress in 1990 with the passage of the Medicaid Frail Elderly Home and Community Care Act, which provides $580 million over five years to make it

103

easier for states to offer long-term care services to the very frail elderly and people with Alzheimer's disease in their own homes and communities instead of nursing homes. Advocates for the elderly see this action as an important precedent that may clear the way for a more far-reaching national long-term care program.[47]

One may be tempted to say (dismissing as hypersensitivity the "stigma" many people associate with being poor enough to have to turn to the state for assistance), "Well, at least everyone is guaranteed long-term care by Medicaid at some point, even if it means using up all one's assets first." It is important to keep in mind, however, that nursing-home beds are not an unlimited commodity, and because Medicaid reimburses at a lower rate than a facility can demand from private-pay residents, many nursing homes are reluctant to accept Medicaid patients. It is also safe to say that one gets what one pays for, and the facilities that do readily take large numbers of Medicaid patients are unlikely to be the finest in the land. At any rate, Medicaid recipients rarely get their pick of their community's nursing homes.

THE OLDER AMERICANS ACT
AND THE "AGING NETWORK"

One further element in the aging-policy arsenal of the United States deserves mention here.[48] The Older Americans Act (OAA), first enacted in 1965 and reauthorized (i.e., reviewed, amended, and renewed) by Congress more than ten times since, provides a wide range of programs and services for the elderly through the Administration on Aging (AoA). The AoA, which is located within the Department of Health and Human Services, was intended to serve as the central focus of the nation's attempts to meet the needs of the elderly. The programs and services authorized under the OAA are far-ranging in their scope, though they have been criticized as directed more at enhancing the lives of middle-income elderly than at meeting the real needs of the poor. The purpose of the Act was to fund programs and services that attempt to enable the elderly to remain independent members of their communities and to avoid institutionalization. Several of the congressional reauthorizations have aimed especially at strengthening services for minorities and for frail and disabled elderly. Service providers are not allowed to determine eligibility on the basis of income or to require payment, though they may request voluntary donations for nutrition and some supportive services.

One of the most significant results of the passage of the OAA was the creation of the "aging network," a multilevel organization established to administer the funds and to coordinate provision of the services authorized by the Act. On the *federal* level Congress amends the Act and appropriates funds, which then are administered by the AoA through its ten regional offices. The *states* (and territories) have 57 central offices or departments of aging that oversee aging programs within their jurisdictions. Most states are further divided into *local* planning and service areas, each under the guidance of one of the 672 Area Agencies on Aging (AAA) nationwide. Frequently the AAA will be part of the county government or located within some kind of multicounty council of government, leading to the appearance that many aging programs are functions of the counties and subjecting them to the political squabbles and turf battles that inevitably occur in that setting. In addition, because of the aging network's emphasis on coordination rather than direct provision of services, some observers have expressed concern about the growth of a large contingent of professional midlevel operatives that noted gerontologist Carroll Estes dubbed the "aging enterprise." These professionals sometimes seem more concerned with justifying the need for their own organizations and programs than with meeting the needs of the elderly.

Among the types of programs the OAA has made available are multipurpose senior centers; employment and job-training services; nutrition programs; in-home services such as homemaker assistance and respite care; adult day care; legal assistance; advocacy; prevention of elder abuse; and the Long-Term Care Ombudsman Program that investigates and resolves complaints by residents of long-term care facilities. Appropriations from Congress for the OAA have tended to be rather limited in light of the need, and thus AAAs have had to seek other sources of funding. This leads to a situation of considerable variation in the kinds of programs and services available from state to state and even from community to community and in the numbers of older people served, especially the poor, frail, rural, and minority elders the OAA targeted.

Despite the problems mentioned above, the Older Americans Act did focus attention on the needs of the nation's older citizens in a way that is at least potentially constructive. The reauthorization process has also periodically spotlighted these concerns and has given older persons and their advocates opportunities to express themselves on a wide range of issues. Although the administrative structure set up by the Act suffers from the tensions, ambiguities, and dispersal of power and authority inherent in the federal system, many of the programs and services made available through the AAAs truly improve the quality of life of many people whose existence would be much poorer without them. Greater support, primarily in the form of better funding, would enhance the ability of the aging network to accomplish the important mission it was originally given by Congress.

CHAPTER 4

CURRENT RESPONSES: ORGANIZATIONS RELATED TO THE ELDERLY

T he elderly are by no means merely passive recipients of public policy made for them by others. Recent years have seen the rise of numerous organizations of older Americans and their advocates. These groups, which are quite diverse and are devoted to a number of different ends, are increasing in prestige and power. Indeed, a commonly voiced fear is that because the elderly are becoming so numerous and vote in much higher proportions than any other age group, once they get really organized they will be able to vote themselves anything they want. Not surprisingly, those who share this fear have also organized to resist the perceived threat of "gray power" and to protest what they see as inequities in current public policy on aging. Three more elements will complete our examination of current responses to the dilemma caused by the "aging of America": a brief look at some of the organizations that speak for the elderly; a consideration of the validity of the fear just mentioned; and a summary of the views of those who see danger in the emphasis on the elderly in U.S. domestic policy.

ADVOCACY ORGANIZATIONS

The archetype of contemporary elderly organizations may well be the Townsend Movement, begun in the early 1930s by Francis E. Townsend, a California physician. Moved by the sight of three destitute old women scrounging for food, Townsend proposed a scheme of public assistance that would both assist elderly people in need by providing a pension of $200 a month to everyone over 60 and revitalize the Depression-devastated economy by requiring the pension to be spent in the United States within a month of receipt. "Townsend Clubs" flourished briefly (with 600,000 dues-paying members at the movement's height) but faded from the scene as the New Deal and preparation for World War II eased the country out of the Depression.[1]

The possibility of organizing older persons around causes of special interest to themselves had been shown to be feasible, however, and such organizing has not stopped since. In fact, according to one count in the early 1980s, when groups that limit membership to older persons are combined with those that are open to anyone but concentrate on issues of aging and the elderly, a total of around 1000 such organizations existed. There is no reason to think the number has declined in the past decade (this total does not include local chapters of national organizations, of which the AARP, for example, has over 4000).

Such advocacy groups tend to fall into several major categories. The largest are the mass-membership, general-purpose organizations like the American Association of Retired Persons (AARP); the National Council of Senior Citizens (NCSC), started in 1961 with support from the AFL-CIO and the Democratic National Committee to carry the banner against the American Medical Association in the fight for Medicare; and the Gray Panthers, founded as a coalition of older and younger people by Maggie Kuhn in 1970 when the United Presbyterian Church forced her to retire from its national staff. Next are groups composed of individuals who have retired from specific occupations, such as the National Association of Retired Federal Employees (NARFE) and the National Retired Teachers Association (NRTA). There are also many smaller bodies created to serve specific constituents among the elderly, including, for example, the National Council on the Black Aged and the National Indian Council on the Aging. Finally, a number of organizations consist primarily of *younger* people who have what might be called "professional" interest in aging and the elderly, such as the National Council on the Aging, the Gerontological Society of America, and the American Society on Aging.[2]

An Example: The American Association of Retired Persons (AARP)

Because it is the organization that is the largest, best known, and most often cited as illustrative of "elder power," the AARP serves well as an example of the potential impact of elder organizations.[3] In 1958 pioneer gerontologist Ethel Percy Andrus founded AARP from the National Retired Teachers Association (which in turn has since become part of AARP) to allow older people other than former teachers to take advantage of the services NRTA was offering to its members (mainly reduced-rate life insurance). Since its founding, AARP has grown steadily until today it numbers some 32 million individuals among its membership, about one-quarter of all the registered voters in the United States. A large majority of these people are white and from comfortable economic backgrounds. AARP has over 350,000 volunteers who offer a wide range of programs and services at more than 4000 local chapter offices.

In addition, the national organization provides a variety of goods and services through the mail, including the world's largest private discount prescription service, insurance (health, home, and auto), a travel service, an investment fund (with over $3.5 billion in deposits), and since 1988 a credit union. Also in 1988, the group's magazine, *Modern Maturity,* achieved the number-one ranking in the country in average circulation. With an annual budget approaching $250 million and a paid staff of 1300, AARP is headquartered in Washington, D.C., sharing with NRTA a modern eight-story office building that has its own ZIP code. The organization also has a legislative staff of 125 in Washington and 20 full-time lobbyists, with 20 more serving on the state level as advisors to volunteer lobbyists. Anyone 50 or older can become a part of all of this for an annual membership fee of only five dollars.[4] No wonder a number of people have expressed concern about the power such an organization might wield if intergenerational relationships develop into the conflict some have predicted.

Accomplishments and Problems

What have groups like AARP accomplished for the older citizens of the United States apart from the services and the sense of belonging they offer? A consensus seems to exist that NCSC played a significant role in the Medicare battle and in the passage of the 1972 amendments to Social Security and that AARP's vigorous support was important in the raising of the mandatory retirement age from 65 to 70 in 1978 and its elimination for almost all workers in 1986. AARP was also prominent in the opposition to the Medicare Catastrophic Coverage Act of 1988 that led to the act's repeal in 1989.

The "gray lobby's" political clout appears to be less than would be expected, however, given the numbers and the organization it supposedly has behind it.[5] Despite the "successes" just mentioned, for example, many observers think that the impetus for most major legislation beneficial to older persons has come from presidential administrations, members of Congress, or bureaucrats who have had their own reasons for proposing and pushing such programs.

Furthermore, little evidence exists that AARP and the other groups have been very successful in controlling or even influencing the way their members vote. In 1980 several major elder advocacy organizations strongly supported the presidential reelection bid of Jimmy Carter, yet a majority of older voters decided Ronald Reagan was the better candidate and voted for him in the same proportion as did younger voters.[6] In fact, 20 percent of the membership of AARP identify themselves as political independents, with the other 80 percent evenly divided between Democrats and Republicans. The general heterogeneity of the elderly discussed in chapter 2 must also be kept in mind, especially in AARP with its low membership age: The concerns and the interests of those barely over 50 tend to differ markedly from those over 80 (or even 70). As Jerry Gerber and his coauthors observe, even on issues that appear to be of common interest to older people, like Medicare and Social Security, "there are differences of opinion about obligations to the young, further government intervention in people's lives, and the responsibility of AARP to act with the interests of society as a whole in mind and not just those of its members."[7]

Another limitation of many of these organizations stems from a characteristic that is endemic to such groups—namely, a tendency to reflect the interests, concerns, and needs of their members (and their leaders). AARP, for example, is overwhelmingly middle-class and white, with only about three percent of its membership coming from minorities. Thus the concerns that AARP has addressed are by and large those of its members, such as the maintenance of Social Security benefit levels and, even more tellingly, elimination of mandatory retirement so that older persons can remain in their (fulfilling) careers. The poor (and especially women, who make up the majority of the elderly poor) have not been particularly well served. AARP, however, has recently begun a "Women's Initiative" (as well as a "Minority Affairs Initiative") and now affirms as part of its "mission" statement in *Modern Maturity* the organization's commitment to "health care and quality of life issues (with emphasis on older women and minorities)." Families U.S.A. (founded in 1980 as the Villers Foundation) is the only one of these groups, though, that targets the poor and vulnerable elderly, and it is a small organization with only a few lobbyists and policy specialists. Robert Hudson and Judith Gonyea evaluate this lack of concern on the part of the "gray lobby" rather harshly (and echo the situation to which the analysis in chapters 1 and 2 of this book pointed): "The differences in well-being in old age between men and women and between couples and unrelated individuals are of such magnitude that any analysis based on adequacy grounds would place the concerns of older women—to say nothing of older minority women—at center stage."[8]

Despite such shortcomings, however, these organizations do possess some subtle forms of power. Apart from whatever real

111

power they may wield, they often have good access to many politicians simply because the official can then say he or she did consult a representative body of the particular constituency of older persons; and as everyone with a product or point of view to sell knows, gaining access to the customer is the first step. Also, aging organizations often are sought out to present their membership's views in other major arenas of influence in policymaking today, such as the media, congressional hearings, and national conferences, thus gaining the opportunity to shape the issues.

Less admirable but equally effective is what Robert Binstock calls the "electoral bluff": Whether or not they can actually deliver large numbers of votes, elder advocacy groups have convinced many politicians that they can, and few lawmakers or other public officials are willing to run the risk of angering such a potentially potent constituency.[9] In fact, the greatest influence of such groups may be of a more negative nature, that is, in protecting certain benefits and perquisites of the elderly from reduction or elimination by cost-conscious legislators. Little doubt exists that vocal opposition from groups such as AARP and NCOA has influenced more than one member of Congress to vote against or at least moderate proposed cuts in Medicare benefits or increases in out-of-pocket costs (the rapid repeal of the Catastrophic Coverage Act of 1988 has already been mentioned). From the viewpoint of many elderly persons in this country, such accomplishments alone justify the existence of these organizations.

"GRAY POWER" AT THE POLLS

This look at organizations related to the elderly would not be complete without a deeper examination of an issue that arouses considerable anxiety among some younger people today—namely, the electoral power of today's older citizens, be it real or imagined. Given the demographics that by now are so familiar to us, the concern is that the elderly will be able to vote themselves anything they want, especially in the future as their proportion of the population grows. This concern is heightened by the documented fact that the elderly vote in much higher percentages than do younger age groups.[10] For example, in the 1980 presidential election, one-third of all voters were 55 or over, and 71 percent of those 55 to 64 voted, a slightly higher proportion than the 69 percent of persons 65 to 74 who cast ballots. This rate of voting by the elderly is much higher than the mere 36 percent of those 18 to 20 who went to the polls. Four years later, the youngest groups voted at only about half the rate of the oldest, and in 1986, history was made as, for the first time, the youngest group of voters (18 to 24) was outnumbered by the oldest (65 and older). In 1988, 69.3 percent of those 55 to 64 voted, 73 percent of those 65 to 74, and 62.2 percent of those 75 and older.

A neutral observer might ask why the impressive voting statistics of the elderly are held up as a virtual *indictment* of them. In other contexts the failure of younger people to go to the polls is deplored; yet in this debate, when the elderly do that which is at the heart of our whole system of government (and, indeed, in the process set an outstanding example for the young), their actions are seen to be in some way sinister, threatening to that very system, and totally self-serving. One is tempted to point out that groups that fear the power of the elderly at the polls could counter it very simply—by voting themselves!

At any rate, as was suggested above with regard to advocacy groups, the elderly, despite sharing the one common characteristic of age, are hardly more likely to vote as a monolithic bloc than are those, say, 18 to 35 or any other age. Granted, certain issues may be seen by the elderly as of greater importance to them, but they are unlikely to agree on what is the best way to deal with any of them. As pointed out in chapter 2, America's older population is quite heterogeneous, differing considerably in income, education, social status, health, life-style, and loyalties to various groups to which they have belonged earlier in their lives.

Furthermore, and often overlooked by those who decry the "poll power" of the elderly, very few candidates run explicitly on

113

what can be identified as an elders' issue or even elders' agenda. If some did, they would not be very likely to be elected on that basis; and even if they were elected, they would hardly be powerful enough as individuals to accomplish that agenda unless it were the will of the majority of the legislators. Even assuming, therefore, a totally self-interested attitude on the part of an elderly voter, it is far from clear exactly *what* would constitute the best (i.e., most self-serving) vote by an older person.

Any segment of a population as large absolutely and relatively as the elderly are becoming must be taken seriously, especially given their level of participation in elections. Over half of all older people live in eight states that represent 40 percent of the electoral votes needed for the presidency, and several of those states are growing rapidly, especially in their elderly populations. Any politician serious about high national office cannot ignore such facts. There appears to be little cause for grave concern, however, that the older citizens of this country are about to stage a "ballot box coup" and establish a gerontocracy that will rule with no concern for the needs of all Americans. When middle-age Democrats and Republicans cannot agree whether a particular candidate or policy is good or bad for the elderly or any other group, it is hard to see how simply turning 65 will erase their life-long differences. Christine Day, after exhaustive research on this issue, offers a judicious and significant conclusion:

> Older people . . . are deeply divided on aging policy issues, particularly along economic and partisan lines. Collectively, they are no more supportive of government benefits for the elderly than are younger adults. Thus, these findings contradict the idea that older people's political attitudes are group-interest based. They also dispute the notion that aging policy is fraught with conflict between the generations.[11]

CRITICS OF CURRENT AGING POLICY

Nonetheless, in recent years a number of vociferous critics of aging policy in the United States have begun to denounce what they perceive to be an unfair advantage currently given the elderly at the expense of other age groups. Before concluding our look at the responses generated by the aging of the United States, we need to consider briefly the main elements of the position taken by these critics.

The increasingly vocal "advocates for generational equity" have utilized various media to assert that, in the words of Harold Fey, retired editor of *The Christian Century,* "The disproportion of public funds paid to the elderly as over against payments and services to children is a scandal, but almost nobody is scandalized." Fey's conclusion reflects a position that appears to have wide support, both in government circles and also in the popular press: "It is simply not right for today's elderly to appropriate for themselves resources and prerogatives in a way that discriminates against their own children and grandchildren."[12]

Echoing this concern but also broadening it, Ken Dychtwald and Joe Flower offer an ominous prediction: "As more young Americans find themselves paying an increasing share of their limited incomes into a questionable Social Security system while they see growing numbers of elders doing well, there is likely to be a generational rebellion."[13] Phillip Longman, the first research director for Americans for Generational Equity, states the point even more bluntly: "The likely result" of the aging of our population and the altered dynamics of the relationship between the generations, "unless many fundamental trends are soon reversed, will be a war between young and old."[14]

An Example: Americans for Generational Equity (AGE)

Such critics are perhaps best illustrated by Americans for Generational Equity (AGE), an organization founded in 1985 expressly to spread the message stated in the preceding paragraph. The founders of AGE included Senator Dave Durenberger (Republican from Minnesota) and Representative James R. Jones (Democrat from Oklahoma), and its first pamphlet included a picture of a young family with the caption "Indentured Servants" and accompanying text that claimed that the American family has been sold into "financial slavery." Although the organization claims to have arisen in response to the increasing inequity between the generations, some observers have suggested instead that "it was AGE, in fact, that *created* the notion that the problem of inadequate societal resources for children was a product of excessive benefits for the aged."[15] AGE is funded mainly by insurance companies and major corporations that face large FICA contributions and growing pension pressures. Several conservative think-tanks are represented on its board, and it receives funds from the Cato Institute, an organization working for the privatization of Social Security. AGE pursues such goals as increased private responsibility for income security in old age and a streamlined Social Security system, without which it predicts the inevitability of the "generational warfare" mentioned above as young and old are forced to compete for their fair share of a shrinking resource pie.

The "Generational Equity" Critique of Current Aging Policy

Among the various criticisms of current aging policy leveled by proponents of generational equity, the one that probably strikes the most responsive chord in younger people is the claim that benefits for the elderly are responsible for the deplorable situation of many of the nation's children. AGE and its partisans make heavy use of this argument. As is sadly familiar to everyone by now, one American child in five lives in poverty (half of all African American children), and by the end of the decade, the number will be one in four if present trends continue.[16] Samuel H. Preston is commonly credited with focusing attention on this issue in a 1984 article entitled "Children and the Elderly in the U.S." To make his case, Preston cites some of the same kinds of data presented in earlier chapters of this book concerning poverty rates among the elderly and children, health-care costs, and voting patterns. He concludes, "Whereas expenditure on the elderly can be thought of mainly as consumption, expenditure on the young is a combination of consumption and investment."[17] Because the elderly no longer produce, no return can be expected on resources devoted to them. Children, however, will repay money spent on them because they can be expected eventually to contribute to "the future productive capacity of the U.S."[18] Near the end of his article, Preston asserts that he does "not want to paint the elderly as the villains of the piece" and declares that he is using them "largely for comparison" in order to express his concern about the plight of children. In the very next sentence, however, he says, "Nevertheless, it is unrealistic simply to wish away the possibility that there is a direct competition between the young and the old for society's resources."[19] This claim has become a central contention of those who predict a coming struggle between the generations.

Of course, the generations expected to participate in the greatly feared "intergenerational wars" are not just the elderly and *children*. Numerous critics of current public policy foresee major conflict also between people who are older now and that mass of 75 million persons who will become old during the next half-century, the baby boomers. The arena of battle here is usually the Social Security program, in terms first of retirement benefits and then of health care. Peter G. Peterson, Secretary of Commerce under Richard Nixon, is a good representative of this concern. Indeed, Peterson basically places the blame for America's slide from preeminence in the global economy to excessive expenditures on the elderly.[20] The essential requirement to restore our role as world economic leader is to reduce such programs. Peterson presents an agonizing litany of the economic failures of the United States over the past several decades and the frightening prospects ahead in the next several. Among a number of specific dangers he cites, he singles out one in particular: "Our budget-cutting efforts during the 1980s have failed because they have allowed continued growth in the one type of spending—for entitlement benefits—that had already risen to unprecedented heights."[21] He concludes that "in any summary discussion of America's prospects in the near, the medium, and the long term, there is one theme that must be emphasized above all others: the indissoluble bond between the

117

economic behavior of one decade or generation and the economic well-being of the next decade or generation."[22] Among his concrete proposals is that "we must above all slow the growth in non-means-tested entitlements, starting with a reform of benefit indexing."[23]

Illustrated in Peterson's approach are several of the major criticisms of Social Security. We see, for example, the threat to the future well-being of the country perceived by some to be endemic in a program that is committed to paying benefits to a rapidly expanding pool of eligible recipients at a time when huge federal budget deficits imperil economic health. Critics of Social Security further claim that funds are being transferred not to the most needy but largely to the middle class or, what is worse, even to the wealthy who do not need them. Elimination of the "universality" of Social Security and greater emphasis on means-tested targeting of the poor would result in more efficient distribution of public funds to those truly in need of them. Another frequent criticism is that the burden of financing the system is unfairly borne because of the regressive nature of the FICA tax. Of course, virtually all of the concerns expressed by advocates of generational equity are made worse, and the fears about the future they voice are made more frightening, by the serious economic woes the United States is experiencing currently.

Underlying the criticism of Social Security (indeed, of practically *all* aging policy) by many proponents of generational equity is an abiding antipathy to government intervention in any area of life and the accompanying desire to shift support of the elderly to the family and the private sector. Such views often lead to proposals to "privatize" old-age insurance, that is, to eliminate compulsory participation in Social Security and to allow workers to invest on their own in whatever financial instruments they determine will best provide for their old age. This position is often supported by appeals to the "unfair rate of return" its advocates believe Social Security yields, as well as to the "coercive" nature of compulsory participation. Depending on the particular proposal, privatization can mean shifting provi-

118

sion of old age security from the government either to the marketplace (to be purchased by individuals) or to voluntary groups, such as family, church, and civic groups of various kinds (to be voluntarily provided), or to some combination of the two.[24] It should be noted that many advocates of privatization do allow for some type of means-tested government program to support the "truly needy." Also, not all critics of Social Security advocate privatization as the only solution to current (and future) difficulties.

Also integral to the position of critics of current aging policy are quite legitimate worries about the future of health care in the United States. People over the age of 65 account for about one-third of all health-care expenditures annually, and the growth in the elderly population suggests that, barring changes in current policy, such costs will only grow. It is undeniable that the health care of children and young adults is inadequate, often because they simply do not have access to such care. Concerns have also been voiced, similar to those raised about Social Security retirement benefits, that when today's young people attain the age of Medicare eligibility, benefits will be markedly lower (if the system has not gone bankrupt). Advocates of generational equity, who see the elderly as a whole as no longer particularly needy or facing major financial obstacles to health care, therefore contend that continued increases in health-care spending on the elderly (especially the "old-old," who utilize health care resources at an especially high rate)[25] unfairly burden the young in at least three ways: Such spending depletes the future assets of Medicare, imposes onerous taxation upon younger workers, and leads to disproportionate concentration of health-care research and technology on ailments that afflict primarily the elderly.

These types of concerns have led to a number of proposals for rationing health care on the basis of age, one of the most controversial aspects of the generational equity movement. Most commentators agree that health care in the United States has always been rationed informally through a number of mechanisms, but calls for official policy that would limit medical care

119

on an explicit basis such as age alone represent a marked change in public debate. Probably the best known of such proposals is that of Daniel Callahan, a philosopher who directs the Hastings Center, a leading bioethical think-tank. Callahan argues that a serious rethinking of the meaning of aging and old age is necessary. Out of his attempt at this reconceptualization comes the concrete proposal that medical care should be limited for those who have reached a "natural life span," that is, "one in which life's possibilities have on the whole been achieved and after which death may be understood as a sad, but nonetheless relatively acceptable event."[26]

Although the concept of a natural life-span resembles the biblical notion of dying "full of years" and possesses some merit, Callahan's suggestion provoked great controversy on two major points. First, he specified a particular age for the natural life-span: by their "late 70s or early 80s" for most people. Second, Callahan advocated the use of the natural life-span as the criterion for three specific proposals:

> 1. Government has a duty, based on our collective social obligations, to help people live out a natural life span, but not actively to help extend life medically beyond that point. . . .
> 2. Government is obliged to develop, employ, and pay for only that kind and degree of life-extending technology necessary for medicine to achieve and serve the end of a natural life span. . . .
> 3. Beyond the point of a natural life span, government should provide only the means necessary for the relief of suffering, not life-extending technology.[27]

Based on the widespread negative reaction to Callahan's suggestions, it seems safe to say that the United States is not likely to implement explicit age-based rationing of health care in the immediate future. As Robert Binstock has observed, however, "The substantial attention that such proposals have received in serious public forums may be the clearest signal that American public policy on the aging is approaching an important crossroads."[28]

120

A Question of Leadership?

A fuller examination of the claims made by critics of current aging policy, as well as a response to them, will come later. At this point, perhaps the most important thing that can be said about the future of intergenerational relationships, especially as the baby boomers enter their old age, is that the direction such relationships take may very well depend on the kind of leaders who emerge and the tenor of the message those leaders convey to their peers. If those who gain the ears of the American people spread a message of conflict, fear, and animosity between young and old, the "age wars" predicted by some may occur. If, on the other hand, leaders at many levels and in many settings concentrate on the need for intergenerational cooperation, concern, and appreciation, it is at least plausible to hope that these more positive attitudes will be the fruit their rhetoric will bear.

An excellent role model for the second type of leader just mentioned is Maggie Kuhn, founder of the Gray Panthers and one of the best known and most effective advocates for the elderly. She evinces clearly the attitude needed: "A healthy society is one in which the elderly protect, care for, love and assist the younger ones to provide continuity and hope."[29] In fact, she sees the old and the young as natural allies because of five things they have in common: marginalization out of the mainstream of society; poverty, near-poverty, or looming threat of poverty because of not uncommon changes in family situation or health status; problems with drugs (though the two groups "have different drugs and different pushers"); bodily changes; and conflict with the middle generation. To play the part of "tribal elder" effectively (Kuhn's preferred model for older persons), she suggests five roles that elderly persons should assume in society today and for which they are especially suited:

- **mentor,** passing on to younger people the wisdom the elders have acquired through their life experiences;

121

- **monitor,** serving as "watchdogs" to assure that the needs of all members of society are met;
- **mediator,** acting as go-betweens and conciliators in various conflict situations;
- **moralizer,** reminding society of the values that really matter in a healthy community; and
- **mobilizer,** calling all people to action in order to accomplish what needs to be done to assure the kind of country we want.

Such an approach surely holds greater potential for a positive future for all Americans than do the cries of impending generational warfare heard today. We live in an age of the "social construction of reality," in which what people *hear* is often what they think *is,* and it is hard to imagine that much good for anybody of any age can come of a situation where the generations are pitted against one another. I am not suggesting that anyone must merely acquiesce and accept a point of view contrary to his or her deeply held principles for the sake of generational harmony. Surely, however, the debate can be couched in less inflammatory terms that contribute to an equitable solution for all, one that assures an adequate standard of living as well.

Our look at the current situation regarding the growing number of elderly persons in the United States and the policies, programs, and organizations that most affect them is now complete. Along the way a number of problems have been suggested, many of which generate the fears of intergenerational conflict described above and raise particular concerns for public policy. It is time now to move on from this exposition to an examination of some of the key values of the Christian tradition that might serve as both motivation and foundation for the more positive approach just suggested.

CHAPTER 5

VALUES:
THE THEOLOGICAL/ETHICAL
DIMENSION

C hapter 3 began with the affirmation that despite appearances to the contrary, the United States has had and does have a public policy on aging. Nonetheless, as Theodore Marmor and his coauthors point out, since the days of the Great Society in the mid-1960s, "there have been few champions of any particular vision of American social welfare policy who have taken it on themselves to explain how that vision is and is not being realized by the current complex of social welfare programs." Thus they conclude, "We have programs, but we seem not to have any principles. And, in the absence of continuous attempts to articulate policy in terms of principles, public understanding is almost certain to be lost."[1] In this chapter, we shall explore some of the ways in which the basic beliefs and values of Judaism and in particular Christianity—the religions that have been dominant in our society since its inception—might offer guidance in the alleviation of this shortcoming in a way that would be consistent with the fundamental tenets of this country and its citizens.

In this regard, philosopher Norman Daniels raises an important issue when he asserts that "conceptions of what is good are *incommensurable* in the sense that we have no perspective from which we can neutrally rank them. We have no view of the good life that transcends all others and by reference to which we can measure or rank all others."[2] This statement carries a valid philosophical insight, but it does not vitiate the claim, made from the Christian perspective, that Christianity's view of what is good does transcend others. What Christianity has to offer the world, in fact, is precisely a "view of the good life that transcends all others and by reference to which we can measure or rank all others." Christians must of course remain sensitive to the fact that not everyone accepts the Christian conception of the good life, however convinced a Christian might be of its validity. Nonetheless, Christians may—indeed must—guide their interpretation of any action that concerns others, as well as their proposals for such action, by the Christian view of the good life.[3]

SOME KEY CHRISTIAN VALUES

What are some of the fundamental values of the Christian tradition that can guide a Christian's discussion of public policy concerning aging and relations among the generations? Many possibilities arise. Indeed, virtually every value associated with biblical religion has some application to this matter. For our purposes, however, we shall try to limit the discussion to those key Christian values that are most relevant to the issue.[4]

Love for Others

From the Christian perspective, one primary and central principle must underlie any view of relationships among the members of a community. Although other value systems stress a lively concern for others, the intensity of this concern within Christianity is illustrated by the fact that it is spoken of there as *love* for others. Although commonly identified with Christianity, this understanding of God's will for human beings derives originally from the Hebrew Scriptures, which were "the Bible" for Jesus and the earliest Christians. Just as Yahweh's nature is manifested to humankind through steadfast love and covenant fidelity, so humans are to treat one another accordingly. The root of this love for others is thus neither some humanitarian impulse nor fear of punishment for disobeying a divine command. It is rather a desire to reflect in human relationships the kind of relationship that exists between God and human-kind, indeed, even to give concrete expression to the "image of God" in which all humans are created. The Holiness Code in Leviticus 19 expresses the perspective of the Old Testament as clearly and as simply as possible: "You shall love your neighbor as yourself" (v. 18).

This verse of course suggests a similar emphasis in the Christian Scriptures, where Jesus' quotation of it (Matt. 22:39) supplies the basic principle underlying everything the New Testament has to say about interpersonal relationships. This theme is repeated throughout the records we have of Jesus' earthly life, and its centrality to his message is well illustrated in John's report of Jesus' farewell discourse to his disciples. Quite simply, if they are to remain in his love, they must obey his commandments, and, Jesus says, "This is my commandment, that you love one another as I have loved you" (15:12).

The content of this love is absolutely clear also, both in explicit expression and in parable. For example, in the passage just cited, Jesus follows his statement of his command to love one another with the sobering amplification, "No one has greater love than this, to lay down one's life for one's friends" (John 15:13). And in the famous parable of the good Samaritan (Luke 10:29-37), Jesus further clarifies what his commandment demands of those who want to follow him. The lawyer asks who his neighbor *is*, but Jesus responds by describing what a neighbor *does*. As Søren Kierkegaard puts it,

> Christ does not talk about knowing one's neighbor, but about one's self being a neighbor, as the Samaritan proved himself one by his compassion. For by his compassion he did not prove that the man attacked was his neighbor, but that he was the neighbor of the one who was assaulted.[5]

125

In a comment especially relevant to the concerns of this book, Paul Ramsey affirms that "the parable actually shows the nature and meaning of Christian love," which is the only ethical viewpoint that "begins with neighborly love and not with discriminating between worthy and unworthy people according to the qualities they possess."[6]

In Romans 13:8-10, Paul expresses the mind of Jesus as understood by the early Church in a straightforward way that can hardly be misunderstood:

> Owe no one anything, except to love one another; for the one who loves another has fulfilled the law. The commandments, "You shall not commit adultery; You shall not murder; You shall not steal; You shall not covet"; and any other commandment, are summed up in this word, "Love your neighbor as yourself." Love does no wrong to a neighbor; therefore, love is the fulfilling of the law.

Paul reiterates this perspective in Galatians 6:2, urging Christians to "bear one another's burdens," an act that he identifies with fulfilling "the law of Christ" (cf. 5:14). This view is repeated by other canonical interpreters of Jesus as well, such as the authors of the epistles of James (2:1-13) and of 1 John (4:11, 19-20) and 2 John (v. 6).

Special Concern for the Needy

What has just been said in general concerning the biblical injunction of love for other persons applies especially to those less fortunate than oneself in various ways. Throughout the Hebrew Scriptures runs a constant strain of compassion for the weak, the oppressed, and the disadvantaged—especially in the legal material and some of the prophets. For example, in Deuteronomy 15:11, Yahweh tells his people, "I therefore command you, 'Open your hand to the poor and needy neighbor in your land.' "[7] Earlier, the Hebrews are told, "For the LORD your God is God of gods . . . who is not partial and takes no bribe, who executes justice for the orphan and the widow, and who loves the strangers, providing them food and clothing"

126

(Deut. 10:17-18). Laws concerning gleaners (Lev. 19:9-10), timely payment of wages to poor laborers (Deut. 24:14-15), provision of the tithe of every third year to the poor (Deut. 14:28-29), the poor's first rights to the sabbatical fruits (Exod. 23:10), the prohibition of taking interest from the poor (Exod. 22:25), and many others amply attest to the law's determination that the people of Yahweh show concern for the needy and the disadvantaged.

The prophets continue this theme in even stronger fashion, with many of their proclamations burning with righteous indignation at the treatment of the poor by the wealthy. Amos warns of the punishment of Yahweh coming to Israel "because they sell the righteous for silver, and the needy for a pair of sandals—they who trample the head of the poor into the dust of the earth, and push the afflicted out of the way" (2:6-7). Later, Yahweh speaks again through the same prophet: "Hear this, you that trample on the needy, and bring to ruin the poor of the land, . . . I will turn your feasts into mourning, and all your songs into lamentation" (8:4, 10). Throughout the book of Isaiah, the widow, the orphan, the deaf, the blind, the hungry, the imprisoned, the brokenhearted, and the afflicted in general receive the special concern of Yahweh and the promise of "everlasting joy" (1:16-17; 3:13-15; 42:7, 18-22; 49:9-10; 61:1-9; cf. Jer. 22:3; Zech. 7:9-10). In Isaiah 58, Yahweh rejects Israel's ostentatious fasting and asserts that the fast that God wants is rather "to loose the bonds of injustice, to undo the thongs of the yoke, to let the oppressed go free, and to break every yoke. . . . to share your bread with the hungry, and bring the homeless poor into your house; when you see the naked, to cover them" (vv. 6-7; cf. Amos 5:21-24; Micah 6:8). It is quite clear from this passage (as it is from numerous others) that the relationship one has with one's fellow human beings (and in particular those in need) has a great deal to do with the state of one's relationship with God.

The Christian Scriptures continue this theme. The Gospels portray Jesus as a Messiah who carried on the concern of the law and the prophets for the weak, the needy, and the neglected in society, and those who followed Jesus appear to have made a very serious effort to practice what he preached (and of course practiced himself). Although Jesus is depicted in this light in all the records we have (cf., e.g., Matt. 25:31-46), the Gospel of Luke in particular stresses his concern for the poor and the needy of his day. Indeed, in the first words of his public ministry, Jesus describes himself as "anointed . . . to bring good news to the poor" and sent by God "to let the oppressed go free" (4:18).

Among numerous parables in which Jesus stresses the centrality of active concern for the needy as demonstration of true faithfulness to God, the story of Lazarus and the rich man (Luke 16:19-31) contains the most uncompromising condemnation of any person in the New Testament. And what is the rich man's offense? He is not an obviously bad or cruel man (as suggested by his concern that his brothers be warned to change their ways lest they share his fate). He does not kick Lazarus as he passes by; he does not order him removed from his gate; he even seems willing to let Lazarus eat from his garbage. The rich man's sin, which consigns him eternally to hell, is this: He never really notices Lazarus, merely accepting him as part of the landscape and considering it perfectly natural, even inevitable, that Lazarus should lie starving and full of sores while he wallows in luxury and self-indulgence. It is a terrible warning to late-twentieth-century Americans that the sin of the rich man is not that he did wrong things but that in the face of human need he did nothing.

As one would expect, the concern of Jesus for the less advantaged members of society continued in those who followed him. For example, in James 1:27 we find the assertion, "Religion that is pure and undefiled before God, the Father, is this: to care for orphans and widows in their distress, and to keep oneself unstained by the world." Widows especially were of great concern to the early Church (1 Tim. 5:3-16; Acts 6:1), and, like today, such women in the first century were surely among the neediest of people. No better summary of the extent to which the early Church followed the clear, though difficult, path of its Lord's teaching can be found than 1 John 3:17-18: "How does

128

God's love abide in anyone who has the world's goods and sees a brother or sister in need and yet refuses help? Little children, let us love, not in word or speech, but in truth and action."

These passages demonstrate an aspect of Christian love that makes it distinctive—namely, its strong element of *compassion,* understood in the original meaning of "suffering with." Just as God assumed human form in Jesus of Nazareth and suffered along with humankind "the slings and arrows of outrageous fortune," so Christians ought at least figuratively to share in the suffering of others and try to alleviate it. Perhaps what is most lacking in current society's treatment of the needy, whatever their age, is this ability on the part of those who are better off to "suffer with" the less fortunate. Christians would appear to have no excuse for such a shortcoming.

In later chapters we shall explore ways in which the values considered here can inform Christian reflection on public policy. At this point it is enough to affirm that, although Christians may not be able to translate God's law of love directly into human laws, "their contribution to the debate on common interest will unavoidably be stamped by the love from which they live. The principle of protecting the weak cannot be obliterated from their understanding of justice."[8] The specifics of the way in which this principle can be applied are open to discussion; that it must be applied is not. Jesus offered no legislative agenda or social policies, but

> the story . . . of Jesus, "anointed . . . to preach good news to the poor," . . . can shape, sometimes has shaped, and always should shape the dispositions of the faithful toward the poor. To follow this Jesus is to do justice and kindness to the poor; to watch for the future reign of God that he announced is to anticipate and already to participate in his blessing upon the poor; to keep faith with Jesus as the one in whom God's cause is made known is to practice hospitality toward the poor.[9]

Respect for the Elderly, Especially One's Parents

Another clear teaching of the Jewish-Christian Scriptures with obvious significance for us also can be seen as a subset of the

129

more general injunction of love for others, with overtones of concern for the needy as well. Respect for the elderly, and especially for one's parents, is a hallmark of this particular religious tradition as far back as the Mosaic law.[10] Leviticus 19:32 provides the clearest expression: "You shall rise before the aged, and defer to the old; and you shall fear your God: I am the LORD." Note the direct connection here between respecting the elderly and fearing the Lord, suggesting that such respect was understood to have a distinct religious sanction.

The best known source on this matter is the fifth of the Ten Commandments: "Honor your father and your mother, so that your days may be long in the land that the LORD your God is giving you" (Exod. 20:12; cf. Deut. 5:16; Lev. 19:3). A great deal could be said about this significant statement, but here only several summary conclusions can be offered.[11] Perhaps most important is clarification of what is meant by the word *honor*. Although usually understood today to refer merely to deferential obedience by young children and general respect by older offspring, Old Testament scholars agree almost unanimously that something more is meant. Rolf Knierim, for example, affirms, "What is less well known, however, is that this commandment refers primarily to the material support of old parents by their adult children." He goes on to conclude:

> The command to honor father and mother must be understood holistically, in the sense of taking care of, supporting, protecting, and respecting parents as long as they live. It reflects a genuine form of social security in which old parents remained part of their families, with dignity and material security.[12]

Such an understanding raises significant questions today about the attitudes of many who consider themselves Christians.

The New Testament does not address the issue as specifically as does the Old Testament, perhaps because the actors and authors of the New Testament assumed the teachings of the Old except where they felt some revision was necessary. Nonetheless, ample evidence can be found that the same respect for the elderly and concern for older parents were present among the early Christian communities. For example, 1 Peter 5:5 asserts, "In the same way, you who are younger must accept the authority of the elders," and 1 Timothy 5:1-2 urges the young minister, "Do not speak harshly to an older man, but speak to him as to a father; treat younger men as brothers, older women as mothers, younger women as sisters—with absolute purity."

Even more significantly, in Mark 7:1-23 (cf. Matt. 15:1-20), Jesus enters into controversy with the Pharisees concerning the practice of "Corban," that is, dedicating one's goods to God. In Jesus' day this religious practice apparently was being used as a way of avoiding one's obligations to support elderly parents. Jesus cites the fifth commandment (along with a "negative" statement of the obligation to "honor" parents, Exod. 21:17: "Whoever curses father or mother shall be put to death") to indicate that not even an act of religious piety like dedicating one's property to God allows the divine command to honor parents to be set aside. Jesus' commitment to this principle is well illustrated by his making provision for the care of his widowed mother even as he hung dying on the cross (John 19:26-27).

That the early followers of Jesus continued their Lord's attitude is demonstrated by the fact that widows, among the neediest older members of any community, were provided for by the Church. James 1:27 has already been cited. 1 Timothy 5:3-16 gives considerable detail about the demands placed upon the Church to honor and to support those whose husbands have died (and, not insignificantly, upon the families of widows fortunate enough to have relatives). Acts 6:1 also attests to the fact that the Jerusalem church made a daily distribution to widows in need.

The last decade of the twentieth century in the United States differs dramatically from the first century of the Common Era in Palestine, and even more so from the nomadic culture that gave rise to the Mosaic law. Even if individual Christians feel obligated to try to apply teachings from those periods to their own lives and family situations, they cannot expect to be able to apply them to their society directly through its public policy.

Nonetheless, if believers are to claim contemporary relevance for their faith traditions, the values articulated therein should inform not only their own individual actions but also their vision for their society. Surely the attitude found in the biblical tradition of respect, concern, and support for the elderly, and especially for one's own parents, is a worthy one to try to convey to this country at this time.

Community

Another central biblical concept, that of *community*, also can contribute significantly to a discussion of public policy on aging. Indeed, this value can be seen as the logical and necessary corollary, or perhaps even outgrowth, of love for others. That is, if I practice love toward you and you toward me (in the sense just described), we must enter into a community fostered by that mutual love as we both strive to meet the needs of the other. Biblical religion, however, affirms that human beings, left to their own devices, always manage to lose sight of "the other" in pursuit of their own interests. Thus some basis for community must be found outside and beyond a mere wish for its existence on the part of human beings. Both Judaism and Christianity find this basis in the notion of a people whose relationships are governed according to their understanding of a God who has created and redeemed them and continues to sustain them.

In the Old Testament, the value of community finds expression first in the creation accounts of Genesis (chapters 1 and 2), both of which depict Yahweh's intention for human beings to exist in relationship to one another. This fundamental fact of human existence is reiterated in the central idea of the covenant "people of God," bound together by the call of a God whose steadfast and unfailing love for them was to be the model for their love for one another. Biblical scholar Norman Gottwald points out, as we saw earlier, that this God "is distinctively a delivering God who takes a strong stand on behalf of the oppressed underclasses that compose Israel." In addition to delivering them, Yahweh also gave them new "social and economic forms of life" that can be called "communitarian."[13]

Such was the import of this communitarian mode of existence that "all the developments in later Israelite history that jeopardize this communitarian mode of life are severely judged by the prophets." Gottwald concludes, "To state it religiously, prophetic theology and ethics are unrelentingly communitarian in their conception of what God wants of all human beings."[14] It is also significant that this covenant community was understood to extend in a very real way *forward and backward in time,* so that one owed a great debt to one's ancestors and carried a heavy responsibility for one's descendants.[15]

In the New Testament the idea of community is present in Jesus' teaching about the "Kingdom of God," in which all the faithful will share fully in God's bounty, but it finds its most vivid expression in the image of the Church as the "body of Christ" (1 Cor. 12:12-31). Although Paul uses this idea to describe the proper relationship among members of the Church, the image can serve as an ideal for the members of any truly healthy society. If we were to see ourselves as members of one body (i.e., "the body politic"), we would be aware that the injury or suffering of one member affects all the others (including oneself), and thus each is well advised to do whatever he or she can to prevent or relieve the pain of any and to assure at least a decent quality of life for all. Viewed in this light, sacrifices that individuals may be asked to make for the well-being of the whole do not appear all that unreasonable or even contrary to their own *self*-interest. This corporate image also includes the sense of continuity with past and future generations noted above in the Old Testament through the concept of the "communion of the saints": All members of Christ's earthly body, whether alive now, dead, or (logically) yet to live, share in the unity that Christ accomplishes for those who believe in him.

An interesting application of some of these ideas to the public arena can be seen in Florida Governor Lawton Chiles' inaugural address in January 1991. Chiles alluded to the value being stressed here when he said, "The difference between a crowd and a community is that in a crowd there is no covenant. People are standing next to each other, but they are looking out *only for*

133

themselves. In a community, people have entered into a covenant to help one another."[16] The religious imagery Chiles used is significant, reflecting the basis for the biblical notion of community—namely, a lively sense of concern for others growing out of a covenant relationship with a faithful and loving God whose actions serve as the pattern for one's own.

A Truly Loving Community?

These first two Christian values—love for others and community—come together in a remarkable way in the description in Acts of the early Christian community:

> And all who believed were together and had all things in common; they would sell their possessions and goods and distribute the proceeds to all, as any had need. . . . Now the whole group of those who believed were of one heart and soul, and no one claimed private ownership of any possessions, but everything they owned was held in common. . . . There was not a needy person among them, for as many as owned lands or houses sold them and brought the proceeds of what was sold. They laid it at the apostles' feet, and it was distributed to each as any had need (2:44-45; 4:32, 34-35).

These passages depict a Christian community that truly embodied the central themes of its Lord's teaching (and life). As Hessel Bouma III and his coauthors put it, "the fact that 'there was not a needy person among them' (Acts 4:34) is a clear allusion to Deuteronomy 15:4-5 and a clear indication that in this sharing community the promises and requirements of covenant are kept."[17]

That a similar level of commitment might be reached today is highly unlikely, even among some kind of consciously intentional religious community. At best, the exceedingly complex arrangements of a modern industrial and technological market economy render direct application of any economic arrangement from a different society virtually impossible. Nonetheless, the biblical example here, as in so many other instances, stands before those who call themselves Christians as an ideal, a challenge, and yes, a condemnation of our unwillingness to live fully the life we profess. This is especially so when one considers how limited the resources of that early Christian community must have been relative to the abundance in this country (much of it in the possession of church members—and churches!). Imagine what a difference there would be in our society if Christians implemented, even minimally, the practices of their early forebears, particularly by influencing the powerful public policy mechanisms now available to us to distribute our resources in ways that better meet human need.

Though it is true that most Americans are not likely to respond favorably to a message of more equal sharing of wealth, it is possible that some movement in that direction may be beginning. Students at all levels are demonstrating a greatly increased concern about environmental problems, as well as other "social" issues like homelessness. An especially hopeful sign is the rapid growth of Habitat for Humanity, a movement that builds inexpensive houses for needy people using volunteer labor and no-interest loans, the repayment of which finances subsequent projects. In just 15 years Habitat chapters have sprung up in 600 cities in the United States and 750 cities in 33 other countries, with a renewed surge of interest recently.

In a speech at the National Council on the Aging annual conference in Miami Beach in May 1991, Millard Fuller, Habitat's founder, expressed a vision that can be expanded to issues beyond housing: "We want to make shelter a matter of conscience. We want to make it politically, socially, morally, and religiously unacceptable to have poverty housing. . . . We have to establish the will in this country. We have the resources."[18] Perhaps the aging of America that has been perceived as a grave danger for our society, threatening warfare between the generations, will become instead a great opportunity that virtually forces us to realize how closely we are all related and how much we need one another, whatever our age, race, gender, or class. As the apostle Paul affirmed from his Christocentric perspective, "There is no longer Jew or Greek, there is no longer slave or free, there is no longer male and female; for all of you

135

are one in Christ Jesus" (Gal. 3:28). This vision, grounded in the values of love for others and community taught and lived by Paul's (and our) risen Lord, can serve to inspire and energize a people to create a society in which individuals can still excel at the same time that the legitimate needs of all are met. If so, the point I made at the very beginning about the Chinese notion of *crisis* will have proved to be true: What appears to be a great danger may turn out to be a tremendous opportunity as well.

Mercy (Adequacy) and Justice (Equity)

In chapter 3 we saw that the major expression of public policy on aging in this country remains the broad and complex Social Security program, that great boon to the elderly that was implemented in 1935 to attack the nagging insecurity caused by the Great Depression but that today seems to some people to threaten the very solvency of our whole political-economic system. This crucial program was founded on the twin principles of social *adequacy* and individual *equity*. It is not altogether clear exactly what those who created Social Security meant by these concepts in 1935 (if *they* even knew for sure). Clarity has not emerged since then. It seems safe to say, though, that the original intent was that the law should treat all participants fairly or *equitably* relative to the contributions that they make, at the same time that at least the minimum needs of all are met *adequately*. After considerable evolution (including the separation of a major adequacy component by the creation of Supplemental Security Income), this intent has come to be met in practice by a system in which workers who pay more in get more out, but those who pay less in receive benefits proportionately higher relative to their payments. Ours of course is a culture that espouses equality of opportunity, to be taken advantage of according to one's ability and willingness to work; equality of outcome has never been high in our scheme of things. In keeping with traditional American values, greater concern has consistently been expressed for assuring equity than for fostering adequacy.

It is striking how similar the two key notions in the creation and evolution of Social Security, equity and adequacy, are to two

136

of the most fundamental principles in both Judaism and Christianity, principles that govern both God's relationship to human beings and humans' relationships with one another. The two religious concepts that correspond closely to adequacy and equity are *mercy* and *justice*. These qualities are attributes of both the good individual *and* the good society as far back as the ancient Hebrews (recall the passages from the prophets cited earlier) and Jesus (read, *inter alia,* the Sermon on the Mount). The religious tradition on which the values of this society depend states unequivocally that an individual who does not manifest these two qualities in his or her dealings with others, especially with those less fortunate than oneself, and a society that does not express both justice and mercy in its laws, institutions, and practices—both such an individual and such a society are simply out of accord with the will of God, who is responsible for their very existence.

Interestingly, one of the major problems many people today have with Jewish-Christian theology is the notion of a God who is both merciful (we have no problem there) *and* just (that is the part we do not like). We do not mind the idea of a benevolent deity who loves humans in a way that gives them whatever they want and allows them to do whatever they want. Let someone start talking about God's judgment upon those who stray from the straight and narrow path, however, and suddenly we hear that that is not the kind of God we can believe in any longer. But both Jewish and Christian Scriptures depict God as demanding certain attitudes and actions of those who claim to follow God, and though God's mercy does not *depend* on proper behavior, that mercy is inextricably linked to God's justice.

From a Christian perspective, the concept of justice gives credibility to incorporating the notion of equity into any nation's public policy, though the definition and implementation of equity must be carefully scrutinized. The centrality of mercy in the Christian scheme of things of course strongly supports the principle of adequacy in social policy, with a question once again about standards of adequacy and their attainment. The central issue, however, from the Christian ethical point of view concerns the relationship between equity/justice and adequacy/mercy: Which is to take priority when both cannot be satisfied completely, and what might such a resolution mean in terms of public policy concerning aging? We shall return to this question in chapter 8.

The Source of True Happiness: Spiritual, Not Material

Our dominant religious traditions contain another concept that can help us in the quest to reconceptualize intergenerational relationships in a more constructive way. Any analysis of the problems our aging society faces in both the short run and the long run suggests that our rampant consumerism is a major contributor to the dilemma. In a society of individuals who must have whatever they want whenever they want, it is small wonder that fear and suspicion become such potent forces when claims are made that there is not enough to go around if one group or the other gets all it wants.

In addition, when coupled with the difficulty of accepting one's mortality discussed below, the consumer mentality can contribute significantly to the crisis of meaning experienced by many older people in the United States: Convinced that the success of one's life is measured by what one has, the stage is set for deep dissatisfaction with a period of life in which one's grasp on possessions of various kinds, including health, is unavoidably loosening. A natural tendency is to try to tighten one's grasp even more, not only upon material possessions but also upon health (and life itself) through overutilization of medical care without regard to the cost to others.

Some guidance in this area can be found, though, in a basic teaching on which not only the dominant religions of our culture agree but also minority religions that are becoming increasingly important in this country, such as Hinduism and Buddhism (see appendix). This teaching is, quite simply, that it is not in material *wealth* that real happiness lies, not in the accumulation and the consumption of things temporal, but in *relationships*, first with

138

the transcendent Being who created us and then with our fellow human beings. Only by rejecting the belief that "the more I have the more I am" can we move beyond the self-centered notion that asserts, "If I have it and you want it, I must somehow be diminished by sharing it with you." In truth I am enhanced and find only in that new vision the peace, the security, and the happiness I have been so desperately seeking in demanding "my due" and insisting on what *you* (or society) owe to *me*.[19]

In the Sermon on the Mount, Jesus addresses the question of the real source of meaning in life in his customary straightforward way. First, he observes, "No one can serve two masters; for a slave will either hate the one and love the other, or be devoted to the one and despise the other. You cannot serve God and wealth" (Matt. 6:24). Then he refers to the material needs that cause so much anxiety for so many people and reminds his hearers of God's bounty. He concludes with a very simple admonition that leaves no doubt as to his priorities: "But strive first for the kingdom of God and his righteousness, and all these things will be given to you as well" (6:33).

Recognition of Dependence

It is difficult for younger people to empathize with those who are older. In theory at least, older persons should better understand the thoughts, feelings, fears, needs, and aspirations of children because they have their own experience to draw on. On the other hand, younger people have not yet experienced old age, with the particular set of emotions, needs, fears, and hopes it brings. They are therefore much less likely to appreciate (in several senses of that word) what the elderly are experiencing. As Greg Arling of the Virginia Office on Aging has put it:

> Childhood is the only stage in the life-cycle in which the individual can appropriately assume the dependency role; and, in that situation, the child can anticipate increasing autonomy with advancing age. The older person must anticipate a further loss of autonomy as he or she ages.[20]

139

Of considerable importance in this regard is another Christian teaching that is at the heart of the faith—namely, the *recognition and acceptance of one's dependence,* in the first place upon God and in a derivative sense upon other human beings. Jerry Gerber and his coauthors, in fact, point to this very issue as central to defining and clarifying the relationship between the generations: "One question that will come up involves something nobody has dealt with adequately because we all avoid it." And that question is, "In a society that emphasizes independence, how can we deal with the issue of dependence in a way that does not demean the one who receives help?"[21] As this question suggests, the problem lies in the gap between the inescapable reality of human existence and our contemporary mythos about our ability to "go it alone."

Compounding the problem is the increasing lack of conceptual resources to deal with the reality:

> Modernity has accomplished many far-reaching transformations, but it has not fundamentally changed the finitude, fragility and mortality of the human condition. What it has accomplished is to seriously weaken those definitions of reality that previously made that human condition easier to bear.[22]

And one of those "definitions of reality" (though put into practice effectively by few people) is the central Christian doctrine that the broken relationship between human beings and their Creator can be restored only through the death of Jesus Christ. Acceptance of this religious truth requires the acknowledgment of one's total dependence upon the freely given and undeserved grace of God. Paul expresses the point clearly when he exclaims, "It is no longer I who live, but Christ who lives in me" (Gal. 2:20), hardly a view most Americans today are comfortable taking. We want instead to be "our own person," to "do our own thing," to "make it on our own." Yet according to the Christian story, it is precisely the recognition stated so bluntly by Paul that is essential for salvation. After all, accepting the totally free grace of God is nothing more than acknowledging utter and ultimate dependence upon God. If we refuse to admit dependence, however, we cannot express gratitude, to God or to fellow human beings, and we tend to concentrate on rights as a way of escaping the acknowledgment of our dependence: If what I am receiving from you is my *right*, then I am not really dependent on you for it.

For a "good old age," of course, freedom is a prerequisite, right in line with our current emphasis on independence, the individual, and the value of autonomy. True freedom, however, comes from security, and this suggests that some other values are also important because security, especially in old age when one's own powers and abilities inevitably decline, depends on others and their willingness to assist. If all of us could recapture a lively sense of our ultimate and absolute dependence, a large step would be taken toward a renewed recognition of our need for one another and thus our necessary *inter*dependence (cf. the discussion of community above). This shift in attitude might make the increased dependence upon other people that accompanies growing older easier to accept.

Acceptance of Mortality

Indeed, the ultimate example of recognizing our dependence upon a gracious, merciful, and loving God is to be able to *accept our own mortality* (and thus that of loved ones), an acceptance that can make a significant contribution toward alleviating some of the problems that have been discussed in previous chapters. As a number of commentators have observed, contemporary Americans do not handle death well. Unlike earlier eras when death was more easily accepted as a fact of life, today numerous factors combine to create a "death-denying" society, one in which death is even dubbed the "new pornography." Alan Harrington bluntly sums up the contemporary American position with regard to death when he proclaims, "Death is an imposition on the human race, and no longer acceptable." Even more tellingly, David Hendin asserts that death "is simply un-American. Its inevitability is an affront to our inalienable rights of 'life, liberty, and the pursuit of happiness.' "[23]

141

This attitude toward death, reflecting as it does an inability to accept our finitude and mortality, contributes greatly to the problem we have acknowledging and dealing with aging. As Daniel Callahan aptly observes, the major hindrance to "any penetrating social vision of the place of the aged" in our society "may be our almost complete inability to find a meaningful place in public discourse for suffering and decline in life. They are recognized only as enemies to be fought: with science, with social programs, and with a supreme optimism that with sufficient energy and imagination, they can be overcome."[24] Thus we are often unwilling to accept the fact of death, either our own or that of others, and we continue to employ aggressive medical treatments long past any real usefulness to the individual. Callahan employs a vivid metaphor—that of a tear in a piece of cloth—to illustrate the point. He says that "no matter how far we push the frontiers of medical progress we are always left with a *ragged edge*—with poor outcomes, with cases as bad as those we have succeeded in curing, with the inexorable decline of the body" (emphasis added). In whatever ways we try to deny our mortality, we will never win "the struggle with the ragged edge. We can only move the edge somewhere else, where it will once again tear roughly, and again and again."[25] In short, at least some of our problems in health-care financing and a great deal of personal suffering result from our culture's "relentless hostility toward physical decline and its tendency to regard health as a form of secular salvation."[26]

It is interesting that we should have developed such an attitude, given the views of the two major religious traditions that have shaped the values of American culture, Judaism and Christianity. Throughout most of the history reflected in the Old Testament, death was accepted as part of life, a natural fate for a creature made of earth (Gen. 2:7). Although certain types of death were seen to be negative—violent, heirless, and especially premature death—the Old Testament view is well summarized in the famous affirmation of Ecclesiastes: "For everything there is a season, and a time for every matter under

142

heaven: a time to be born, and a time to die" (3:1-2). Even in Isaiah's magnificent vision of "new heavens and a new earth" (65:17-25), expressing the prophet's understanding of the universe as *God* intended it to be and would someday restore it to the faithful, death is *not* eliminated; rather, a full life-span is guaranteed to all (v. 20).[27]

In the New Testament, which on the surface may appear to offer a different attitude toward death, the fundamental message remains the same. Granted, the apostle Paul does call death the "last, great enemy," but he never denies its reality or its necessity in this life. In fact, in his great analogy of 1 Corinthians 15, Paul makes very clear his real attitude toward death: Only as this body (the seed) *dies* can the human being come to know the eternal life (the plant) made possible through Jesus Christ. A careful reading of that passage hardly allows it to be taken as a plea to eliminate death itself, and certainly not as support for an attitude that fears death so much one will do anything to put it off as long as possible. Paul's acceptance of mortality, of course, is yet another reflection of his absolute confidence in the reality of Jesus Christ: "So then, whether we live or whether we die, we are the Lord's. For to this end Christ died and lived again, so that he might be Lord of both the dead and the living" (Rom. 14:8*b*-9).

What does this reassertion of a biblical understanding of our mortality have to contribute to the concerns addressed in this book? Basically, such a shift in our prevailing attitude could allow a move toward a social climate in which "caring for the elderly and the dying" can take on new meaning. As we saw in the earlier discussion of Medicare, our health-care policy is currently structured to provide virtually unlimited acute care and almost no long-term, supportive care. One result is that a great deal of expensive life-sustaining technology is used merely to extend lives that have no capacity to enjoy the extension. A healthier sense of our mortality, of the inevitability of aging and death, might allow us to ask an often neglected question: Just because we *can* do something, *should* we do it? We need to learn to see aging and death as inevitable and acceptable aspects of

143

human life, and for the sake of the one who is suffering, to let that person go when the time has come (or, when it is our time, to be willing to go without vast expenditures on *futile* treatment). As surgeon Perry Stafford of Bethesda Naval Hospital observes, "Most of the elderly would probably accept that idea. It is usually their families who have this tenacious hold on anything that will prolong life. It is hard for people to see that at some point, you are prolonging death, not life."[28]

Even before the point at which death becomes imminent, however, acceptance of one's mortality can be helpful. Ken Dychtwald and Joe Flower warn:

> We would be unwise to forget that above all else, the [baby] boomers are the "youth" generation. They love their youth. . . . In fact, we might expect that because they love their youth so much, they will do everything possible to take it with them into old age.[29]

Because it seems unlikely that even unforeseen advances in medicine will be able to eliminate or even seriously retard the inevitable process of aging, it is not unreasonable to suggest that policymakers (perhaps especially those in the area of public health) encourage people to face up to and accept their aging. This is not to say that one should not strive to stay active as long as possible, only that at *some* point the realities of aging can no longer be denied, covered up, or escaped; and the overall mental health of our society will be enhanced if we can accept who we are and quit striving irrationally to be who we can never be again. A potential indirect benefit of this might be a reduction in the unnecessary but very large expenditures on cosmetic surgery, pills, potions, and other such ineffective ways to deny the inevitable fact that one is aging and therefore approaching death.

The Old Testament offers a superb image that conveys well the point being made here. In Genesis 25:8, we are told that Abraham "died in a good old age, an old man and full of years." If one can accept the basic fact of mortality, that description is a

Values: The Theological/Ethical Dimension

beautiful expression of what all humans surely would want for the inevitable outcome of their lives. But what does it mean? To die "full of years" seems to suggest that one has reached one's "capacity for years of life," just as a cup can hold only so much water before it becomes "full of water." Most people readily recognize the folly of continuing to pour water into a cup already filled to capacity. Thus we should ask a simple question of our current policy and practice regarding the elderly: What is the point of trying to force more into a vessel already "full of years" unless the capacity of the vessel can be expanded?

Please note that I am not arguing against reasonable efforts to "expand the capacity" by enhancing health in later years and by finding ways to give older persons some meaningful role to play in modern society. I am simply suggesting that from a biblical point of view the goal should be not merely *more* life but *better* life, even if the absolute length is shortened. We must take seriously the fear often expressed by old and young alike of ending up "hooked up to all those machines and tubes"—unnecessary and excessive high-technology life extension, which merely postpones what all the major religious traditions teach is the inevitable fate of the human being. The approach advocated here can contribute to a "good old age," to use a very apt biblical phrase. By allowing us to move beyond inappropriate uses of technology, acceptance of our mortality and willingness to die when our life is "full" may enable us to refocus on more personal care and even free up some resources that can be devoted not only to such care but also to further research and education that would make old age even better.

The Munificence of God

Still another concept that may help us re-vision intergenerational relationships is important in both Judaism and Christianity. Let me introduce this idea with a story. A hiker stopped at a rest stop, bought a cup of coffee and a newspaper, and sat down to relax and to enjoy some cookies he had brought with him. There were not many seats in the crowded rest stop, and he had to share a small table with a woman who gave him a pleasant

145

smile when he sat down. After reading his paper for a few minutes, he took a cookie from the package on the table and out of the corner of his eye saw the woman do the same. This bothered him a little—after all, they *were* his cookies, and she didn't even ask!—but he decided not to say anything. He took another cookie, and she did too. Then he saw her take the last cookie, and as she did, she caught his eye. She smiled again, broke the cookie in two, and offered him half. Incensed, he grabbed his backpack and paper and stomped out, muttering to himself about the gall of some people. He paused outside to put his unread paper in his backpack, and as he did so, he reached in and found *his* unopened package of cookies!

From the perspective of biblical religion, this story describes perfectly the situation in which all humans find themselves when it comes to the things we so loudly declare to be "ours." From the proclamation of Psalm 24:1, "The earth is the Lord's and all that is in it, the world and those who live in it" (quoted by Paul in 1 Cor. 10:26; cf. Ps. 50:12: "for the world and all that is in it is mine"), to the description of God's Logos in John 1, "all things came into being through him, and without him not one thing came into being" (v. 3), scripture testifies that God is the Source of everything. Not only does everything exist through God's creative energy, but God has freely given of this incredible bounty to humanity. All our "cookies" are in fact *gifts from a gracious and giving God,* though most of us have had them so long that we cannot acknowledge any longer that they do not really belong to us. If we can accept the fact that everything we "possess" is freely given by God, we do not need to grasp so desperately at whatever we want or cling so firmly to whatever we have. A return to the biblical perspective makes it considerably easier to share what we mistakenly think is our rightful due with others who have just as much claim to it and perhaps a much greater need for it.

Our difficulty in acknowledging God's gracious gifts manifests itself not only in regard to material possessions but also in other areas relevant to our interests. As John Arras and Robert Hunt aptly observe, "Today we expect not only to be cured of ills that were previously incurable but also to be prevented from experiencing a variety of infirmities and misfortunes that were once the common lot of humankind. *And we feel wronged if these expectations go unfulfilled.*"[30] When taken in conjunction with the acceptance of our mortality discussed above, a more conscious recognition of life itself as a gift from God might make a difference in some health-care decisions in the later stages of life.

The Value of Work

As we saw in earlier chapters, improvements in health care, nutrition, and working conditions have increased the active life-spans of Americans dramatically in this century. Sociologist Amitai Etzioni thus aptly observes that "defining people as old at 65 is obsolescent. That age limit was set generations ago, before changes in life styles and medicines much extended not only life but also the number and quality of productive years."[31] Yet current public policy and overwhelming public opinion still recognize 65 as the official beginning of old age, qualifying a worker for full Social Security retirement benefits and Medicare.[32] As chapter 2 showed, many Americans take advantage not only of this opportunity but also of the chance to retire as early as 62 with 80 percent of full benefits.

Although mandatory retirement has been eliminated and the retirement age will increase very gradually early in the next century, many observers consider the change too little and too slow to help very much in addressing the burden the baby boomers will place on Social Security when they begin retiring. Furthermore, on a more personal level, Robert Morris and Scott A. Bass fear that with a larger number of people facing long retirements, a "situation is being created that leads to what we call a 'new class' without function, or a generation *inutile,* struggling to find a purpose or use in modern society."[33]

Another important concept of Christian theology can contribute to a reorientation of our thinking on these issues. One of the hallmarks of the Protestant Reformation was its distinctive notion of *the nature and value of work.* The very first chapters of

147

Genesis make clear that work is a legitimate part of human life. After all, humans are created in the image of a God who worked without rest until the glorious task of creation was complete. That same Creator gave to humankind work in the garden in which they lived, "to till it and keep it." By the Middle Ages, however, the Roman Catholic Church had come to stress the superiority of religious vocations over others. Certain types of work were more pleasing to God and therefore more valuable.

Martin Luther and the other Reformers, reacting at least in part to this view, shifted the notion of "vocation" or "calling" to apply to any type of work, as long as it was done for the "greater glory of God." God has called the Christian to the ordinary and mundane chores of daily life no less than to priestly activities, and the manure-spreading of the peasant could be as God-pleasing as the prayer and the fasting of the monk. Indeed, no work is demeaning or degrading if done in the proper spirit—a spirit of faith and love, of service to God and one's neighbor. All people, no matter how lowly their work and how menial their chores, have a vocation—they are "called" by God to their responsibilities. Luther went so far as to say, "God wants people to work. . . . We must note well the words of the Lord. He does say: Do not worry! But He does not say: Do not work! Worry is forbidden, but not work. . . . God does not want man to be idle."[34] Writing from a contemporary Roman Catholic stance, Joe Holland eloquently reflects a broader Christian view of work:

> All work is profoundly religious, even if we are not conscious of that fact. Work is nothing less than human participation in the divine creativity expressed in the creativity of the universe. Work is a fundamental cultural way by which we reveal God's actively creative love. Work is a fundamental cultural place where we express our dynamic rootedness in the rest of our natural world, and ultimately in the Creator.[35]

Does this perspective provide a religious warrant for encouraging people to work longer (i.e., to retire later)? If Christianity is concerned with promoting human fulfillment and meaning in life, perhaps the time has come for the churches to raise some questions about retirement: Is retirement as currently practiced an unmitigated good, especially given the uses to which many people put it? Is "leisure" the purpose for which God created us? Might not our later years be much richer if we continued to do that which for most of us serves as one of the major sources of self-identity? Norman Daniels puts the matter into perspective when he observes, "For many individuals, including elderly individuals, being productive or pursuing meaningful work is a central element of well-being. Work is much more important than as a mere means to income."[36] The truth of this observation is well illustrated by the fact that many people who have been eagerly anticipating retirement find themselves very dissatisfied with life after work because they are accustomed to being busy and feeling productive (national surveys show as many as half of all retirees find themselves in this situation). As Morris and Bass observe:

> This is not to say that all retirees are finding dissatisfaction in retirement; however, for many, the lack of a significant social or economic role for a long period of relative health can lead to a sense of disillusionment and dissatisfaction. Further, it raises the more significant question of whether such uncertain roles in society square well with a national ethos of activism and a constant desire for the improvement of human conditions.[37]

Other remedies for this problem exist, such as countless worthwhile volunteer opportunities, but continuing to work should be seen as another option that has much to recommend it. As Amitai Etzioni suggests, "One might recognize that many of the 'elderly' can contribute to society not merely by providing love, companionship and wisdom to the young but also by continuing to work, in the traditional sense of the term."[38] Morris and Bass concur, adding that "left to our imagination, with modest financial incentives, some able older people would be interested in performing useful societal tasks that marketplace activity alone cannot perform."[39]

Please note that I am *not* advocating taking away anyone's

149

freedom to retire, although the logical policy result of the case I have made would be to render retirement, especially early retirement, less attractive. Nor am I saying that people should work until they drop. I am well aware that a great difference exists between white-collar, personally satisfying careers and unfulfilling, physically deleterious, degrading jobs (though the notion of Christian vocation could help on this last score). One of the most significant advances of modern society in human terms is the possibility of ceasing work, especially unfulfilling work, before one becomes disabled or dies.[40]

Nonetheless, if the churches were to resurrect the classic Reformation doctrine of vocation, putting work in a better light as part of a Christian's "calling," at least some people might find greater satisfaction in continuing to work. At a minimum, they would postpone the time when they become, in society's eyes and thus in some sense most likely in their own, "*inutile*," without purpose or function. Apart from this personal gain, society would benefit more directly as well. Lengthening the productive period of a person's life and shortening the nonproductive part would both increase that individual's contribution to retirement funds, public and private, and reduce the support he or she would need from others. Choosing to work longer thus appears to have much to recommend it from several practical perspectives and to be in line with basic Christian doctrine.

The Purpose of Government

A final theological/ethical issue of considerable importance for Christians in the public policy debate concerning the elderly demands attention—namely, *the role of government*. After all, government is the source of public policy, and public policy reflects the values of government. The nature and the purpose of government are of course a hotly debated political question; one need only recall the recurring attacks on "big government," especially by recent administrations, and note that virtually all challengers to the incumbent president ironically also run "against Washington."

Consideration of the nature and the role of government is

150

more than political, however. For the Christian, it is a question with deep religious overtones. Why, theologically speaking, is there government? What should Christians want their government to be and to do with regard to older people? Although this is not a book on the Christian view of government, a few words on just one function of government may be helpful.

Romans 13:1-7, the classic text on this issue, does not legitimate any particular form of government (or even any function of government, except perhaps the power to tax!). The passage rather seems to be a basic statement that Christians are to submit to government because it is one of the structures or "orders" that God has ordained for the world. Among the roles that government can play in a Christian view of the world seems to be one with some significance for our particular issue.

According to biblical anthropology, human beings are finite, fallible, and self-interested, or in theological terms, sinful. We refuse to acknowledge the limits that our loving Creator has placed upon us for our own good, and we insist that "we can do it better" our own way. Genesis 3 expresses this view rather starkly early in the Hebrew Scriptures, and Paul especially reiterates it often from the Christian perspective. Left to ourselves and our own devices, we are more likely to do what benefits us (or at least those most like us) than what is best for everybody and certainly what is best for those very unlike us. It is for this reason that rational, "civilized" people have banded together and relinquished some of their autonomy to what we today call "government." In short, government can help us to do some things that we need to do in order to live together in society, and perhaps that we even want to do, but that we find difficult to do on our own because of self-interest.

In Romans 7 Paul elaborates on Jesus' undeniable insight into human nature that "the spirit indeed is willing, but the flesh is weak" (Matt. 26:41b). In a description of his own inner moral life that any self-aware person cannot help recognizing, Paul laments, "I do not understand my own actions. . . . I can will what is right, but I cannot do it. For I do not do the good I want, but the evil I do not want is what I do" (Rom. 7:15a, 18b-19). Paul

151

makes clear that there is only one real solution for this inner conflict ("For the law of the Spirit of life in Christ Jesus has set you free from the law of sin and of death," Rom. 8:2). In the absence, however, of universal acceptance of the salvation offered in Christ and the liberation it brings (cf. 2 Cor. 3:17*b*: "where the Spirit of the Lord is, there is freedom"), Paul appears to recognize the necessity of earthly government to keep human self-interest in check: "For rulers are not a terror to good conduct, but to bad. Do you wish to have no fear of the authority? Then do what is good . . . . But if you do wrong, you should be afraid, for the authority does not bear the sword in vain! It is the servant of God to execute wrath on the wrongdoer" (Rom. 13:3-4).[41]

In a sense, then, government helps to accomplish one of the basic wishes of God for humankind: It allows us to live together in some sort of community. If we all could submit to God's will and thus love one another as we love ourselves (as Christ commands us to do), then we would not need government. Alas, we seem unable (and/or unwilling) to do so, and therefore we need the external constraint of government. Abraham Lincoln expressed the point well when he said, "The legitimate object of government is to do for a community of people whatever they need to have done, but cannot do at all in their separate and individual capacities."[42]

To give a concrete illustration of this function of government relevant to our concerns, let us examine briefly one of the common criticisms of the Social Security system as it exists today. Some critics contend that the system is coercive and requires people to participate who would prefer not to and who could get a higher return on their investments elsewhere. Whatever the merit of this last claim, giving up current consumption for economic security in old age is not easy for most people, and individuals utilize any number of methods to try to get themselves to save more for this purpose. The problem is that contracts one makes with oneself cannot be enforced. The Social Security system simply imposes a discipline "that most people find useful, even if grudgingly so."[43]

Granted, this is a type of "self-paternalism," to use Marmor's felicitous term, and those who conceive of individual liberty "as expressible only in uncoerced private transactions"[44] may have problems with it. Given a democratic system, however, the voters always have the right to change what the government is compelling them to do. In the case of Social Security, however, there seems to be little desire to do so (recall the survey figures cited in chapter 3 that showed overwhelming support for the system, even to the point of paying *more* tax to sustain it).

Marmor's argument is further illuminated by a concept that biologist Garrett Hardin introduced in 1968 in the context of the ecological debate then heating up. In his provocative essay, "The Tragedy of the Commons," Hardin suggests that there might be some things that we need to do for the common good but that we just cannot bring ourselves to do on our own (although he would reject the theological explanation for this human trait presented above, it is relevant here). Hardin therefore proposes that we implement a policy of "mutual coercion, mutually agreed upon by the majority of the people affected."[45] This approach honors the important principle of freedom of choice (after all, *we* have decided what we want, and *we* have mutually agreed to it), but it also "helps" us to accomplish what it is that we want (an early example of this principle, though in this case more *self*-interested than mutual, is Ulysses' ordering his crew to tie him to the mast and then to ignore his entreaties to be released so that he can listen to the Sirens' song without endangering himself and his crew). Hardin argues that although "the word coercion implies arbitrary decisions of distant and irresponsible bureaucrats," this element hardly seems relevant if those affected agree to it. Furthermore, "to say that we mutually agree to coercion is not to say that we are required to enjoy it, or even to pretend we enjoy it. . . . But we accept compulsory taxes because we recognize that voluntary taxes would favor the conscienceless." [46] Among the methods that Hardin suggests to implement this approach to public policy is obviously taxation. Social Security thus can be seen as an excellent example of Hardin's proposal, a proposal that is quite in line with the theological case made above.

Indeed, to bring the matter back full circle, it is arguable that virtually everything government does is "self-paternalism" or "mutual coercion, mutually agreed upon," from zoning and traffic laws to taxes. The coercion is agreed upon because it makes the overall quality of life better for everyone, even if as individuals we give up some freedom to do as we please (the simple illustration of traffic lights makes the point quite clearly, at least for residents of metropolitan areas). Once again we are brought face-to-face with a basic theme of this book—namely, that what lies at the root of our problems in aging policy (as in so much else) is not the difficulty of finding mechanisms to accomplish what we want but rather of finding agreement about what it is that we do want. As Marmor and his coauthors put it, "It makes a big difference in political life whether a disagreement concerns the appropriateness of a particular goal or the appropriateness of a particular strategy for achieving an agreed goal."[47] In short, we see again that the central issue concerns the values that people hold. Until change occurs at this level, no lasting solution will be found.

Books about public policy on aging are becoming commonplace. What has been lacking is the analysis of the situation from an explicitly Christian perspective. The pieces are now in place to consider what this perspective can contribute to the discussion.

CHAPTER 6

VALUES: UNDERSTANDING THE POSITIONS

As we saw in chapter 3, undeniable problems exist in the programs that most reflect United States public policy concerning aging, especially Social Security and Medicare. Many individuals and groups have stepped forward in recent years to offer both explanations for the origins of these problems and various suggestions for their correction. Not surprisingly, these commentators have disagreed strongly in both areas. The disagreement has not arisen for the most part over the "factual" information presented in the early chapters of this book, information that is necessary to provide the context for meaningful discussion of aging policy. As suggested earlier, it is instead *interpretation* that usually plays a larger role than data in the differing conclusions reached both by the supporters of current U.S. aging policy and by an increasingly vocal group of critics of that policy (and of the elderly themselves).

Interpretation, of course, reflects the values of the interpreter, and the previous chapter has now provided a basis from which to consider the values of those who comment upon public policy on aging in this country. In the next chapter I propose a "value congruence analysis" that may be used to evaluate this policy and suggested revisions of it. First, though, it will be helpful to review the positions taken by both critics and supporters of U.S. aging policy and to offer an assessment of the situation in this country that underlies and gives shape to much

155

of the controversy. As we do so, we can begin to identify explicitly the values that have played and continue to play such a central role in this discussion.

A NEW VIEW OF THE ELDERLY

Chapter 4 contained a summary of the criticisms made of current aging policy by various individuals and groups like Americans for Generational Equity (AGE). In a remarkably brief period of time, such criticism has succeeded in bringing about a major shift in popular thinking about the elderly from that which was widely accepted for roughly the first three-quarters of this century. No longer are the older members of the population seen as generally destitute and barely surviving; now they are perceived as the age group in the best financial shape, especially given all the special breaks and benefits they receive. No longer are the elderly merely a small group of people on the margin of society, to be dealt with primarily as targets of individual or local charity; now they are a rapidly growing, well-organized, monolithic mass concerned only with their own well-being. In fact, they are increasingly portrayed as "greedy geezers" who are determined to use their newly discovered political clout to continue to drain more and more from the shrinking resources of society, thereby depriving other groups (especially children).[1] Articles about the elderly appear regularly with headlines like "The Tyranny of America's Old," "Consuming the Family," and "Soaking the Young To Enrich the Old," and serious questions are raised constantly about the future ability of our nation to afford such a burdensome responsibility. Anxiety is especially high with regard to health care, and some form of "rationing" (read "limiting expenditures of various kinds for the elderly") is thus increasingly proposed as the only viable solution.

Such claims contain an undeniable element of truth. Many older people are in much better financial condition than ever before. Greedy elderly persons exist as surely as do greedy younger ones.[2] The increasing numbers of older Americans will put considerable pressure on our system, especially as it is now structured and operated, and even more so as the proportion of elderly in the population grows. Some changes and even restraints are almost certainly going to be necessary if the promise of the good life to which everyone aspires is to be realized. It is my contention, however, that the issues go far beyond a simple matter of age. In fact, by focusing on the question of age alone (or even primarily), advocates of generational equity obscure the real problem, which, as I argue shortly, is an economic disparity much broader than that between generations.

THE OTHER SIDE

Despite the wide-ranging criticisms offered by the generational equity movement, public policy on aging as currently practiced in the United States is not without its ardent supporters, and not just among the elderly who are accused of selfishly "working the system" to such personal benefit. The American Association of Retired Persons (AARP) and other advocacy groups described in chapter 4 come most readily to mind. The arguments of these champions of current policy have largely been set forth already in chapters 2 and 3 and need not be repeated here because they are basically an affirmation of the fundamental success of current policy. That is, public policy on aging, as manifested primarily through Social Security and Medicare, is seen to have accomplished its primary purpose of providing a certain measure of security in the later years of life (adequacy) in a fundamentally fair way (equity). For example, Janet Otwell and Janet Costello of the Illinois Department on Aging assert, "It's a major policy coup in our country that, during the past five or six decades, we have provided millions of elderly Americans with basic income protection and access to health care. Older persons in our nation are, in general, better off than the elderly of former generations."[3]

Social Security has played the major role in this improvement. For example, some three-fifths of those 65 and older receive at least half their income from the program, with one-quarter relying on it for 90 percent or more. Among the older poor and near-poor who live alone, Social Security is the sole source of income for four out of five. Indeed, without Social Security benefits, the proportion of the elderly who lived in poverty in 1989 would have risen from 14.4 percent to 54.9 percent.[4]

Thus Robert Hudson and Eric Kingson call the criticism that "universal" programs do little to eliminate or reduce poverty "mistaken." In fact, "Social Security . . . does substantially more to reduce income inequality and poverty than either the American tax system or public assistance programs, despite the latter's being explicitly targeted to that goal." They acknowledge that such programs do benefit the middle class and that improvements could be made in benefit allocation, but they assert that "the critical and indisputable conclusion remains that these programs cannot be somehow understood as 'middle-class entitlements.' "[5] Because of the interaction of the program's adequacy-equity principles, high-income workers receive higher absolute benefits, but low-income workers have a much higher percentage of preretirement income replaced by Social Security. In 1991, for example, a person retiring at 65 who had earned one-half the national average throughout his or her working years received about 55 percent of preretirement earnings from Social Security; a worker who earned the maximum taxable under Social Security got approximately 24 percent.[6]

The record of Medicare is less impressive but still laudatory, as we saw in chapter 3, though no one denies the grave threat posed by rapidly escalating medical costs. In response to the criticism that the elderly are responsible for the high inflation rates in health-care expenditures, defenders of current policy contend that attention should instead be directed toward those who charge older people for that care—namely, "the health care providers, suppliers, administrators, and insurers."[7] As far as not meeting the needs of the poorer elderly, Medicare provides the same benefits for all recipients even though the higher earners have paid considerably more into the program. In addition, the greater need for health care by the poor means that on average they will receive more benefits through the program. Despite its flaws, then, supporters of current aging policy maintain that without Social Security Hospital Insurance, the state of health (both physical and fiscal) of the nation's elderly would be considerably worse than it is now.

Nonetheless, even the most ardent defenders of the current programs for the elderly readily admit that numerous flaws and shortcomings exist, a number of which were mentioned in chapters 2 and 3. In fact, many contend that not less but even more assistance is necessary if older Americans are not to live out the last years of their lives in constant anxiety of impoverishment. Speaking to the closing general session of the 1992 annual meeting of the American Society on Aging in San Diego on March 17, U.S. Commissioner on Aging Joyce T. Berry asserted that current programs do not adequately address the needs of large numbers of older persons, especially minorities. She pointed out that 91 percent of elderly black females living alone are poor, marginally poor, or economically vulnerable. Berry concluded that "vulnerability should be the determinant of need," not poverty as currently defined. Recent efforts to increase cost-sharing, for example, especially in health care through Medicare Part B premiums and other copayments and deductibles, cause grave concern because the tendency toward "flat" rates in this approach affects the poorest beneficiaries most heavily. Also, the failure of the Medicare Catastrophic Coverage Act of 1988, which required wealthier elders to contribute toward the benefits of their poorer peers, raises questions about the political viability of any program that attempts to fund benefits for the poor by directly taxing the wealthy when the latter see little in it for themselves.

THE VALUE QUESTION

Although a more complete analysis of the interaction between values and aging policy must await the next two chapters, a

159

preliminary comment can be made here. Advocates of generational equity, as the appellation suggests, appear to stress the
principle of equity (or justice) over adequacy (or mercy) and the
value of work over the other values identified in the preceding
chapter. They are concerned that a certain segment of the
population, no longer seen as a generally needy group, appears
to be getting more than its fair share, much of which cannot be
considered "return on investments" based on earned income.
This situation is especially problematic because the "inequity" is
seen as depriving other truly needy groups, particularly
children and young adults, of what society owes them. There is
also a concern that today's workers, who are making significant
payments into Social Security and Medicare trust funds in
anticipation of security in their own old age, will be short-
changed when that time comes. To many of these critics of
current policy, a system that allows people to "make their own
arrangements" for their old age thus seems preferable.

On the other hand, supporters of current policy, including
most of those identified as "advocates for the elderly," appear to
stress the value of adequacy (or mercy). Although not insensitive
to the call for basic fairness, they consider the needs of the
poorer members of society to take precedence if both values
cannot be served equally. Values like concern for the needy,
recognition of dependence, and the importance of government
in redressing basic inequities show through in this stance. These
people are aware of the shortcomings and potential dangers in
the current programs, but they believe that the system overall
has worked well and, with minor adjustments, can continue to do
so. The notion of a "privatized" approach to old age security is
troublesome because it undermines the commitment to universality that serves as the basic foundation for current policy, thus
weakening the sense of community also considered important.

This book is not the place to try to evaluate in any kind of
exhaustive, technical fashion the claims and counterclaims made
by critics and supporters of current aging policy in this country.
Entire books have been devoted to such analyses,[8] and I suspect
that one's evaluation of the positions presented depends more

on the values one holds than on the strength of the various authors' arguments (as the old farmer once put it, "What you see depends on where you stand"). What can be said here is that the United States faces some serious problems in the near future with regard to caring for its aging population, that those problems may lead to some form of conflict between the young and the old, and that now is the time to begin to consider from many different perspectives ways to deal with the situation that confronts us.

INTERGENERATIONAL RELATIONSHIPS: A "ZERO-SUM GAME"?

Before presenting a model for the more thorough analysis of the interaction between values and public policy, I want to outline what I consider to be the basic value orientation of our country that has led in large part to the threatened intergenerational conflict. Specifically, I submit that recently we have come to conceive relationships between the generations in terms of what is called in the branch of mathematics known as game theory a "strictly competitive two-person game," or more popularly, a *two-person zero-sum game*. The views of those who foresee "age wars" in our nation's future illustrate this position: If one generation receives a piece of the public resource "pie," it keeps another generation from having it, a classic example of the zero-sum game. Although not so marked in the position of elder advocates, some of the same attitude shows through in their determination to hold on to all the benefits currently available to older persons. Before we can examine this assessment further, we need to know something about game theory.

A detailed examination of game theory is unnecessary because game theory itself is incidental to the real thrust of this section. I am using the notion of the zero-sum game as a *metaphor*, an image that helps us to understand one entity through seeing it as something else.[9] This metaphor is especially instructive in describing increasingly common attitudes toward intergenerational relationships and in proposing a possible resolution to the perceived conflict. Undoubtedly, economic balance between the generations must be considered, and hard allocation decisions may have to be made along the way. Nonetheless, the best hope for resolution of the problems the United States faces today and over the next half-century is to discover a new way to envision the situation created by the aging of our population and to replace the zero-sum view with a new metaphor that offers a different vision of the future. To set the stage and to provide the terms in which I want to consider the issue, then, some familiarity with the basics of game theory is necessary.

Game theory has been defined as "a model for situations of conflict among several people, in which two principal modes of resolution are collusion and conciliation."[10] Kenneth Boulding has commented that "game theory is an intellectual X ray. It reveals the skeletal structure of those social systems where decisions interact, and it reveals, therefore, the essential structure of both conflict and cooperation."[11]

As mentioned previously, our primary interest lies with the "two-person zero-sum game." Obviously, we are not dealing with only two persons in a literal sense here, but according to Luce and Raiffa, in game theory "any decision maker—a single human being or an organization—which can be thought of as having a unitary interest motivating its decisions can be treated as an individual."[12] Although generations are more heterogeneous than this quotation suggests, current popular thinking seems to see each generation as united enough in its interests to justify this analysis. At any rate, in game theory the "zero-sum game" assumes that the interests and preferences of the players are strictly opposing. As Luce and Raiffa describe it, "It is, therefore, a game in which cooperation and collusion can be of no value. Any improvement for one player necessitates a corresponding loss for the other."[13] Thus in their choices, the participants end up in practice, if not in intent, striving to hurt each other because the situation dictates win/lose terms: If you win, I necessarily lose, and vice versa. Even more bluntly, Anatol Rapoport describes the player in a zero-sum game as one who "looks out for his own interest only. . . . He does not have any concept of collective interest. In comparing two courses of action, he compares only the payoffs, or the expected payoffs, accruing to him personally."[14]

Let me interrupt this description of the zero-sum game briefly to make clear that *I* do not believe the relationship between the generations is a zero-sum game. If it were, as we have just seen, little room would be left for anything but competition based on one's own self-interest, because that is the very definition of a zero-sum game. My point is rather that various participants in the "game" of intergenerational relationships are mistakenly perceiving and *defining* it as zero-sum and thus setting up a "playing field" and proposing rules, so to speak, that do not reflect the realities of the situation. If, however, we were to perceive the situation differently, as I shall suggest shortly, not only the "rules" but also the whole understanding of the game would be changed for the better. Presumably such a change would lead to rather different attitudes, actions, and outcomes.

Utility

A central concept of game theory, and one that will be crucial for the reconceptualization of the relationship between young and old just mentioned, is *utility*. The use of this word in game theory must be distinguished from other more familiar uses of the term, such as that of John Stuart Mill in his ethical theory that has come to be known as "utilitarianism." In game theory, utility is defined as "that quantity whose expected gain . . . is attempted to be maximized by a decision-maker." [15] Of no great surprise, then, a fundamental assumption of game theory is that "each individual strives to maximize his utility."[16] Furthermore, the *self*-centeredness of the zero-sum game is evident here as well because in such an environment, "the problem of assigning utilities to the several possible outcomes reduces to the problem of assigning only one's own utilities."[17] No concern is given to others' desires and interests because they are perceived to be diametrically opposed to one's own.

It is crucial for our purposes here to understand that, unlike

163

Mill's fairly specific definition of *utility* as "the greatest happiness for the greatest number," in game theory the term does not connote any specific meaning in and of itself, any "objective" reality apart from the *individual*'s desire to maximize something, which by definition becomes his or her utility, which therefore is what he or she seeks to maximize. Although this may appear to be circular reasoning, upon close examination it can be seen not to be, and clarity about this concept is central to the application of game theory to our topic. The key point of the definition is that *utility* can refer to a virtually unlimited range of entities, both material and otherwise. Although money is the most often used utility (and is certainly basic to the generational equity debate), "outcomes of decisions are not always associated with monetary payoffs."[18]

Utility in this scheme is intensely personal and therefore subjective. Rapoport points out that "the given payoffs are assumed to reflect the psychological worth of the associated outcomes to the player in question,"[19] and he asserts that "how one assigns utilities to outcomes is the decision-maker's private affair."[20] In short, what is important to one person may not be to another, and one's ideas of what *is* important can change over time with new information, experience, and insight (not to mention advancing years).

Game theorists stress that preference precedes utility. That is, we do not say that someone "preferred A to B because A has the higher utility; rather, because A is preferred to B, we assign the higher utility."[21] Similarly, Rapoport asserts that the assignment of utility is "to be presumably *discovered* from the decision-maker's preferences among all possible" choices.[22] This point is important because it further affirms the subjective nature of utility and therefore (important for our purposes) its ultimate malleability.

Dominant American Values

So far I have suggested that the zero-sum approach has become the controlling metaphor in our understanding of the relationships between young and old in the United States, especially as we look into the not-too-distant future when the number of older persons will increase dramatically and resources will apparently be less abundant. Robert Reich, however, in his hopefully titled *Tales of a New America*, suggests that this attitude extends far beyond intergenerational relationships to our fundamental political mythos, an assessment with which I agree. Indeed, Reich points to our nation's basic political problem in words worth quoting at length because they express so well several of the key points of this book:

> The common error [of the prevailing American political mythology] is the rigid delineation of "us" and "them." Modern liberalism—as distinct from its more balanced New Deal ancestor—is too ready to coddle the other; modern conservatism, to defy him. Both tend to envision human encounters as blunt conflicts of interest in which one party improves its lot and the other . . . concedes. The conservative morality tales speak of the other's strength and deviousness; the liberal morality tales, of his weakness and need. Neither variant of the basic mythology features stories of mutually rewarding encounters, or common efforts to overcome perils. The tension between a basic stance of accommodation or one of confrontation excludes the middle ground of negotiations and collaborations that both assert "our" interests and comprehend "theirs." It is here, in the premise of generally opposed interests, that the prevailing myths serve worst as guides to reality.[23]

In a similar vein, Anatol Rapoport points out that, by definition, in a zero-sum game, "if one of two possible outcomes is preferred by one of the parties . . . , the other outcome is sure to be preferred by the other in the same degree." Thus, if the only options available are those of a zero-sum game, "clearly no negotiated agreement can simultaneously benefit both parties."[24]

This zero-sum approach to political relationships, seeing as it does all "human encounters" in "us/them" terms, may in fact reflect an even more fundamental set of values, values that have always been present in our tradition but recently have come to

165

dominate the "American" way of life. There can be little question that the hallmark of American culture is its emphasis on individualism, autonomy, and the freedom of each person to pursue his or her own ends, limited only by the avoidance of overt (usually physical) harm to others. These values fueled this country's rise to a place of political, economic, and military preeminence in the world, and they still motivate numerous individuals to exceptional achievements of many kinds in many arenas of life. They are not, however, without their dark side, and medical ethicist Larry Churchill expresses this aspect well: "The genius of the American self-image—individualism, self-reliance, progress, and prosperity—predisposes us to an ethical individualism and makes us forgetful of our interdependence and social connectedness."[25]

Independence: Privacy, Equality, and Economic Autonomy

In an insightful article that deserves more attention than I can give it here, ethnographer Andrei Simic examines the ways in which these values are inculcated through American childrearing practices and the impact they have on generational relationships. He cites as of "particular significance" the concept of independence, manifested both in "the idea of privacy [notably lacking in many other cultures] with its connotation of the right, pleasure, and necessity of being alone"[26] and in the orientation away from the family through peer-oriented activities like school, sports, clubs, and so forth. Simic observes, "The reality is that in many American homes children and parents actually see very little of each other during the most formative period of a young person's life"[27] (he does not mention that the parents' often compulsive commitment to work causes *them* to be absent frequently when the children might be at home).

The democratic ideal of equality is also crucial, breaking down traditional deference toward those who are older (both parents and siblings) and reinforcing the independence and "doing for oneself" already mentioned. The push toward individual autonomy also tends to limit expressions of affection between

166

parents and children, especially with the onset of adolescence. And contrary to the pattern in more traditional cultures, American parents today have serious reservations about just how responsible they are for the actions of their children.

Not surprisingly, these same values appear in an economic guise in several ways. Children are encouraged from an early age to earn money, often justified as a way to teach the child "to manage one's own finances." Children soon learn, however, that having one's own source of income greatly reduces dependence on parents, at least for the "luxuries" of life. Seldom are children expected to contribute to the family treasury, and even many husbands and wives now retain control over their own earnings rather than have a joint account. As Simic notes, "Implicit in this value system is the presumption that the economic fate of one family member is not necessarily the concern of others."[28] Even when parents provide financial support to their children, it is often considered a "loan" expressly for the purpose of allowing the younger member of the family to gain independence. The same attitude carries over into the later years, and at a time in life when in more traditional cultures older people expect to be cared for by their younger relatives, "what the American elderly seem to fear most is 'demeaning dependence' on their children and other kin. Rather, the ideal is to remain 'one's own person.' "[29]

This is not the place to enter into discussion of American childrearing practices, nor do I want to argue that the dominant values encouraged by those practices are totally detrimental. The results of such an approach, however, should be noted. Not only are Americans taught from the beginning of life to cherish for their own sakes their independence, privacy, freedom from authority, and sense of self-worth based on economic productivity; their sense of commitment, responsibility, and obligation to other family members, especially perhaps to those who are older, is also undermined by these very values and the strong emphasis on peer-group orientation and "social adjustment." As Simic concludes, "All of this reflects a conceptually weak corporate image of the family and fails, in many cases, to provide the basis for a lifetime of cooperation and reciprocity linking the generations."[30]

Competition and Success

All of the dominant American values discussed so far come together quite fittingly in a major motif of life in this culture, competition. From birth most Americans are imbued with the notion of "games," and in general these are games in which one side wins and the other loses (i.e., zero-sum). Efforts to remedy some of the excesses of this indoctrination have been made (e.g., "Y-Winners" soccer and the like, where every child must play one-half and winning is not [supposed to be] emphasized), but they appear to be part of a *losing* effort! Because so much of American life is cast in the form of competition for something (grades in school or admission to the best university, a job with the right firm or promotion to a certain position, the closest parking space or the office with the best view), it is not surprising that the zero-sum metaphor for intergenerational relationships strikes a responsive chord.

Flowing naturally out of this approach to life is another dominant ideal of our society—namely, success, almost always understood as *self*-advancement and usually measured in terms of money, power, and fame. Consider the "heroes" of contemporary culture—Donald Trump, Mike Tyson, Madonna—all individuals who, in the competition for fame, power, and money, arguably have put personal "success" far ahead of any sense of concern for the well-being of the society in which they live. It is not at all surprising that when these dominant cultural values appear in the context of a debate over benefits for the elderly versus benefits for those who are younger, the values express themselves in terms such as "watching out for myself," "getting all I can," "wanting what's mine," and "getting what's due me." A bumper sticker, that classic American medium for "making a statement," puts it well, expressing clearly both this attitude of preoccupation with self and the zero-sum mentality outlined earlier: "It's not whether you win or lose . . . it's whether *I* win or lose."

168

The basic problem, as Robert Bellah and his associates put it, is that "we have committed what to the republican founders of our nation was the cardinal sin: we have put our own good, as individuals, as groups, as a nation, ahead of the common good."[31] As a result, "the American dream" has become a very individualistic one, a dream of coming out on top, of being the "star," to whom all those who do not quite have what it takes must look up in envy.[32] We want what is ours, what we have coming to us, and we rebel against any suggestion that we would all be much the richer for sharing, for helping those less able to help themselves in order to have a better community for all. Indeed, we seem increasingly incapable of that basic activity of community, sharing, because our zero-sum mentality leads us to believe that when someone else gets something, it is necessarily at our expense.

The conclusion Bellah and his coauthors reach is right on target, and profoundly sad: "Since we have believed in that dream for a long time and worked very hard to make it come true, it is hard for us to give it up, even though it contradicts another dream that we have—that of living in a society that would really be worth living in."[33] Indeed, they go so far as to express the fear that "this individualism may have grown cancerous—that it may be destroying those social integuments that [moderate] its more destructive potentialities, that it may be threatening the survival of freedom itself."[34] Little wonder that when it comes to the relationship between the generations, all the forces discussed previously that tend to separate younger and older people are magnified by the belief that *I* am all-important and that any good that comes to someone else must cost me.

In fact, it can be argued that the most significant failure to date in the "American experiment," a failure that lies at the heart of the generational equity controversy, is our loss of a sense of integration, of interdependence, of community, and thus of commitment to the common good. We no longer remember what is the essential basis for any meaningful society—namely, a lively sense that "we are all in this together," that, as suggested in

169

chapter 5 in the Hebrew notion of "corporate personality" and in Paul's "body" imagery, what helps others helps me and what hurts others ends up hurting me because we are all part of the same "body politic." And even if the help or hurt is not directly personal (perhaps, for example, I will no longer be around by the time my self-centeredness really costs anybody anything, or my willingness to give up some current income to make the last days of some older people more humane does not improve *my* quality of life), nonetheless I should have enough concern for the well-being of the community, understood to extend forward and backward in time as well as in space, to act in a way that is for the good of all.

MOVING BEYOND THE ZERO-SUM GAME

I am suggesting, then, that we need to redefine (or reconceptualize) the "game" of intergenerational relationships so that win/lose becomes win/win, so that *your* gain is not seen as *my* loss, indeed, so that we no longer think in "you/I" (or at least "them/us") terms at all. Luce and Raiffa describe the zero-sum game:

> Given the choices of each of the players, there is a certain resulting outcome which is appraised by each of the players according to his own peculiar tastes and preferences. The problem for each player is: what choice should he make in order that his partial influence over the outcome benefits him most? He is to assume that each of the other players is similarly motivated.[35]

Here we run head-on into a problem that has been mentioned several times already in our discussion—namely, the so-called social construction of reality. Theodore Marmor and his collaborators point out that a great deal of misunderstanding of public policy exists within the United States. The reason "may simply be that certain ideas are more hospitable than others." Significantly, they observe that "people believe *what they want to*

170

believe, and no amount of haranguing by well-intentioned fact-grubbers is likely to change their minds."[36] Concerning the particular topic of intergenerational relationships, as we have seen, the analyses that lead to various positions, and the "facts" on which they are based, are not universally accepted. That there actually *is* a conflict between the generations may not even be the case at all, or at least that there *must* be one does not seem to me to be proved.[37] But the *perception* of conflict is certainly abroad, and, unfortunately, history shows that people often act according to their perceptions, whatever the facts are.

If, however, we could modify what people "want to believe"—those "peculiar tastes and preferences" mentioned above by Luce and Raiffa—if we could find a basis for changing them in certain ways, for instilling in the players a new vision of the desirability of various outcomes, then perhaps the whole game could be seen in a very different light. In game theory terms, the perceived "utilities" or "payoffs" of the various outcomes need to be redefined for the players in the game, a modification that we have seen to be possible because utility is subjective and therefore amenable to redefinition. What can be said about this possibility?

As suggested earlier, one of the major problems with the current zero-sum mentality in intergenerational relationships is that the only utilities that seem to matter are economic. The driving consideration appears to be how much money each individual, group, or even generation is going to get. And if one gets it, the zero-sum argument goes, another cannot (or, more to the point, if *they* get it, *we* cannot!). Thus, as Marmor and his coauthors suggest, economists are the contemporary "policy gurus," believed able to predict the results of public policy changes on the basis of the central tenet of economics, to wit:

> People behave rationally. If you increase or decrease the economic rewards of particular activities, you will get more or less of those activities, *unless,* of course, something else happens simultaneously to alter behavior in a different direction.[38]

171

Too many people overlook that crucial "unless," the effects of which are much harder to predict than isolated, more easily measured economic variables. Thus Marmor and his collaborators conclude that it is simplistic to assert that economic forces alone drive human actions in an area as complex as intergenerational relationships. In their words, "Not only are there many confounding factors, but people also may interpret what has happened very differently than we would have imagined. The world is not so simple: Incentives are not behaviors."[39]

What this means for the concerns of this book is that—as suggested earlier in connection with the notion of utility—the best approach to resolving intergenerational conflicts may lie in that "unless," in trying to assure some revisions in people's ideas of what outcomes are most beneficial. In short, we need to strive to get individuals of all ages to redefine their utilities so that even if they receive fewer dollars, for example, this perceived loss is more than made up by gaining more of other things that come to be seen as equally or even more important (of course, realism requires that we acknowledge that economic incentives will always remain important).

As an example of the redefinition of utilities being proposed here, consider *community*, one of the values described in the preceding chapter and discussed just above, a value that is particularly relevant to this discussion but that has little readily apparent economic value for many people. Although the theological basis for community presented earlier is significant, this value has traditionally held a high place in our nation without explicit religious sanction, and the payoffs from a rediscovery of community might seem very attractive to many people who are suffering alienation and *anomie* in our individualistic society. One aspect of a renewed sense of community that would be particularly helpful in the case of relationships between the generations, for instance, is the possibility of improved *communication* between young and old (note the common root of the two words).[40] As Anatol Rapoport points out concerning so-called nonnegotiable games, of which the zero-sum game is an example, "Players who cannot communicate must depend entirely on guesses about what the other is going to do,"[41] an accurate description of our current situation. Furthermore, in a zero-sum environment such as many think we have reached today between the generations, these guesses are not likely to lead to positive feelings or interactions. In such a situation, Rapoport suggests, "Security levels are determined *in ignorance* of the other's payoffs or, to put it another way, by assuming the worst about the other player, namely that his interests are diametrically opposed to one's own." He concludes, significantly for our concerns, "If, however, the payoffs of the other are available, decisions can be made on another basis."[42] Clearly, better communication growing out of an increased sense of community can lead to healthier decision-making in aging policy because even in game theory, abstract as it is, Rapoport affirms that "trust begets trust; distrust begets distrust."[43]

A New Starting Point

Archbishop William Temple once said:

When I read any description of an Ideal State and think how we are to begin transforming our own society into that, I am reminded of the Englishman in Ireland who asked the way to Roscommon. "Is it Roscommon you want to go to?" asked the Irishman. "Yes," said the Englishman, "that's why I asked the way." "Well," said the Irishman, "if I wanted to go to Roscommon, I wouldn't be starting from here."[44]

Similarly, I submit that if this country desires to reach the destination we all seek—a truly just, equitable society in which the needs of everyone are adequately met—we must no longer start from "here." We must abandon our fervent demands characterized by such statements as "what *I* (or those in my age group) deserve," "what *you* owe me," "what *I* have earned," and so forth. In short, we must transcend the zero-sum attitude described earlier. Our desired destination will be more attainable if we reject the categories that define the current

173

debate (old versus young, mine versus yours, us versus them) and seek instead a different vision that requires us to consider more seriously the kind of nation we want to *be* before we try to decide what we have to *do*. This will require an examination of the kind of people those who make up the nation want to be, which in turn involves analysis of our values and revision of our utilities. To continue the journey motif, the point is well made by the Cheshire cat's reply to Alice's inquiry, "Would you please tell me which way I ought to go from here?" The cat, doubtlessly grinning, said, "That depends on where you want to get to."

Theodore Marmor and his colleagues recognize this fact, along with the difficulty it entails. They assert that social welfare policy contains an unavoidable ideological element, because the way we structure such programs discloses a great deal about our national identity and beliefs. In fact, this aspect of the matter is largely responsible for the emotional nature of much of the debate on the topic. They conclude, " 'What shall we do?' in talking about social welfare provision also implies 'Who are we?'—a question that almost no one confronts with complete equanimity."[45]

Interestingly, Daniel Callahan arrives at the same conclusion using a rather different approach. He suggests that we analyze the problems in our health-care system at three levels. The first is the "technical," those "institutions, mechanisms, and systems already in place to deliver health care." Next comes the "entitlement" level, referring to fair allocation of resources in terms of who gets what at government expense and who must pay for themselves. The third level Callahan calls our "way of life," by which he means "our political values, our understanding of health and its place in our individual and national life, and our understanding of illness, decline, and death." So far, he asserts, our efforts at reform have included some "tinkering" at the second level but have been confined primarily to the first, where "politicians and administrators feel most comfortable" because that level avoids "deep, disturbing moral questions, questions that begin to touch on some fundamental American political and social values."[46]

After stating the obvious, that changes at the first two levels alone are inadequate and thus "the crucial and determining level is that of the third level," Callahan asserts, "At that level we must change public opinion and expectations about what we can afford and what we need." He concludes, "What I am suggesting is that we should now have a national debate at the third level, about the place of health in our way of life." In other words, the time has come that continuing to try to address the problems that have been delineated previously in this book by devising new programs based on the same assumptions and approaches will simply no longer work. The only viable alternative is to go farther, move deeper, and face up to those "disturbing moral questions" that we have largely avoided up to this time.[47] As I have suggested, Callahan also asserts that the "most important future task is that of transforming public opinion and the values that lie behind it."[48]

It is noteworthy that even a game theorist like Anatol Rapoport, on the final page of *Two-Person Game Theory*, reaches basically the same point. After acknowledging the inadequacy of "rational analysis . . . to tell us how we ought to behave," he goes on to express very much the perspective that I am advocating:

> Too much depends on our choice of values, criteria, notions of what is "rational," and, last but by no means least, the sort of relationship and communication we establish with the other parties of the "game." These choices have nothing to do with the particular game we are playing. They are not *strategic* choices, i.e., choices rationalized in terms of advantages they bestow on us in a particular conflict. Rather they are choices which we make because of *the way we view ourselves, and the world, including the other players* [emphasis added in this sentence]. . . . Game-theoretical analysis, if pursued to its completion, *perforce* leads us to consider other than strategic modes of thought.[49]

One critical element is lacking in these various analyses, and that is the answer to a fundamental question: Where might we turn for guidance in trying to find these "other modes of thought"? We need a source for the values and motivation to

175

address questions such as proper intergenerational relationships and the place and role of the elderly in our society in terms
more useful than the zero-sum approach currently in vogue.
Fortunately, this book is a joint venture of the Churches' Center
for Theology and Public Policy and Abingdon Press, an imprint
of The United Methodist Publishing House. And churches
(unlike game theorists) have never been shy about explaining
and attempting to correct people's perceptions of reality and
thus their desires, their preferences, and their understandings
of "utility" (value).[50]

It is apparent from much that has gone before that the
evaluation of and approach to the relationship between the
older and younger generations in this country are greatly
influenced by the way in which one conceptualizes that
relationship and the terms one uses to describe it. I have
suggested that intergenerational relationships in the United
States today are largely conceived in purely economic terms as a
"zero-sum game," and the perception that if one generation
"gets something" the other must necessarily lose something is
very real. I have also claimed that the brightest hope for the
future of an aging society approaching a time of scarcity is to
reconceptualize the basic nature of those relationships. We must
recognize the truth that Robert Reich well expresses:

> There are few encounters in which one side wins and the other
> loses, apart from sporting events, litigation, and quick wars on
> small islands. The general case is for interests to overlap, if not
> completely; for all parties to gain or lose together, if not all to the
> same extent; for each to depend on the other, if not all to the same
> degree and in the same encounter. This holds for international
> commerce as well as for international diplomacy, for dealings
> between managers and workers as well as dealings between the
> poor and the prosperous.[51]

We can safely add to Reich's last sentence "for intergenerational
relationships" and "for dealings between the young and the old."

Centuries ago, a very wise anonymous author in the Middle
East stated bluntly, "Where there is no vision, the people perish"

(Proverbs 29:18 KJV). Today in the United States, we need a new vision, in which the well-being of all citizens—young and old, children and the elderly, black and white, rich and poor—is understood to be essential for a society worth living in. And such a new vision (which is really not so new after all) is possible. I submit that this new vision, in which interests are seen to overlap and all parties to gain or lose together, may best be realized by revising the utilities attached by each generation to various outcomes. To be sure, some amount of economic competition may be inevitable as different groups lay claim to diminishing resources. But we must also suggest other values in place of the chiefly monetary ones that have come to dominate our culture, and we must make the "payoffs" accruing from implementing those values more attractive than the threats of generational warfare currently held out as our likely future. Only as our vision expands beyond "the way things have always been" to encompass "the way things should be" can we hope to ensure genuine intergenerational equity.

THE EIGHTEENTH CAMEL

An old story illustrates quite well much of what I have said so far in this book concerning the misconception of intergenerational relationships and the role that Christian values can play in revising that conception in a positive fashion. Many years ago a Middle Eastern sheikh died, leaving all his possessions to his three sons. According to the customs of that time and place, the eldest son inherited one-half of all his father owned, the middle son one-third, and the youngest son one-ninth. Everything was going along quite smoothly until they came to one of the dead man's most valuable possessions, his herd of camels, which unfortunately numbered seventeen. Try as they might, the three sons simply could not find an equitable way to divide seventeen camels into shares of one-half, one-third, and one-ninth. The family was threatening to come unraveled when someone suggested they visit the oldest man in the village, who was widely renowned for his wisdom. After hearing their story, he smiled at them and said, "I am sorry, but I have no solution to your dilemma. I do, however, have one camel that you are welcome to borrow for a while." Not wishing to offend the old man, the brothers took his camel home and decided to try once more to resolve the problem. Standing outside the camel pen, they counted the herd again, and lo and behold, there were now *eighteen* camels in the pen. Immediately they determined that the eldest son would get one-half or nine, the middle son one-third or six, and the youngest son one-ninth or two, for a total of seventeen, leaving the eighteenth camel to be returned to the village sage—who had had no solution for their problem.

The sons represent our prevailing "zero-sum" mentality—that justice (as each perceives it) must be served, that each is entitled to receive his or her "rightful" share, perhaps even that certain goods of life should come one's way with no effort on one's part. The village sage offers a different perspective from which to analyze the values relevant to the situation, thus allowing the limited resources to be divided in a more equitable way. The old man in fact demonstrates the truth embodied in the Christian message: In being willing to share what one has with others who need it—whether or not they have any claim whatsoever to it—the true "utilities," the real payoffs for all, are greatly increased.

It seems to me that what we may be about today in the debate over intergenerational equity is very similar to a search for that eighteenth camel, and for people wise enough to recognize it—and to notice that the percentage shares in the story do not total 100! Indeed, perhaps in that example of the storyteller's naive license lies further corroboration of the point just made—namely that those who have even legitimate claims to the world's goods should be willing to take a little less than their "rightful" share if doing so promotes the general well-being of the community, however defined.

Indeed, the clearest message stemming from our examination in chapter 5 of the key Christian values relevant to public policy concerning aging is that Christianity's vision for human community is definitely *not* a purely economic zero-sum game. At the heart of the faith is the explicit affirmation that it is only in giving of oneself, in refusing to buy into the values that have come to dominate contemporary American society, that one can find true fulfillment, satisfaction, and, yes, happiness.

Jesus leaves no doubt that the zero-sum mentality has no place in the lives of those who would be his disciples. For example, in Luke 12:15 he warns, "Take care! Be on your guard against all kinds of greed; for one's life does not consist in the abundance of possessions" (cf. Matt. 6:21: "For where your treasure is, there will your heart be also"). Among numerous other expressions of this admonition, the Sermon on the Mount contains perhaps the clearest statement of Jesus' view:

> And if anyone wants to sue you and take your coat, give your cloak as well; and if anyone forces you to go one mile, go also the second mile. Give to everyone who begs from you, and do not refuse anyone who wants to borrow from you. (Matt. 5:40-42)

That is about as far as one can imagine from the "what's-mine-is-mine," zero-sum mentality abroad in our society today.

This remarkable attitude of Jesus receives secondhand corroboration in a statement by Paul that also demonstrates the apostle's acceptance of his Lord's teaching on this matter. In Acts 20:35 Paul quotes a statement of Jesus not found in the Gospels but obviously known among his early followers: "It is more blessed to give than to receive." It is worthy of note that Paul introduces the quotation by saying, "In all this I have given you an example that by such work one must support the weak," reiterating a major teaching of the dominant religious traditions of our culture.

And what is to be the reward for those who can put into practice values so radically different from the ones dominant in their society? Significantly, it is not the miserable existence envisioned by many, especially by those who advocate intergenerational struggle to get one's due, but exactly the opposite. "I came that they may have life," Jesus says, "and have it *abundantly*" (John 10:10, emphasis added).

CHAPTER 7

SHEDDING LIGHT: A "VALUE CONGRUENCE ANALYSIS"

THE "ETHICS-ACTION GAP"

In an editorial entitled "Narrowing the Ethics-Action Gap," James A. Nash, Executive Director of the Churches' Center for Theology and Public Policy in Washington, D.C., discusses the need for lively and constant interaction between "scholars in the theological-ethical disciplines and advocates in the political combat zones." He rightly observes that "the Christian social mission urgently needs the interpenetrating benefactions of both." In order to move toward "this combination of contributions and competencies," Nash says that "we probably need a model of *Christian ethical action*" that "would combine coherently the essential elements in both social ethics and social action."[1]

Such a model, Nash continues, requires several elements:

1. fair and accurate presentation of relevant data, never easy in its own right but which, as we have seen, can be "complicated by the claims of competing partisans";
2. elucidation of the theological/ethical/philosophical foundations of a particular social concern;

3. determination of the central moral issues, "particularly the moral values and norms at stake";
4. suggestion of "corrective policy options" that apply Christian values to the social problem while recognizing political reality "(always remembering that a prime moral duty is to seek the expansion of the parameters of the politically possible)";
5. inspiration of Christian social action through "education, communication, and motivation"; and
6. application of political wisdom to achieve the ethical goals desired.

This book has already addressed several of the components of Nash's outline of a "model of Christian ethical action." Chapters 1 and 2 laid the foundation for a consideration of public policy on aging by setting forth the demographic data and social changes in the United States that will have a profound impact upon American society in the next half-century. Chapters 3 and 4 described existing public policy and organizations that constitute the major elements of the response to these changes and reported some of the problems with that response. Chapter 5 identified major values and norms in the Christian tradition that are particularly relevant to the issue of aging policy. And in chapter 6 we saw that the growth in the number of the elderly, the increased costs associated with health care, and pressures on government at all levels have created an environment in which decisions about allocation of resources have come to be viewed by many as a "zero-sum game," in which what one group (or generation) receives invariably comes at the expense of another. This "win/lose" approach to intergenerational relationships both reflects and finds philosophical grounding in the fundamental value orientation of American society, with its extreme emphasis on independence, individualism, and personal success measured in material terms. Because utilities (what one wants to "win" in the game) are subjective, however, the possibility exists to devise options that will reorient the understanding of utilities so that win/lose can become win/win. The Christian values described in chapter 5, I submit, offer a way to bring about and to guide this redefinition of utilities along lines that are both historically acceptable in this society and faithful to the God who calls Christians to further God's reign on earth.

I am not so concerned in this book with advocating particular strategies and policies as I am, first, to argue that Christians should utilize the resources of their faith in public policy debate and, second, to suggest a way that policy can be evaluated in light of values I consider central to a Christian understanding of human life. I intend for my effort to be a step toward treating, in Nash's words, "ethical and strategic considerations not as separables, alternatives, or dispensables"[2] but as necessary partners in a Christian approach to public policy. The critical question is how to apply the theological values identified in chapter 5 in an explicit and systematic way when the programs described in chapter 3 and the positions presented in chapter 6 are evaluated and when new policies and programs are proposed.

In particular, is it possible to develop an approach that ensures that each strategy,[3] existing or proposed, gives due consideration to values identified as relevant and important to the social concern under consideration? People engaged in public policy debate are hardly objective and disinterested. Usually those on each side of an issue concentrate on the parts they want to stress, and they ignore (or, what is worse, distort) the rest. Imagine a nighttime landscape: If a light is directed at the foreground, a stream is illuminated; if the light is aimed farther away, a rustic cottage appears. The point is that both the stream and the cottage are part of the landscape, but very different pictures appear depending upon where the light shines. What we must strive for in ethical considerations of public policy on aging, and what I hope to help provide, is a method to achieve a broader illumination that allows us—indeed, forces us—to see *both* the stream and the cottage.

VALUE CONGRUENCE ANALYSIS

Purpose

Toward this end, I propose an approach that I call *value congruence analysis,*[4] which is designed to encourage discussion about and systematic evaluation of policies and programs in light of Christian (or other) values. A brief description of value congruence analysis is necessary before seeing how it might be used in this critical endeavor, but first one thing needs to be clearly understood: The primary value of the analysis lies in the *process* it offers, not the *product* it produces. That is, the model is not intended to be a method for making public policy decisions. Instead, the process required by the model demands the consideration of values in public policy debate by identifying those values relevant to the various policies and programs under consideration, analyzing their importance for the social concern at hand, and evaluating the congruence of the policies and programs with the values. This process helps to identify the strengths and weaknesses of a given policy or program in relation to a set of values that have been identified as relevant and important, but it does not determine policy.

In short, the end result of the analysis, though not unimportant, is much less significant than what the participants in the process do in the application of the model. I have more to say shortly about what this means in practice, but I cannot stress the point too strongly here at the very outset. If the analysis I am proposing is misunderstood to be some kind of method for quantifying values and reaching "scientific" conclusions about policy, little good will come of it. If, however, value congruence analysis is seen for what it is, a *heuristic instrument* that helps us understand the complex interaction of values and policy, then it can be a powerful tool for bridging the gap between ethical reflection and embodiment of that reflection in advocacy for particular policies and programs.

183

Methodology

The value congruence model that I am proposing is a seven-step process. Although the analysis can be done profitably by an individual, it is most effective when it is utilized in a group setting, preferably by those who are involved in public policy advocacy, formulation, and/or implementation. The reason for this will become apparent as we look at the model itself.

1. *Understand the dilemma.* The first step in analyzing any public policy issue is to understand the dilemma that gives rise to the need for such policy. Although one might be tempted to treat this step lightly and superficially because the dimensions of the problem often seem to be well known and obvious, a serious and thoughtful analyst will seek and examine all relevant data from as many perspectives as possible. In order to know what values are appropriate and how they apply to the issue, one must understand all facets of the dilemma.

2. *Describe current responses.* Similarly, it is essential to identify and evaluate existing policies, programs, and organizations that address the dilemma in order to have a comprehensive understanding of the policy environment.

3. *Identify relevant values.* The purpose of this analysis is to infuse an explicit consideration of values into the public policy process. This step requires the analyst(s) to develop a list of potential values, using two criteria. First, the values chosen will be those that are considered to be most important. Clearly this judgment is subjective and reflects the basic value orientation of the persons involved. For most people reading this book, values from the Christian tradition will be dominant.[5] The second criterion is relevance to the policy issue under consideration. Some values may be cherished by a given individual or group but simply not relevant to the matter at hand.

In this step, it is important to be thorough and to compile as comprehensive a list as possible. After the list of values has been determined, it is useful to rank them from most important to least important. The purpose of this "weighting" is so that, when specific strategies are evaluated later, one may be willing to compromise on some aspect of a particular policy or program in a way that reduces congruence with a less important value but increases it with a value deemed more critical.

It is at this point that the significance of *group* involvement first comes to the fore, not only in ensuring that the list of values is as exhaustive as possible but also in enriching the determination of the relative importance of the values, about which group members may well disagree. It should also be noted that members of the group may have different understandings of the exact *meaning* of some values, such as, for example, justice, love of neighbor, or the value of life. Discussion of these differences during this step is a valuable benefit of the more goal-oriented process of policy analysis.

4. *Select strategies for analysis.* The analysis can be used to evaluate existing strategies for dealing with the dilemma that was identified in step 2, to compare such strategies with alternative strategies, or to assess proposed strategies. Thus value congruence analysis can be used either retrospectively (to consider programs and policies that already exist) or prospectively (to examine proposals that are not yet implemented).

5. *Assign congruence ratings.* The next step is to develop a value congruence matrix (grid) in which the values identified in step 3 are the row headings and the strategies selected in step 4 are the column headings (see exhibit 7.1). A value congruence rating showing the degree of congruence between the strategy and the value is entered into each cell of the matrix using the following seven-point scale:

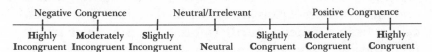

The seven-point scale, although arbitrary, allows not only an indication of positive, negative, or no congruence but also some differentiation in the strength of congruence. A scale with fewer values may be used if this level of distinction is not desired.

EXHIBIT 7.1
VALUE CONGRUENCE MATRIX

STRATEGIES

VALUES	Strategy 1	Strategy 2	Strategy 3	. . .	Strategy m
Value 1					
Value 2					
Value 3					
.					
.					
.					
Value n					

Two passes through the matrix are made. First, ratings are assigned one column at a time (i.e., all congruence ratings are assigned for one strategy before proceeding to the next strategy). Then, after all the strategies have been rated, another pass is made through the matrix, looking at one row at a time, in order to determine whether the relative ratings for each strategy are appropriate (i.e., is the strategy that received the highest rating, for example, really the one that is most congruent with the value when compared with the other strategies?). If necessary, any ratings in question are changed to reflect the appropriate *relative* congruence. This second evaluation provides an opportunity to check the validity of the ratings assigned the first time through. Incidentally, some passage of time before the second evaluation can often reduce bias toward a particular rating that may linger from the first rating.[6]

Like the value identification in step 3, this rating process is undeniably subjective (as are values by definition and therefore *any* discussion of them). Furthermore, ratings assigned from the point of view of one subpopulation affected by the policy may be quite different from those of another subpopulation (e.g., the poor and the wealthy with regard to non-means-tested retirement benefits). If necessary, multiple ratings can be used to reflect the different perspectives and/or situations of different subpopulations. Note also that at this step the group

186

process becomes central once again. The group members will most likely differ in their ratings, fostering discussion as each member explains his or her ratings and questions those of others in the group.

6. *Determine the strategy with the "best" congruence pattern.* The strategy that has the largest number of positive ratings on the congruence scale (especially "highly congruent") and the smallest number of negative ratings is by definition most congruent with the values identified in step 3. If two strategies have a large number of positive ratings, preference is given to the one rated higher on the more important values as decided in step 3. It may be helpful here to prepare a table with the distribution of ratings for each strategy (see exhibit 7.2). For each column in the congruence matrix, the number of times each rating appears is counted (i.e., the number of HCs, MCs, and so forth) and the totals are entered in the new table showing the distribution of ratings.

7. *Reassess values and strategies.* At this point, it may appear that the analysis is complete. It is essential, however, to do two more things. First, the value congruence matrix in step 5 is examined in order to determine if any *strategy* (column) has few or no positive ratings. If this is the case, the analyst(s) may have begun the process with a bias against the strategy in question. Such a bias can lead to two results. First, the strategy may simply be rated unfairly. It is axiomatic that the results of an analysis of this kind are only as useful as the ratings assigned; unfair ratings lead to unfair conclusions and can short-circuit the most valuable part of the process, frank and open discussion of *all* policy options. A second and more subtle distortion also may have occurred—namely, values that support the strategy in question may have been neglected. After all, people are apt to identify as essential those values that support their own positions rather than the views of others, especially if those other people do not agree with them. Additional values, therefore, some of which may come from outside the Christian tradition, should be identified in order to give a fair assessment of other points of view. It is also interesting to ask at this point whether any values

187

EXHIBIT 7.2
DISTRIBUTION OF CONGRUENCE RATINGS

STRATEGIES

RATINGS	Strategy 1	Strategy 2	Strategy 3	. . .	Strategy m
Highly Congruent (HC)					
Moderately Congruent (MC)					
Slightly Congruent (SC)					
Neutral/Irrelevant (N)					
Slightly Incongruent (SI)					
Moderately Incongruent (MI)					
Highly Incongruent (HI)					

are being implicitly appealed to, values that have not been identified and articulated in step 3. In a discussion of a particular program or policy, remarks like "That's just not right . . . " often reveal an underlying value that has not been brought to the surface. If such values are discovered, they should be made explicit and added to the list. Steps 5 and 6 can then be repeated with these new values included in the analysis.

Second, the value congruence matrix is reexamined to see if any *value* (row) has few or no positive ratings. An absence of such ratings would suggest that none of the strategies being evaluated addresses that particular value. If the value in question is considered important, new strategies should be proposed (or existing strategies amended) to reflect the value.

An Example

With the basic outline of value congruence analysis before us, and recalling the caveats about its purpose and goals, we can now

188

consider how it might be applied to an issue in the realm of aging policy. A personal note is in order first, though. I have wrestled seriously with the question of whether or not to include my own ratings of some real programs. Recall that the *outcome* of the value congruence analysis is not what is important. Instead, it is the *process* of identification, deliberation, and revision that gives the analysis its value, and that process cannot be adequately related or experienced merely through a presentation of the final value congruence matrix. Nonetheless, I have decided that an illustration of how the value congruence model works is necessary to give life to the abstract description above.

It should be noted that this matrix represents at least my fourth effort[7] to rate these policy approaches in terms of their congruence with my understanding of relevant Christian values. During that process of rating, re-rating, reflecting, and re-rating again, some of my ratings changed as much as from "highly" to "slightly" or vice versa. I am not sure that I exactly enjoyed the process, either: It is hard work deciding what one really thinks about programs as complex and problematic as these, then reevaluating them in terms of one another, and finally articulating one's reasons and defending them in discussions with others. Also, some discomfort is usually involved any time one is forced to face up to one's own basic assumptions and to examine seriously and systematically the values used to justify positions held on matters of importance to that person.

Chapters 1 and 2 of this book serve as step 1 of the model, which calls for a thorough understanding of the dilemma that prompts a policy response. Step 2, a description of the existing response, is carried out in chapters 3 and 4. The identification and explication of the values I find most relevant to the issue at hand (step 3) begin in chapter 5; for me these values come from the Christian faith. Chapter 6 also contains a discussion of dominant American values and how they are reflected in the positions taken by many of those involved in the current debate about aging policy. Step 4 calls for selection of the strategies to be analyzed. I consider first the basic Social Security pension program, Old Age and Survivors Insurance (OASI). Next I look at Supplemental Security Income (SSI), the means-tested program that is designed to assist those of any age who fall below certain income levels but is often resorted to by the poor elderly. Both of these programs have been described in chapter 3. Finally, I apply the value congruence model to the "privatization" of old-age insurance discussed briefly in chapter 4, an alternative to current programs that has been proposed by a number of advocates of "generational equity."

The value congruence matrix created in step 5 of the analysis appears as exhibit 7.3. Although I will not attempt to explain or justify all of my ratings, nor to recount the numerous revisions I made in them or the reasons for those changes, several examples will be helpful for illustrative purposes. The first time through the matrix, I rated each of the three programs separately on each value. Later I went through again, looking at the three together in light of the relative ratings I had assigned for each value. My first revisions occurred at this point as I decided, for example, that if OASI deserved a "moderately congruent" rating for "love of others," then SSI had to be raised from my original rating of "slightly congruent" because it exemplifies even more than OASI the value of unmerited giving with no expectation of return. Similarly, my original ratings on "justice/equity"[8] changed several times, upward for privatization as I decided that that value is at the heart of this strategy and downward for SSI as I realized that it does not embody equity at all. Interestingly, I noticed that my ratings in general were higher the first time through and then lower on subsequent iterations.

I also discovered that I simply might have overlooked a significant consideration in assigning a rating, as when I originally gave privatization a "neutral/irrelevant" on "acceptance of mortality" because I did not see how the proposed strategy incorporated the value at all. In a subsequent iteration, however, it struck me that urging people to plan consciously for their later years by having to arrange old-age insurance for themselves acknowledges one's aging and thus ultimate death more than programs that make such provisions automatically and, for most

EXHIBIT 7.3
VALUE CONGRUENCE MATRIX
FOR AGING POLICIES

| | STRATEGIES | | |
| | Existing | | Proposed |
VALUES	OASI	SSI	Privatization
Love for Others	MC	HC	MI
Concern for Needy	MC	HC	HI
Respect for Parents/ Elderly	HC	MC	MI
Community	MC	HC	MI
Mercy/Adequacy	MC	HC	HI
Justice/Equity	SC	HI	HC
Source of True Happiness	N	N	SI
Recognition of Dependence	MC	HC	MI
Acceptance of Mortality	SC	N	MC
Munificence of God	N	SC	SI
Value of Work	SC	MI	HC
Purpose of Government	HC	HC	MI

HC Highly Congruent   HI Highly Incongruent
MC Moderately Congruent   MI Moderately Incongruent
SC Slightly Congruent   SI Slightly Incongruent
N Neutral/Irrelevant

people, without their even realizing it. My "neutral/irrelevant" thus changed to a "moderately congruent."

Exhibit 7.4 summarizes the distribution of my final congruence ratings, the basis for step 6 of the analysis. An examination of the table suggests that of the three strategies analyzed, OASI and SSI are most congruent with the Christian values I deem essential in the evaluation of strategies intended to provide for people in their later years. Although SSI receives more "highly congruent" ratings, OASI receives more positive congruence ratings overall. Because the analysis is not intended to be precisely quantitative, probably the best that can be said in this

EXHIBIT 7.4
DISTRIBUTION OF CONGRUENCE RATINGS
FOR AGING POLICIES

STRATEGIES

RATINGS	OASI	SSI	Privatization
Highly Congruent (HC)	2	6	2
Moderately Congruent (MC)	5	1	1
Slightly Congruent (SC)	3	1	0
Neutral/Irrelevant (N)	2	2	0
Slightly Incongruent (SI)	0	0	2
Moderately Incongruent (MI)	0	1	5
Highly Incongruent (HI)	0	1	2

particular case is that both programs are quite congruent with the identified values. Note, however, that even if, say, OASI had received ratings that made it clearly most congruent, SSI and even privatization would still rate more congruent on certain values. Remember also that these ratings are relative, not absolute. The fact that one strategy is *more* congruent than another does not mean that it fully reflects the values identified as critical. Revisions or alternatives may easily produce a program that is even more congruent and therefore embodies essential values more adequately.

One clear conclusion does emerge from this analysis: It would appear that privatization has little to recommend it in comparison to the existing old-age insurance programs. Step 7 of the analysis, however, suggests that such an outcome means that one's value congruence analysis is not complete and that not enough effort has been made to understand this particular strategy. Advocates of privatization might contend, for example, that my list of values overlooks some that they consider essential to any discussion of Social Security. Privatization might well embody such cherished values of the "American way of life" as independence, individualism, privacy, and striving for success earned on one's own merit (see chapter 6), none of which I would want to reject totally. Indeed, such advocates might argue that privatization reflects even a Christian value like concern for others. After all, one of the goals of such an approach is to avoid a situation in which large numbers of older people in the future are counting on Social Security to fund their retirement, only to find the system bankrupt because of current inequitable benefit structures and increasing dependency ratios.

Stewardship is another important Christian value that has been omitted from the analysis so far, and, although I would argue that for Christians economic considerations cannot be finally determinative, any sensible and serious contribution to public policy discussion from a theological perspective must recognize the economic realities. Privatization then can be seen as a response to a legitimate concern about allocation of resources when there may not be enough for everyone under certain conditions of distribution. In short, completing the value congruence analysis requires me to recognize that a strategy that appears at first to be largely incongruent with most of my values may deserve further examination.

Not incidentally, this discussion points up once more the importance of utilizing the value congruence approach in groups, within which give and take, challenge and response, can occur. Someone who advocates privatization could present more values in support of such a proposal and perhaps even point out ways in which this strategy reflects more of the values I identified as important. In conversation with such a person, I would have to clarify my reasons for holding the values I hold and for advocating the policies and programs I advocate, perhaps even modifying some of them as I receive new information from both within and without. I would hope that the process would lead anyone who disagrees with me to do the same.

Furthermore, reference to exhibit 7.3 shows that four of the values from step 3 ("source of true happiness," "acceptance of mortality," "munificence of God," and "value of work") scored quite low for the two existing programs. This suggests that these values, which I identified as important and relevant ones, are not being expressed well in either of the existing programs considered in this analysis. If one wants to maintain the significance of these values (and I do), step 7 of the analysis again urges consideration of alternative strategies that will better reflect them.

Let me conclude this example by acknowledging my awareness that few readers will agree with my interpretations and ratings. This comes as no great surprise. In fact, my purpose in offering this value congruence analysis will be best served if that is what happens! If the reader concludes this section by saying, "How could he give *that* value *this* rating?" or "Why does he think *that* value is more important than this one?" or "What does he think that value means or that program does?" then he or she will have begun to engage in precisely the process that I am advocating and that the value congruence model facilitates. In that process, the reader will also have begun to discover and to appreciate the usefulness of the model (though I must reiterate here that value congruence analysis is most effective when employed in a group setting that allows a multiplicity of opinions, perspectives, experiences, and value orientations to be expressed).

Some Comments

Several things remain to be said about value congruence analysis as proposed in this chapter. The first is a word of warning. A characteristic of any model is the oversimplification of reality, and I do not want to give the impression that the approach described here represents a way to take into consideration every facet of an amazingly complex situation. Nonetheless, in the very process of simplifying whatever policy issue is chosen for analysis, some of the hard choices have to be made that begin the movement toward understanding the values that underlie the position to be taken on the issue. At the end, however, it must be remembered that the complexities of virtually any issue are too great to be dealt with adequately in a

194

model, which again demonstrates that the process of reflection, articulation, and especially discussion is the most important contribution of value congruence analysis.

In fact, the example above should make clear that one of the strengths of this type of analysis is its "dynamic" nature. That is, although the model provides a systematic and orderly framework within which to relate values and public policy, it also requires frequent adjustments to evaluations made in previous steps and contains several built-in checks that help to prevent unfair assessments, especially in steps 5 and 7. As we have just seen, when one policy came out with uniformly low congruence ratings, I was forced to reconsider my own point of view in an effort to be fair, and when several values failed to garner any high ratings, I have had both to ask if those values really are important in this context and to seek strategies that might better embody them in our society.

Value congruence analysis demonstrates flexibility in another sense as well. I am using explicitly Christian values in this book, but the analysis allows for the utilization of values derived from any source or discipline, such as medicine, economics, or philosophy. Indeed, the most effective application of this method of analysis might well be with a group in which several different value orientations are represented. The model provides a way to take all of these various perspectives into account and to incorporate their insights into policy discussion, evaluation, and formulation.

Note also that value congruence analysis can be applied much more broadly than just to the evaluation of particular strategies for public policy on aging. For example, in chapter 6 I was interested in examining not so much policy strategies themselves as the positions of the critics and the supporters of current aging policy. My assessment of the values that underlie those positions was written after applying value congruence analysis to the two positions. In fact, *any* moral issue can be profitably examined using this methodology, and an interesting exercise might be for groups, or even individuals, to apply value congruence analysis to, say, their personal attitudes toward abortion or termination-of-treatment decisions, rating them according to the values deemed relevant for the issue.

Moving beyond methodology, the value congruence approach to the evaluation of public policy has one outstanding advantage: It provides a mechanism that requires people always to keep values in mind because it states explicitly exactly what the values are that are being addressed and insists that all programs and policies be evaluated systematically and comprehensively in light of the complete set of values that have been identified as relevant. Without some method to ensure such comprehensiveness, an individual or group may be strongly committed to one particular value (or even limited set of values) and therefore may tend to "keep the spotlight" on that value alone. To do so, however, can lead to a loss of awareness of the overall picture (recall my image earlier of the stream and the cottage) and thus to neglect of values and persons that should be considered. For example, those who see generational *equity* as the only value worthy of implementation in proposed aging policy can overlook the genuine needs of people who are not in a position (and never have been) to take advantage of such a value. On the other hand, to concentrate solely on *mercy* toward some limited group can be to lose sight of legitimate stewardship concerns and end up being unfair (and perhaps even unmerciful) toward some other people.

Value congruence analysis thus encourages recognition not only of one's own guiding principles but also of those of others with whom one may disagree, and this is a second major advantage of the approach. Indeed, one of the major problems with much recent public debate about aging policy is that the participants are approaching the issues from totally different starting points. Their presuppositions, assumptions, and basic values are different, but these diverse starting points go unrecognized and unacknowledged in the heat of often acrimonious charges and countercharges. Such discussion is not fruitful. Utilization of value congruence analysis, however, forces examination of the basic assumptions, the fundamental values on which the positions of others, as well as one's own, are

196

based. By formalizing evaluation of the values that underlie various policies and programs, such analysis can help to produce healthier compromises as the various parties discover that their basic values may not be all that dissimilar. Any individual or group serious about influencing public policy in a pluralistic democracy must be willing to move toward an acceptance of some of the values of others, provided that those values are not so alien to one's own as to be completely incompatible. Without such willingness to try to see the situation from the perspective of others, it is hard to imagine any policy formulation that can respond to the needs and wishes of as broad a representation of the population as possible.

At the very least, a systematic process of value identification, explication, and discussion such as that offered by value congruence analysis ought to show us that our opponents are not always evil people just because they disagree with our policy analyses and recommendations. Perhaps they simply hold values different from ours, values that mean as much to them as ours do to us and that they can defend as well as we can defend ours. We demand and expect acknowledgment of the validity of our values because they are the foundation upon which our whole understanding of reality rests. Serious analysis of our values, as well as of the values of those with whom we disagree, should lead us to grant the same respect to them.

A third advantage of value congruence analysis, one that should hold special appeal to religious bodies, is its opportunity for growth in knowledge of self and group. The systematic nature of the ranking and rating, coupled with the requirement for frequent reevaluation and discussion of those judgments, encourages personal and group maturation as participants in the analysis are forced to put their values in order of priority and to engage in a process of comparison, explanation, and reevaluation. Furthermore, values come to be understood even better when strategies are rated according to how well they fit each value: During this step of analysis closer attention must be paid not only to the meaning of each value in relation to its application in life but also to its relevance to a particular strategy for responding to a problem. The result of this systematic

197

twofold encounter with an individual's or a group's values is an important one: At the end of the process, instead of just *thinking* (or believing, or even "feeling") that one value is more important than another or that one strategy is preferable to another, one should have discovered *why* he or she thinks so. As I said above in the discussion of the example, it is hard work as one confronts one's own most deeply held and all-too-often unexamined beliefs and values (i.e., assumptions).

Value congruence analysis can lead to another positive outcome. One of the problems with much contemporary ethical discussion is that values, though given lip service as central to the ethical enterprise, often seem to disappear when concrete action plans are devised. What, one often wants to ask, is the connection between the values articulated as important and the proposals made? One reason for the effectiveness of Jesus as a moral teacher is that he always gave concreteness to the values he taught, either by embodying them in his own life or by applying them in parables. The translation of values into behavior was high on Jesus' list of religious priorities (witness his running feud with the Pharisees!). In rating strategies by each of the values identified as the guiding principles for the analyst(s), the participant(s) in value congruence analysis must identify the real values that are motivating behavior and must give them concrete application to the specific issue at hand.

Of course, decent and honorable people will disagree on what the critical values are, which of those values are most important, and what specific programs and proposals best implement any particular values. Speaking practically to religious groups for a moment, though, it seems that if such groups harbor any hopes of influencing public policy, they need to work very hard to agree among themselves about which values ought to be maximized. Policy proposals can then be analyzed in accord with these values and supported or not supported depending on how well they are in accord with them. Obviously, the value congruence analysis proposed here lends itself very well to use in various group settings within the churches (as well as in "seniors groups" of all kinds).

In conclusion, I want to repeat that the real value of this approach to public policy analysis lies in the *process* that it encourages and guides of identifying, articulating, and applying those values that are most important to the group's self-understanding. Having done the hard work required by the model—both of learning about the dimensions of the dilemma and of hammering out agreement on the values that ought to be embodied in aging policy—a religious group can speak intelligently and forcefully in the public arena.

LOOKING BACK—AND AHEAD

In the introduction I made the case that the churches have a legitimate and important role to play in the public policy process in the United States, despite our historic commitment to separation of church and state, our religious freedom and tolerance, and our increasing religious diversity. At that point the role of the churches had to be described in abstract terms because we did not yet have the information necessary to permit concrete analysis and interpretation. Now we have gained such knowledge through an examination of the demographic, economic, and social situation this country faces as its population grows increasingly older over the next half-century. We also have been reminded of one of the distinctive marks and potential contributions of the churches, a deep commitment to a set of values that Christians claim reflect God's loving will for humanity. Finally, we have learned about a method for relating those values to the information gathered earlier.

Our discussion therefore can now take a more concrete turn. The last step of value congruence analysis focuses special attention in three areas: first, strategies or positions that do not at first appear very congruent with the original list of important values; second, new strategies that embody these values better than the strategies under consideration; and third, new values that have been omitted from the analysis. Chapter 8 offers some further thoughts that arise from my reflection upon these areas.

SHEDDING LIGHT: FURTHER THOUGHTS ON THE CHURCHES AND PUBLIC POLICY

THE IMPORTANCE OF VALUES IN DISCUSSIONS OF AGING POLICY

The question of values lies at the heart of any discussion of public policy. More and more observers of contemporary America in general and of the coming demographic dilemma in particular agree that solutions to our social problems lie less in the realm of facts and figures than in the arena of values. We have heard several such statements already. Robert Reich summarizes the position well when he points out that the usual extremes of political discourse in this country—at the one end "the transient moods elicited by political advertising or lofty rhetoric" and at the other "the detailed policy prescriptions manufactured by the inhabitants of Washington think tanks and universities"—neglect the major area in which social problems are defined and public goals discovered, "a realm of parable and metaphor. . . . To dismiss this realm as 'ideological'—meaningless because irrational and unempirical—is to miss the point that value, not fact, is the currency of the realm. It is to neglect the importance of values for motivating a society."[1]

Thus values are critical to what we are about because, as I

suggested in chapter 6, relationships among the generations appear to be governed increasingly by values that reflect a "zero-sum" attitude: If one generation receives something, it must be at the expense of another. Furthermore, I have claimed that the best hope for overcoming this "zero-sum" approach to intergenerational relationships is to change the "utilities" or payoffs that the players in the game are seeking to maximize. This again is a matter of values because the utilities that a person adopts are reflections of what he or she considers worth striving for—that is, what is believed valuable. Recall that "preference precedes utility": What is favored, sought, chosen is a person's utility, which he or she seeks to maximize. Perhaps we can say simply that what we strive to get is, not surprisingly, a function of what we want. If we can change underlying preferences—assessments of what is important—utilities will change and behavior will be directed to different ends. Reich once more: "Public problems don't exist 'out there.' They are not discrete facts or pieces of data awaiting discovery. They are *consequences* of our shared values."[2] Again, it appears that if values can be revised, definitions of "public problems" can change, and with changed definitions can come new insight into solutions.

In our particular case, it is pointless if not impossible to talk about "public policy on aging" in any meaningful sense without realizing that the situation that demands such policy merely reflects the social structure of society in general, mirroring the values, power relationships, and inequities that exist much more broadly across and through all age groups. The difficulty is that these fundamental values and the utilities that stem from them usually remain unrecognized and unarticulated, precisely because they are so basic, what the German theologian Helmut Thielicke once called "the things an era takes for granted." The centrality of values to the being and activity of the churches, however, gives the churches precisely the perspective and expertise that are needed in today's public policy discussion. Along with these advantages comes an abiding responsibility to foster such discussion and to offer viable alternatives to the commonly held utilities that lead to much of the controversy about relationships among generations.

ADEQUACY AND EQUITY, MERCY AND JUSTICE

Adequacy and Equity

We have seen in previous chapters that recent public discussion of aging policy has become polarized into two camps, one that largely endorses current policy (though recognizing the need for some adjustments) and another that considers that policy to give too much to the elderly, especially to those who are not needy, at the expense of others who are needy, especially children. Analysis of this tension between supporters of current aging policy and its critics suggests that the major source of their disagreement stems from the fundamental value that each side considers primary and thus upon which their assessment of existing (and proposed) policy is based. Supporters, well exemplified from among a number of elder advocacy groups by the American Association of Retired Persons (AARP), appear to stress the value of "adequacy," underscoring the vulnerability of the elderly and the need for a civilized society to assure them adequate income that will allow for a decent standard of living.

Critics of current policy, on the other hand, best represented by Americans for Generational Equity (AGE), emphasize, as their name suggests, the value of "equity" in their critiques, arguing that the generations are treated inequitably (or unfairly) by the existing imbalance in public expenditures, an imbalance that they project to be even worse when the "baby boom" generation reaches retirement age beginning in 2012. As in most such controversies, more common ground probably exists than either side recognizes (or is willing to grant), and confusion about the nature and the purpose of existing policies and programs contributes further to the tension.

Indeed, because of the fundamental values of our culture, some of this same tension and confusion is inherent in United

States aging policy itself and, in general, throughout all of our social policy. Again, Social Security illustrates the point well. As we saw in chapter 3, the founders of Social Security were sensitive to both "adequacy" and "equity" when they created the program, and they knew that the two values in conjunction possess an inner dynamic that needs to be kept in some sort of balance.[3] Throughout its existence, therefore, Social Security has been a program that neither serves simply a welfare (adequacy) function nor is merely an insurance (equity) program. From its inception it was meant to serve both purposes at once. This dual thrust, however, has led to confusion about what Social Security is intended to accomplish.

Theodore Marmor and his coauthors, for example, point out that critics of American welfare policy (and of Old Age and Survivors Insurance [OASI] in particular) "typically confuse the pursuit of an alternative purpose with a failure to achieve their own favorite welfare state goals."[4] Such confusion of purpose with result reflects the critics' value assumptions and thus expectations. For instance, because Social Security is *not* fundamentally an investment scheme (although the element of "putting aside for one's retirement" is part of the structure), there should be no expectation of return equivalent to what one might achieve through private investment. Rather, because of the complex interplay between the adequacy and equity principles, OASI is really an intergenerational agreement among all the working citizens of the country to help those more needy by allowing a portion of the greater wealth of some to be redistributed to others. Furthermore, this redistribution occurs in a way that allows those less well off to retain as much dignity as possible because it comes in the form of a return on their contribution (even if it represents a greater return for poorer workers than for those better off). Most of those who participate in this agreement do so largely unknowingly (and some others somewhat unwillingly), but that Social Security is so designed demonstrates the wisdom of those who devised the program. Whether they consciously intended it or not, the structure of the program they created embodies a heartening vision of intergenerational community.

Unfortunately, it is precisely this aspect of Social Security's fundamental nature that offends those for whom equity is the controlling value. Receiving one's due—whether that be a greater return for greater contribution or a smaller return for smaller contribution, even if one has little or no control over the conditions that lead to the magnitude of contribution or to current need—is seen to be the overriding consideration. But a one-sided emphasis on equity, whatever its motivation or however sincere its proponents, of necessity leads to a neglect of the needy. The poor (and near-poor) will never fare well in a system based on a return of what they have been able to contribute financially to any retirement system.

From a Christian perspective, however, the problem goes even deeper, to a basic difference in the understanding of justice itself. After all the rhetoric and the philosophical rationalization are set aside, the "equity" demanded by some critics of Social Security is simply *self*-centered. Equity has come to be seen as equivalent to getting what is due *us, our* fair share, what *we* want. This element, as we have seen, is part of the basic value structure of Social Security and reflects the original concept of equity, that is, that benefits are to be based to some extent on what the worker pays in.[5] But the equity principle was intended to be balanced by the adequacy principle, and this balance seems to have been lost by those who urge the dismantling of Social Security.

The view of equity mentioned above seems to be what is meant when the cry "generational equity" is raised: The elderly are getting too much, certainly more than they deserve or have contributed, and thus too much of *our* money. The stage is thus set for a "zero-sum" view of intergenerational relationships because our "utilities" are seen largely in terms of economic goods that benefit *us,* which we will lose if you get anything we think we deserve.

Mercy and Justice

From a Christian point of view, the parallel between justice and equity that has seemed so natural up to this point breaks

204

down here. Theologically speaking, justice—like virtually every-thing else in human experience—is turned completely upside-down and inside-out from the Christian perspective. According to the apostle Paul, anyone who is "in Christ" is a "new creation" (2 Cor. 5:17), controlled by the "love of Christ" who "died for all, so that those who live might live no longer for themselves, but for him who died and was raised for them" (vv. 14-15). And what better description is there of what living for Christ means than John 15:12-17: "This is my commandment, that you love one another as I have loved you." (v. 12)? From this vantage point, justice now means making sure *others* get what is *their* due, what *they* need, even if it "costs" *me* (cf. Jn. 15:13). Paul Ramsey expresses the point well when he affirms that "just as any who are [merely human] are apt to exercise partiality when judging their *own* cause, so Christian love (which is self-love inverted) judges with partiality the *neighbor's* cause, treats his case as exceedingly dissimilar from one's own."[6] Clearly we are dealing here with radically changed utilities from those expressed earlier.

Ramsey states bluntly the revision in the view espoused by advocates of generational equity that a Christian value orientation demands:

> We must wrench our minds around from supposing that all the poor and weak of the earth need is "equality before the law" or justice in the sense of equal opportunity and the devil take the hindmost. . . . Instead, partiality for them lies at the heart of the biblical notion of justice.[7]

In fact, in the final analysis adequacy and equity, mercy and justice are not so separate and opposing as they at first appear or as we may try to make them, at least not for Christians. God's justice in fact appears to *demand* our mercy, as both the prophets and Jesus make very clear, because that divine justice is directed toward redressing the imbalance between those who have and those who have not, and God's followers on earth are the ones who are commanded to implement that justice. Amos's plumb line (7:7-9) is clearly intended to represent divine justice—what else does a plumb line do but "judge"?—and the rest of Amos makes clear that what is out-of-square, not straight about the people to whom he is speaking is at least in no small part their lack of mercy and compassion for those less fortunate (cf. 2:6-7, in which God vows to punish Israel "because they sell the righteous for silver, and the needy for a pair of sandals—they who trample the head of the poor into the dust of the earth, and push the afflicted out of the way").

Indeed, for Christians God's justice *is* mercy. The way God chose to exercise divine justice in dealing with human sin, which justly deserved the harshest punishment, was through mercy, a love so profound that the just God suffered in God's own person the ultimate punishment for our sakes.[8] There was no *justice* in this saving act on God's part; it resulted from God's unbounded *mercy*. In this light, Paul Ramsey's assertion rings true: "Jesus Christ must be kept at the heart of all Christian thinking about justice—and precisely that sort of justice which should prevail in the 'world of systems,' in this world and not some other."[9] From a Christian point of view, the only true justice (equity) lies in mercy (adequacy at least).

To sum it all up in a simple yet profound sentence, the *motivation* for justice comes from mercy. To put it another way, mercy brings us to practice justice. Implementing this divine requirement may of course mean giving up to others some of what we can claim as our own (recall the notion of the munificence of God, which reminds us that all that *any* of us has comes as a freely given gift from God). Indeed, the scriptural evidence is strong that this compassion for the needy is the basis upon which our faithfulness to the risen Christ will be judged (cf., e.g., Matt. 25:31-46).

Old Testament scholar Norman Gottwald offers an apt summary of both the roots and the challenge of the biblical notions of mercy and justice:

> The truth is that the cruelty and neglect suffered by the poor and deprived of the earth continue in our time without any surcease. . . . On this point the Bible is as contemporary a

document as can be imagined. Without giving specific instruc-
tions, it says again and again in stunning ways that something
must be done about mass economic injustice in our world if this is
to become God's earth and we are to be God's people.[10]

This statement draws us back more directly to our public
policy concerns, and the conclusion of our consideration of
adequacy/mercy and equity/justice[11] can be summarized simply:
From a Christian perspective, any public policy that does not
concern itself with meeting the needs of the less fortunate of
society, that serves instead to enhance the financial situation of
those who are already comfortably situated, is unjust and
therefore unacceptable.[12] Clearly Christians need to look at
aging issues not from the first understanding of equity described
above, that of getting what is due *us*, but rather from the second,
that of assuring that *others* get what is due them, or even more if
that is necessary for a decent life. Such a commitment would
preclude any possibility of taking a zero-sum approach in which
we believe that your gain must be our loss and would result in
some very different utilities as we no longer seek to maximize
only our own benefits.

A final consideration to come out of this analysis can be
mentioned here. Adequacy and equity are the basic values that
policymakers decided from the beginning should be embodied
in Social Security, indeed, the values upon which the system is
based. Thus it is hardly inappropriate to advocate them in a
pluralistic, diverse society, even if one bases one's understanding
of them on religious beliefs and emphasizes one over the other.
After all, others do the same thing, only stressing the other
value! By appealing to a theological basis for values that are
recognized throughout society as foundational, those who are
concerned with living out their faith in life can find guidance
and motivation meaningful to them without fear that they are
trying to impose values upon society that are not widely shared
within it or are even alien to it.

In fact, this same line of reasoning can be applied to the overall
approach taken in this book. From the beginning I have based

my analyses and suggestions on my avowed Christian values, values that are often suspect in the public policy arena. I have argued that any significant improvement in intergenerational relationships, and any useful policy approaches to the demographic dilemma we face, will have to be based upon a fundamental shift in the dominant metaphors we live by. In short, we must move beyond the "zero-sum" mentality and see beyond narrow self-interest to a heightened sense of community based on genuine concern for others that embodies both justice and mercy. The recognition of a number of other values identified earlier will also facilitate this shift. These values and this argument are clearly Christian, *but* they are *also* in the best interests of the nation as a whole. On this last affirmation we can rest the validity of our values, analyses, and suggestions in dialogue with "objective" observers and analysts.

IS AGE REALLY THE PROBLEM? OR IS *AGE* THE PROBLEM?

With this general discussion of the values that underlie the call for "generational equity" as background, a more specific response to the claims made by the movement's proponents is in order. As I have suggested several times, current policy is not above criticism and revision. The bulk of the criticism leveled at it by advocates of generational equity like AGE, however, and perhaps even more the *tone* of that criticism appear to me to be misdirected and thus only obscure the real issues and distract attention from them.

In the first place, the claim that the elderly are not productive and therefore represent only a drain on society's limited resources is untenable from the Christian perspective, in which *all* persons are deemed worthy because they are God's children and because Jesus Christ died for them. In fact, as we have seen, the elderly are even accorded a special place of honor in this tradition. Beyond theological inadequacy, though, this view of the elderly seems to fall short on economic grounds as well. In the first place, many older people do still work in various ways,

208

including countless volunteer hours without which many institutions in this country could hardly function.

Even more significant is an argument advanced by gerontologist Vernon L. Greene that the elderly represent "human capital," which he asserts determines a society's economic well-being more than physical capital does. Just as other forms of capital are created by postponing immediate consumption for the sake of future productivity, the elderly gave up spending financial resources and free time on themselves when they were younger in order to make available to today's workers the knowledge, the skills, and the attitudes of the labor force that generate current production. In short, older people created human "capital" by "investing" *themselves,* primarily in the creation and continuation of the educational system, formal and informal, that produced today's workers.

Greene asks who the human capitalists are who "sacrificed their earlier personal consumption and potential for private savings to invest in the vast enterprise of human-capital creation to which our society owes its physical comfort and economic wealth." The answer, of course, is "those same 'greedy geezers' who . . . many now say should have been putting money into personal savings (instead of squandering it on taxes for the next generation's care and education) so that they wouldn't be such a 'burden' to us now," that is, "the elderly."[13] A human capital perspective, Greene claims, refutes the charge that *any* benefits the elderly receive can be called "welfare." Such benefits are instead "but the claim of major investors to a return on the human capital that they sacrificed to create."[14] Greene concludes, "On balance, they have probably taken better care of us than some of us now wish to take of them." This argument does not answer all the claims made by the generational equity movement, and it is not without its own problems. It does seem to me to represent a change in values that moves beyond a zero-sum attitude and leads to a more helpful way to think about the situation.

The second thing to be said by way of response to proponents of generational equity is the introductory statistics instructor's first, frequently repeated, and probably most important remark to students: "Correlation does not prove causation." That is to say, merely because two events occur simultaneously or even in conjunction with each other does not mean that one *caused* the other or even had any meaningful influence upon it. Leaving aside for the moment the serious question of whether the two events under consideration here—the relative improvement in the condition of our oldest citizens and the relative decline in that of our youngest—are correlated at all, it is naive, simplistic, and downright mean-spirited to assert that bringing one group (many of the elderly of this nation) up to some decent standard of living is to blame for the unconscionable plight of another group (our children) and that the best solution to the problem of child poverty is to implement policies that are likely to return many of those older persons to poverty.

Philosopher Norman Daniels echoes the judgments of a number of authorities when he asserts simply, "The issue is miscast if it is portrayed as competition between children and the elderly."[15] The resources of this country are expended on much more than programs for the elderly and for children. I will say again, then, especially given recent changes in the world political situation, that if resources are limited and there must be competition for funds, it should not be between programs that help elderly human beings and those that help young human beings but between programs that help *all* human beings and those that help none.

A third concern with the generational equity view has to do with motivation. The position taken by AGE and its supporters seems at best an uninformed and misguided mixture of fear and of admittedly legitimate concerns about potential problems facing our nation in the next century, but at worst it can be seen as a "cynical and purposely divisive strategy put forth to justify and build support for attacks on policies and reductions in programs that benefit all age groups."[16] The real problem is that many advocates of generational equity appear to have misstated the situation to serve their own political ends, which appear to grow out of the traditional conservative antipathy toward

210

government in general and public assistance for those less fortunate than themselves in particular.

The appeal to important and generally accepted values like fairness, equal treatment under the law, and concern for children seems instead to mask a different agenda. In fact, despite AGE's claimed commitment to improving the plight of poor children, the organization has offered no policy proposals to do so. Furthermore, it is of more than passing curiosity that many of the individuals, corporations, and organizations that have recently become ardent in their call for generational equity are precisely ones that traditionally have shown virtually no concern for the poor children of this country or for the welfare of future generations, instead criticizing *all* government programs that assist the needy and calling for cutbacks in such spending, especially those aimed directly at children, such as Aid to Families with Dependent Children (AFDC).

Indeed, in addition to Norman Daniels' warranted skepticism that "dismantling the protection we have afforded the elderly poor will really be followed by more adequate transfers to the remaining poor,"[17] a basic flaw exists in the central tenet of generational equity that government transfers to the elderly hurt children. In the absence of such transfers, the only other reasonable source of support for the elderly is family, meaning primarily their adult children (who, as we have seen, already provide the majority of direct care). Such care, however, does not tend to involve much financial support: Fewer than 1 percent of the elderly in recent surveys receive their major financial support from children or other relatives, and fewer than 5 percent receive enough to list as "income." If public benefits to the elderly were restricted, however, families would have to make up the difference, thus reducing the resources available to further their children's welfare. In addition, the impact on the elders' self-esteem should not be overlooked: Of the 5 percent mentioned above who received financial help from family, fewer than 20 percent considered it appropriate and desirable.

The French writer Bernanos once observed that "the worst and most corrupting of lies are problems wrongly stated." By allowing AGE to "state the problem" in this case, we have created a zero-sum mentality that deflects the harsh light of truth from the real issues. The fundamental problem with the view of those who paint America's current and future problems in the hues of intergenerational conflict, in which the elderly are the villains because they have it "so much better" than younger people, is that the real issue is not one of *age* at all, though the demographic data presented earlier definitely complicate the matter. The true problem is the age-old one of unequal distribution of wealth, with all the inequities that creates between rich and poor of any age. It is not so much a question of taking from the young to support the old, or robbing children of basic necessities to provide the elderly with luxuries, as it is a matter of assuring that all who have legitimate needs are enabled to live a decent life, whatever their age. That is not a "generational" issue at all.[18]

Unfortunately, couching the debate in terms of *inter*generational equity can blind us to these inequities *within* each generation and throughout society at the same time that it keeps us from pursuing seriously our nation's avowed goal—honored more in its failure than achievement—of justice for those of any age who are most needy. That many of the elderly of our society (bearing in mind the large number who still live in poverty or on its very edge) have been enabled to count on a minimally decent standard of living in their later years is hardly a fact to be lamented. Rather, attention should be directed to the increasing disparity in economic resources among all generations that denies an acceptable quality of life to many, both young and old.

Our national character contains more fundamental failings than an old-age insurance program that admittedly contains some inequities. Trying to take resources away from the elderly will hardly rectify these shortcomings. In a country as wealthy and supposedly civilized as ours, the logical approach is not to advocate retrenchment with regard to the elderly but to use as models the programs that have been successful for them and to work for similar programs for children (and any other truly needy persons). In short, the question we really need to ask is well put by Gary M. Nelson, Director of the Center for Aging

Research and Educational Services at the University of North Carolina School of Social Work: "How do we best ensure that all members of society, irrespective of age, have equal access to a fair share of society's social spending in order to sustain life at a decent standard of humanity?"[19]

However valid the claim that age lies at the heart of the issues we have been discussing, it should be noted, recalling a point made often in chapter 2 especially, that one of the major roots of the problem may be found in a distinction even more fundamental than that between young and old—namely, that between male and female. What happens to men and women as they journey through life differs markedly in ways too numerous even to mention here, and surely this lifelong trail of variance leads to some markedly different experiences. We have already seen this to be true when it comes to life expectancy, income security, prospects and responsibilities for care in the later years, and the like. Thus, although aging itself is a universal phenomenon, the *experience* of it, and certainly the impact it has upon a person socially, psychologically, and financially, may be more dependent upon gender considerations than is usually recognized.

As Beth B. Hess points out, in the 1950s the elderly poor were mostly male heads of families and unemployed workers, and major increases in old-age benefits received high priority. Today, however, women and people of color make up a large majority of the poor elderly, and there is a rising tide of sentiment that programs for the elderly lie at the root of all that threatens the continued well-being of the United States. It is hard to avoid the conclusion Hess draws: "Because the life course is played within systems of stratification, sex and race distinctions will remain crucial to understanding the process of aging in any society as long as gender and racial equality remain distant goals."[20] Sadly, she aptly describes the United States of America in the last decade of the twentieth century.

One last point before moving on: I mentioned earlier the "tone" of much of the recent writing on intergenerational relationships, with its almost vicious condemnations of the

213

elderly for their purported greed and lack of concern for anybody but themselves. Epithets such as "greedy geezers" appear regularly. This attitude raises a disturbing question in light of the traditional American concern for the disadvantaged members of society. One is tempted to ask what has happened to our country in this arena. People who as *individuals* are good people, who give to charity and probably even volunteer some of their time for various civic or religious causes, write as if *public* policy that assists other people who may need help in one way or another is beyond their ken, is something no reasonable person would even consider. What are we missing? Where is the connection that will allow us to put into practice in our public policy the basic goodness that so many people in this country still demonstrate privately?

Perhaps the answer lies (and it comes as no surprise to those who are familiar with Christian theology) in a comment made by that astute observer of human nature, Mark Twain, many years ago: "In any community, big or little, there is always a fair proportion of people who are not malicious or unkind by nature, and who never do unkind things except when they are overmastered by fear, or when their self-interest is in danger."[21] In this case, both of Twain's reasons come into play (and also help to explain the misstatement of the case by advocates of generational equity described above): the fear that the needs (and desires) of the elderly will overwhelm the resources of younger generations available to meet them; and the self-interest of those same younger people as far as an increased tax burden today and lack of provision for their later years are concerned. This self-interested fear causes people to build walls, to install locks, so to speak, to hold on to and to protect what they consider to be theirs. It is hard not to think here of the statement in 1 John, "There is no fear in love, but perfect love casts out fear" (4:18). The change in utilities described earlier, from self-directed to other-directed (recall Paul Ramsey's definition of Christian love as "self-love inverted"), of necessity reduces the self-interest that causes so much of our fear. We do not usually fear those with whom we communicate, cooperate, and work together to build community.

IS *AGE* ALL BAD, THOUGH?

AGE has just taken a beating, it would seem, perhaps even looking a little like a "straw man." The philosophy of the value congruence analysis presented in chapter 7, however, requires reevaluation of any position that appears to be totally unacceptable. Therefore we need to pause for a moment here to see if something valuable in the position taken by AGE and its supporters has been overlooked. We have already seen that a major difference exists in fundamental values between that stance and the one suggested in this book, but perhaps there is something more that we have missed.

The Plight of Children

In fact, advocates of generational equity raise several valid claims (some of which I have made throughout this book), and some aspects of their proposals have much to recommend them. The children of this country are suffering terribly, and we are running a grave risk with our future if their situation is not addressed soon and seriously. A child of a single mother (divorced or never married) is over five times as likely to be poor as a child in a two-parent family, and around 30 percent of American families are now single-parent. In fact, one-quarter of American children are born to single parents, leaving little room to wonder why over 20 percent of all children live in poverty. Interestingly, just as the importance of the family as the primary source of support for the elderly (financially at least) has declined steadily during this century because of the growth of various social insurance programs, the same divestment with regard to children seems to be occurring now, largely as the result of some of the factors just mentioned. For example, the large increase in the number of children born outside of marriage means that fewer fathers assume ongoing responsibility for them, as is often the case in divorce situations as well. The problem is that the government has not seen fit to step in and fill the gap in supporting children as it has with older people. The generational equity movement's focus on the plight of our

215

nation's children is significant and welcome. Practically any value one can think of—equity, adequacy, concern for the needy, community, common decency—cries out for attention to this problem.

Problems with Social Security

AGE also has rightly pointed out that many elderly who do not need Social Security benefits receive far more than they paid into the program, subverting not only the principle of equity but also decreasing adequacy: If they received less, more would be available for the truly needy. How best to rectify this situation is a technical question beyond my competence to answer. The recent move to tax Social Security benefits above a certain level seems reasonable. In fact, given that these benefits have taken on the nature of "wage replacement" as the program has evolved, perhaps they should simply be taxed as ordinary income. A similar proposal has been made with regard to the cash value of Medicare benefits. Certainly the regressivity currently embodied in the FICA tax must be reduced or preferably eliminated.

Raising or removing the cap on income subject to Social Security taxation and "flattening" the benefit formula to give an even higher rate of return to low-income workers relative to high-income workers also seem in line with the values presented in this book. Changes in the indexing (COLA) formula have also been proposed. As it works now, with automatic adjustments made based on the consumer price index, retirees are protected from the inflationary pressures everyone else in the country suffers. Some therefore propose a system in which certain inflationary elements that affect the elderly very little (like new housing costs) are excluded from the calculation of the COLA.

Some of the suggestions for a two-tier Social Security system may hold promise as well. Such a system separates the equity function into more of a straight "investment" program, with return tied directly and uniformly to amount of contributions, and the adequacy function into a means-tested program that targets the truly needy. Any such proposal would need to be scrutinized very carefully, however, to ensure that it was not a camouflaged attempt to "privatize" old-age insurance and eviscerate the adequacy function. One of the interesting things about many of these proposed revisions is that they serve both equity and adequacy functions at once: The contributions of those who are financially secure are more in line with their ability to pay (and/or the benefits they receive are also more appropriate relative to what they paid in), and more funds become available to distribute to those who need them.

The Crisis in Health Care

I hesitate even to raise the issue of health care, and true to my promise in the introduction, this discussion will be mercifully brief. Much of the problem in provision of services for the elderly, especially with regard to health care, comes from our unwillingness to face up to some difficult questions. It is undeniable that *de facto* rationing of health care has taken place in the United States, but it has not been done in an explicit and rational way. Instead, we have developed a health-care system that, in David Stockman's apt phrase, favors "strong clients with weak claims" over "weak clients with strong claims," or, in Stephen Crystal's words, "those who are better able to negotiate the system and to 'leverage' public resources with their own."[22]

Advocates of generational equity claim they want to inject some rationality into the rationing, and they generally seem to support proposals such as Daniel Callahan's outlined in chapter 4. Callahan, recall, suggests rationing health care based on age (the "natural life span") in order to free more resources for younger people. As a reflection of heightened acceptance of one's mortality (which in Callahan's case, at least, I am convinced it is), this approach has some merit. One cannot help wondering, however, if it is not acceptance of *somebody else's* mortality that is being suggested in many of these schemes. And that is the problem: Once again those who would suffer would be the poor and near-poor (and probably more of the middle-class than are aware of it today). The wealthy will be able to buy whatever care they need (or desire).

217

AGE and its supporters may be surprised at the outcome of the discussion of health care they have helped foster because the policies and programs that arise out of it may accomplish purposes quite different from their intention. AGE and like-minded people want to reduce government outlays for "futile" medical treatment of older people who no longer contribute to the nation's productivity. It seems more likely, though, that some form of national health insurance will have to result from the attention that AGE has helped to direct to the issue[23] (a result that should have occurred long ago). From a Christian perspective it is clear that a civilized society can no longer tolerate a situation in which costs continue to escalate wildly while millions lack health insurance and/or access to basic health care in the midst of the most technologically advanced medical system in the world.

Indeed, one action—not simple by any means—that would do more than perhaps any other to "defuse" the generational equity debate and the fears of intergenerational "warfare" is the implementation of some form of universal health care, guaranteed to all regardless of age or any other characteristic. If no one had to worry about whether he or she could get basic health care when needed, it would greatly reduce the zero-sum charges that others are getting resources to which one has a better claim. This is especially the case with children, who suffer inadequate health care in disproportionate numbers. A rather significant change in utilities—directed previously at getting one's fair share, or feeling cheated if there is a perception of not getting it—could result from the assurance that a person and those he or she cares about will not have to worry about basic health care.

Again, the form that such a program should take is beyond the scope of this book. I would suggest, however, that based on the values identified in chapter 5 as important for public policy considerations, several characteristics are appropriate. As noted above, basic services should be available to everyone. The emphasis should be on prevention/wellness, starting prenatally and continuing through the life-span, and not on acute care.[24]

Similarly, some provision must be made for long-term care, not only for the person needing it but also to support family members who often lose their health through the rigors of constant caregiving.

Beyond routine care, the operative principle should be that if a person can afford to pay, he or she should pay. That seems to me to be the just, equitable thing to do, and inasmuch as it makes more resources available to those who have less, it is also a compassionate approach. Individuals must be willing to assume a fair share of the costs of health care programs and to ask no more than an appropriate share of the benefits. On the other hand, if a person cannot afford the care that is needed, the community should provide such care in a way that is fair, sensitive to the differing needs of different people, and not demeaning. The compassionate nature of this approach is obvious, and in truth it serves a greater justice as well. In short, for our country to ensure both equity and adequacy, justice and mercy, to all its citizens, we need to direct increasingly burdened public funding of health care *away* from those with less economic need and/or more private resources and *toward* those with greater need and/or fewer private resources. Such an approach seems to me to be in keeping with the cardinal values of both the major religions of our culture, Judaism and Christianity, as well as of other religions that are increasing in importance in this country.

The Question of Work and Retirement

The emphasis placed by AGE on equity suggests that complementary importance is also given to the value of work. After all, equity in this view is based on a close linkage between contribution and benefits. In recognizing the importance of work, AGE affirms one of the values articulated earlier in this book. Apart from simply urging that benefits be dependent upon having worked for them, however, critics of current policy make several other work-related proposals (various ones of which receive support from many people who definitely do not

219

want to be considered members of the generational equity movement). Some of the key elements of this issue were addressed in chapters 2 and 5. Here we need only summarize a few of the suggestions.

One of the most common recommendations is to postpone the age for full retirement benefits, already being implemented in gradual steps to 67. Some have said 70 would more accurately reflect today's increased life-spans. The advantages of later retirement are an improvement in the dreaded dependent-to-worker ratio, an enlarged labor pool and increased productivity, a reduction of the burden on the Social Security trust funds by delaying the time when benefits begin, a rise in payments both into those trust funds through continued FICA contributions and into general revenues through income taxes, and longer retention of self-esteem and independence by older people. Reduction or elimination of the "earnings test" is also suggested as a way to encourage more older people to continue working (or even to return to work), with the same advantages just listed. Yet another recommendation is to create a two-tier system, in which retirement at any age before 70 would require a means test (such as low income or disability) for benefits, which would be granted in full with no eligibility criteria once the age of 70 is reached.

Based on the exposition in chapter 5 of the value of work from a Christian point of view, most of these ideas appear to be appropriate, representing as they do a recognition that work is a positive aspect of human existence. Still, any new retirement policy should recognize the variations in types of work and their different potentials for personal fulfillment and degradation. In addition, any rise in age of eligibility for benefits will have to be coupled with job protection for older workers and enhanced opportunities for employment for those looking for work. Otherwise we will re-create a situation similar to that which existed before Social Security, with large numbers of older unemployed people who can only wait for retirement age to collect benefits.

In sum, it appears on the one hand that AGE has fundamentally misstated its case, emphasizing minor inequities between age groups while ignoring major and increasing inequities in income distribution across all age groups. Its expectation that every generation ought to be able to make it on its own without subsidies from those of a different generation, with whom it is locked in unavoidable competition for limited resources, is in keeping with certain aspects of the dominant American mythos. It is not, however, an accurate reflection of the heterogeneity of each generation in terms either of needs or of resources to meet those needs. Such a view is certainly not in keeping with the dominant values of the Christian faith, whose values, not incidentally, are largely reflected in our most important public response to the dilemma of an aging population, the Social Security program.

On the other hand, some older persons do act in ways that give credibility to the charges leveled by advocates of generational equity. From a Christian point of view, both parties in the debate fall short of what God requires of God's human creatures. Indeed, the problem is that both AGE and those they criticize operate out of the zero-sum mentality that can see only their own utilities—that is, what they want and think they deserve. Heightened awareness of the value stance from which they are operating, coupled with more open and honest conversation with those who see things differently, could contribute to a change in utilities and thus greater cooperation.[25] I do not agree with the presuppositions of the generational equity movement. I do think that, despite their fundamental error, they have done the nation a service by helping to force discussion of the matter. The churches can play an important role in channeling that discussion in constructive ways, as we shall see shortly.

RESPONSIBILITIES OF THE ELDERLY

A number of the matters just discussed raise a point that must be addressed explicitly. Just as the elderly have certain claims upon a just and compassionate society for care in their old age, so they also have responsibilities that no more end at a particular

221

age than do those claims. So far we have focused on responsibilities *to* the elderly. We need to consider now some responsibilities *of* the elderly.

As we saw earlier, elder organizations have influence in the policy arena and at the polls, even if not as much in either area as their critics think. So far, however, this strength has been used in ways that primarily and directly benefit their own age group. The Christian values we have identified argue for a different approach. The elderly ask for recognition that the community extends *backward* in time when they want their past accomplishments and contributions to society acknowledged now as at least part of the basis on which they claim society's concern and current resources. Older people, however, need to develop a deeper appreciation of the community's extension *forward* in time as well and thus recognize their obligation to future generations. Again, we see the importance of a change in utilities away from those that promote a zero-sum approach to intergenerational relationships and toward those that foster greater interdependence, mutual concern, and true community.[26]

In short, the financially "comfortable" elderly must be willing to recognize the needs of younger people (and of other older people less well off than they) and be willing to moderate their demands if necessary to help provide for these others. Indeed, one of the best ways to defeat the "generational equity" charge of rampant greed and self-concerned abuse of growing political power on the part of the elderly might well be for older people (and the organizations that represent them) to begin to use that power to advocate strongly and with united voice for those whom the elders' improved situation is accused of harming so unfairly—namely, the nation's children (and the poor of any age). Apart from deflecting criticism, such a campaign would simply be the right thing to do to make this country a better place for all.

The possibilities for such action are practically endless. On the individual level, tutoring at local schools, serving as "foster grandparents" for needy children, and working to elect officials or pass bond issues that would benefit younger members of the community might make a significant difference in the futures of particular children. On the organizational level, elders' groups might invite public officials to their meetings to discuss the problems faced by children as well as by elders. If the "gray lobby" has anything approaching the power often attributed to it, that influence should be just as effective in advocacy for the young as it is alleged to be in quest of perquisites for the old. Several national organizations like the American Society on Aging have begun to hold special sessions at their annual meetings to draw attention to the needs of children and to explore areas of mutual concern to both old and young; in fact, the theme of the 1992 annual meeting of the American Society on Aging was "Generations at Risk: We Walk on Common Ground," and many of the sessions highlighted the *inter*dependence of the generations. Strong advocacy for a comprehensive national health insurance program represents one of the clearest points of correspondence in the interests of the elderly and children. As gerontologist Meredith Minkler urges:

> At a time when the elderly and their advocate organizations are being unjustly characterized by the mass media as a wealthy and self-indulgent interest group, let's beat them at their own game. Let's show the media and the nation that . . . organizations that focus on the concerns of the elderly recognize that the needs of our nation's children are one of our foremost "age issues."[27]

Indeed, the responsibility (and opportunity) of older members of society for positively influencing public policy extends beyond the narrow area of the welfare of children. The elderly should organize and speak out on the "larger" questions of the day beyond narrow, self-interested, age-related issues. Matters of peace and justice throughout the world, the terrible destruction we continue to wreak on the environment, and the gross inequity in the distribution of wealth, not only within this country but internationally, are all pressing concerns that demand the attention, time, energy, and effort of everyone. Apart from their wisdom and experience, the elderly have in

223

abundance one essential item for accomplishing almost anything that most younger people covet, the *time* to do so.[28] Not all older people will agree on these issues any more than they agree on those that affect them more directly. Still, they have been around long enough to gain some understanding of life, and their voice is one that needs to be heard in the public arena.

Toward this end, it is useful to note that in the churches recently, emphasis has been placed on ministry *with* (and even of) the elderly instead of ministry *to* the elderly. Similarly, advocates for the elderly have been urging for some time that aging policy should be aimed at empowering the elderly and not rendering them dependent and helpless. In light of these two emphases, I suggest we need to rethink our dominant and long-standing practice of formulating public policy *for* the elderly to policy *of* (and by) the elderly. What better way is there to empower the elderly than to get them more involved in formulating the policies and programs that have such an impact on their lives? In fact, this revision may soon become a necessity because of the demographics reported earlier: Before the middle of the next century, one of every four or five Americans will be 65 or older. We will need the personal resources the elderly have to offer, especially given the fact that if current trends continue, those elders are likely as a group to be the best educated citizens of the United States. For this approach to be effective, of course, the older members of society will have to be willing to accept such heightened responsibility, perhaps requiring a reassessment of certain attitudes toward work, retirement, and "leisure."

Some unexpected but wholly positive effects might result from a greater role for the elderly in formulating public policy. Of course, merely being older does not automatically free one from the zero-sum attitude and misdirected utilities described earlier (witness recent presidential administrations), so the churches will still need to work to bring about the changes advocated in this book. Those older persons who have learned the lessons to be gained from living long and experiencing much, though, can assume an especially meaningful role in changing the utilities that the zero-sum metaphor dictates.

For example, their own situation, as well as the deaths of many people important to them, gives them a perspective from which they should be better able to accept their mortality than are younger people for whom the ultimate effect of that mortality is usually farther away. Also, as their own strength declines, the elderly can develop a more realistic acknowledgment of their dependence on others and perhaps even a greater recognition that throughout their lives they have been sharing in God's limitless bounty instead of achieving solely on their own. For the same reasons, the importance of a supportive community should become more apparent.

By "modeling" such changes in values in their own families, churches, places of employment and recreation, and public forums, older people can demonstrate the power and attractiveness of this approach to intergenerational relationships. And because of their numbers and at least potential political strength, the elderly are also in a position to demand that the utilities reflected in public policy be revised away from the current win/lose perception toward a win/win situation. Indeed, even the value of respect for the elderly can be seen to be served by this strategy: By demonstrating their sense of responsibility to other generations and by taking an active, positive role in society, older people are showing that they have value and are overcoming the very perception that leads to cries for "generational equity."

Incidentally, it should be noted that I am not asking of the elderly anything that I do not ask of other age groups. I am merely suggesting ways in which I think older persons may be particularly suited to embody certain values that our society has largely lost sight of and thereby provide models for those who may have more trouble grasping those values. Indeed, as I have argued throughout recent chapters, it is only as *all* of us revise our utilities in light of neglected values such as the munificence of God, the inability of the material to provide true happiness, the value of work, and so forth that we can extricate ourselves from the zero-sum trap into which we have fallen.

225

A story told by the respected actor Ossie Davis at the annual meeting of the American Society on Aging in New Orleans in March 1991 ties together very well the points I have just made concerning the responsibility of the elderly:

> A group of Jews fleeing Germany during the Holocaust had to cross a mountain to reach safety. Some of the older members of the group began to tire and asked to be left behind to fend for themselves rather than endanger the rest of the group by slowing them down. A number of the younger members of the group, fearing for their own safety, were quite ready to agree.[29] A wise younger person in the group, however, countered by saying, "We realize that you are old, tired, and infirm, and that you just want to sit down and rest. But we have these young women with babies, and they are so tired from carrying them this far. Will each of you take a baby and just carry it as far as you can before you give out? Then we'll leave you there." Everybody in the group made it across the mountain!

Today we need a greater recognition on the part of young and old alike, private citizens and policymakers, that the older members of society have not only claims upon that society but continuing responsibilities to it. They do have a contribution to make, not least of all by helping younger generations "make it." In the process, the older persons will be given new purpose and meaning, and they will find a satisfaction in continuing to live that many people may feel old age has stolen from them.

THE ROLE OF THE CHURCHES

It is time now to explore a little more explicitly some of the ways in which the churches can contribute in the realm of public policy on aging. The revision in utilities that I have suggested must take place to overcome the zero-sum attitude toward intergenerational relationships will not happen by itself, and there are ways that the churches can help. I do not intend here to get into theoretical questions about models of advocacy and the like.[30] Instead, I want only to offer a few of my thoughts that have arisen in the course of my research, analysis, and reflection.

The Churches Must "Be the Church"

One indisputable conclusion arises from what has gone before, and it sounds rather simple: If the churches want to have the right to speak at all on these issues and to advocate the values they espouse as essential to good public policy, *the churches themselves must embody those values in their own lives and actions*. In short, the churches must become true communities in which what they advocate for society is lived out and their members are empowered to demonstrate to the world that the best way to live is according to what the churches believe and say it is. At the heart of Christianity stands the Incarnation. This central doctrine suggests that in God's scheme of things, if one wants to accomplish something (whether it be the salvation of humanity or the implementation of a certain set of values in public policy), one does more than *tell* others about it or how to do it; one *embodies* it. Linked inextricably with this fact is Paul's magnificent image of the Church as Christ's earthly body (which is an awesome responsibility, if taken seriously). With this model of human relationship to strive for, it is imperative for the churches to embody the values that they affirm are the result of faithfulness to their Risen Lord. Indeed, without such living out on their own of what the churches profess, in obedience to the One who himself incarnated those values, it is hard to understand what they mean by "faith."

In short, the churches should just "be the Church," the *koinonia* and *ecclesia,* the "earthly body of Christ" they are called to be, loving all their members and everyone else (even their enemies) as commanded by their Lord. In doing so, the churches *show* the world, "the principalities and powers," the power elite, and the uncaring what kind of community can exist. This is one thing Christians can do with no qualms and no debate about their "proper" role in society. Until they do it, their pronouncements of respect for the elderly, concern for the needy, the importance of community, and so forth will always ring hollow.

227

Is this all the churches can do? Certainly not, but it is preconditional. In addition to embodying the values they espouse and thus showing that those values can form the foundation for a real human community, the churches can engage in various sorts of advocacy in accord with their own historical traditions. If active participation in the political process is an option, something like the value congruence analysis suggested in this book can be fruitful in helping a congregation (or larger denominational body) engage in a systematic examination of the particular aspect of the dilemma being addressed, the values considered important in addressing it, and the directions in which it can be addressed that will be most congenial to that particular church's values. Again, let me stress that it is the process that the model facilitates that is its real value. It does not make policy. Churches seem ideally suited to use such a process, and if our claim for the power inherent in the Christian message has validity, the very act of identification and discussion of the values contained in that message should have a profound impact upon any church and its members that engage in such a process.

The Family

Another important role that the churches can play in regard to public policy on aging is to strive to develop ways to *strengthen the family*. It is striking but not surprising how often the impact on aging policy of some matter related to the family has arisen in previous chapters (especially chapter 2). New marriage and divorce patterns, changes in childbearing and childrearing practices (especially an alarming trend toward single-parent families), and other alterations in traditional patterns have had various effects upon the family and its ability to provide the care of its elderly members that it has offered in the past.[31]

This concern has two primary aspects. First, the family traditionally has served as the source of values for children. Not only was there explicit teaching of the values of the particular family and reference group; the family was also the place where the child learned "tacitly" from seeing values lived daily, values like sharing and community, recognizing one's dependence, forgiveness and unmerited love, being valued not for what one does but for who one is, perhaps the importance of work, and even respect for parents and other elderly persons. If there is no family, however, as is increasingly the case today, children must turn elsewhere for their values. The most likely source is "society," whose values, we have seen, leave something to be desired from a Christian point of view. Even if the family is relatively intact, the values that are taught may not encourage intergenerational bonding and obligation (recall Simic's analysis of American childrearing in chapter 6). It may be more than coincidental that the deterioration of the family and the rise of the zero-sum attitude described earlier have occurred at roughly the same time.

If the churches are serious about promoting the values that have been identified here as important in considerations of aging policy, a good place to start would be the family. This is not to say that we should go back to any particular past model of the family, which has had its negative aspects that were glossed over in my idealized account above. Also, care must be taken that an appeal to "traditional family values" not be used as a way to undermine public responsibility for addressing problems that are beyond the ability of families to handle. Still, functioning families seem to be virtually essential in a democratic society to produce healthy individuals with positive self-identity and a sense of social obligation.[32]

The other major area where changes in the family have a significant impact on aging policy concerns care of the elderly, which we saw earlier is still primarily a family affair. But when the changing demographics reported in chapters 1 and 2 are coupled with the changes in the family reviewed just above, serious questions arise. Despite an ongoing effort by many individuals and organizations, this country still does not have any kind of meaningful long-term care program. We remain willing to pay for institutionalization when virtually everyone agrees it is the least desirable option, but we are not yet willing to make decent support services available, such as respite care to allow caregivers to "recharge" occasionally and tax incentives or work credits to ease their financial burden.

Even from a strictly economic point of view, given the extremely high costs of institutionalization cited in chapter 2, putting a great deal more of our resources into supporting home care would be much cheaper than continuing to expand institutions (two-thirds of the budget for Medicaid, originally designed to provide basic health care for the poor of all ages, now goes to institutional care of indigent elderly). Apart from these considerations, churches may well want to make this a priority on their advocacy agenda because of the toll that lack of long-term care provision extracts from the primary caregivers for frail or chronically ill elderly, particularly those with dementing illnesses like Alzheimer's disease.[33]

As long as no public program is in place, the churches should once again do more than merely express their opinion or speak out in favor of governmental assistance. They can embody their commitment to families caring for elderly members by, at the least, devising respite programs that will allow caregivers to get out occasionally without financial burden or concern about finding a short-term replacement who will care about the patient. As seems so often to be the case in situations like this, the benefits are mutual. Churches in the United States have large proportions of older members, and many of these well elders complain of loneliness and lack of fulfillment after retirement and/or death of a spouse. A program like this would help to overcome both of those problems at the same time that it provides a greatly needed service to caregivers and meets a need of society.

Some will say that if the private sector mobilizes and provides a service, there will be less pressure and/or incentive for the government to do so. This may be the case (and if the private sector mobilization is extensive enough to meet the need, who can say that is all bad?), but I doubt that the move toward some kind of public long-term care program will be sabotaged by the churches' meeting the needs of their members (and others in the community, if possible). At any rate, it seems rather more utilitarian than Christian to let people suffer who may not need to in order to keep the pressure on the government to develop a long-term care policy that should have been in place for some time.

In this context, the disproportionate burden borne by elderly women, especially widows and those of color, merits mention once more. The burden goes far beyond the fact that women are the major caregivers for the elderly in our country, and enough has been said earlier in this book about the situation of older women to need no recapitulation here. Beth B. Hess summarizes the problem well (and reflects a further concern voiced in chapters 5 and 6 of this book):

> The position of older men or women in the various status hierarchies of our society is a reflection of the importance of gender in past and present systems of work and family life and a reflection of a value system based on an essentially masculine work effort in which *peoples' moral worth is measured by their market value.*[34]

Here again, the churches have a special responsibility. Their primary value of love for others, especially as manifested in special concern for the needy and respect for the elderly, coupled with their understanding that one's worth as a human being does not depend on "market value," demands a lively and far-reaching response to the plight of older women. Indeed, specific scriptural warrant exists as well in the activities of the early Christians on behalf of the widows of their communities. Once more, the churches must work for changes in society's utilities that will address the problem on a systemic level. At the same time, however, they must also strive to devise ways to meet better the challenge they find in their own tradition to address the special needs of elderly women.

Education

Another unquestionably appropriate role the churches can play with direct and significant relevance to public policy

231

formulation in the United States is to take the lead in the *education* of at least their own members and perhaps others concerning some important issues. Three directions in which this effort might proceed come readily to mind from what has gone before.

1. Some of the problems raised by the generational equity movement stem simply from interpersonal *ignorance*, both that of the old toward the young and of the young toward the old. It is easy to misunderstand others' motives, intentions, and values if one does not know the other people, and by and large the generations in the United States today do not know one another. Because of a number of the social changes mentioned in chapter 2, coupled with the pervasive "ageism" of the past several decades, less interaction takes place in this country today among younger and older people than ever before in human history. A great deal of what each generation knows of the other is mediated through presentations of each on television, in newspapers and magazines, and through statements made by both elder advocates and those representing a "generational equity" perspective. No wonder there is a great deal of mistrust and even hostility among the generations today! The churches can perform a real service here through more explicit intergenerational programming for their own members and by taking an active role in promoting more general opportunities for the generations not only to interact but also to learn what mutual benefits exist in cooperating on matters of mutual concern. Leading an intergenerational group through a value congruence analysis of Social Security would be an enlightening (and challenging) adventure for everyone involved!

2. Beyond this more general education of the generations about one another, another type of education can prove very helpful in addressing the problems outlined earlier in this book. Recall that in chapter 7, my example of a value congruence analysis suggested that several of the Christian values I had identified as important for aging policy received low congruence ratings with current aging programs. We have already seen at several places in this chapter that greater awareness and

appreciation of those values might facilitate the change in utilities necessary to overcome the zero-sum attitude our society has developed with regard to intergenerational relationships. In general, if people recognized the munificence of God and reduced their conviction that happiness depends on what they possess, the quality of life for all would improve markedly. Also, as mentioned in chapter 5, a return to the Reformation notion of the value of work could enhance many people's enjoyment of a necessary component of life and perhaps even contribute to alleviating some of the perceived pressures on Social Security in ways outlined earlier.

The other "missing value," acceptance of one's mortality, lends itself especially well to meeting a glaring need in society, the need to educate people better for their own aging. More of us live to be old—and we get older—than ever before. Acknowledging that fact is essential to dealing with the aging of the individual and of the society. Historian W. Andrew Achenbaum asserts that "continually scrutinizing our assumptions about the nature and dynamics of growing old(er) is imperative in a society that continues to be at the cutting edge of worldwide modernization."[35] Harry R. Moody also wisely observes that human beings *will* age and die, and this "residual existential tragedy of old age and death" means that the difficulties of aging will never be completely amenable "to any complete solution in the policy arena." If we stress the tragedy, we tend toward "benign neglect" of the elderly because there is nothing we can do for them; if we put too much emphasis on public intervention into these difficulties, we create false hopes that can lead only to disillusionment. No policies, no health-care programs, no amount of service provision will stave off the ultimate deterioration and death of the human organism.[36]

Yet what are we doing to teach members of our society how to handle their aging, older years, and impending death? Issues of benefits, financing, and so forth aside, would we not have a much better society and much happier citizens if we prepared ourselves adequately for a worthwhile, productive, fulfilling old

233

age? Faith communities have a special responsibility for such preparation because the issue is ultimately a theological one, involving the "big questions" like the very meaning of human existence and of death that have always been the special province of religion. Here again the churches are well situated to play this significant role because they are widely understood to be concerned about such matters and have a number of vehicles through which to address them, such as sermons and adult education.

3. Finally, an even more specific form of education, directed especially at older persons (though useful also to younger people who will some day be old), seems helpful. Considerable ignorance and misinformation exist about a number of issues of great import to the elderly. Social Security seems to be at the center of this problem, not surprisingly given its complexity. A good illustration is one of the festering problems underlying some of the antagonism of the generational equity debate. Many older people act as if they are not getting back what they put into Social Security (or at least act as if they deserve to get back more). Such remarks often strike younger people, who may be worried about whether they are going to get *anything* when they retire, as unjustified whining or greed, and the zero-sum attitude is reinforced. In fact, as we have seen, today's retirees are already getting back *more* than they put in and therefore do not have a *right* to demand more. For example, for an average couple who turn 65 today, the husband can expect to live 15 more years and the wife 19. Their FICA taxes, their employers' taxes, and a reasonable rate of interest will combine to cover 8 years of benefits.[37] People who became eligible for Medicare in 1983 made an average total contribution of $2,690. Their estimated benefits were $34,000 if female and $28,000 if male.

The use of a method like value congruence analysis in church or seniors groups would be an excellent way to address this issue. In the first two steps of understanding the dilemma and describing current responses, necessary information to clarify the situation might well arise. If the problem is not resolved at this point, however, such a concern would likely arise as various values are examined and their relevance to the issue discussed during the value identification step. This would be another opportunity to foster better understanding of the facts and perhaps to encourage a heightened acknowledgment of one's dependence and the need for appreciation for society's largesse. This situation, then, illustrates a case in which better information, augmented by a look at relevant values (especially Christian ones), could lead to a change in a person's utilities and thus a considerable improvement in relationships among the generations.

The Value Question Again

Finally, before leaving this consideration of some ways the churches can influence aging policy, we return for a brief reprise of a theme that has been heard throughout this book. Of all the institutions of our society, the churches are most concerned with questions of value. They do not have to apologize for this, gloss it over, or be embarrassed about it. It is, in fact, what is expected of them. Therefore it is the responsibility of the churches to take the lead in assuring that the value question be taken seriously in the discussion of any social issue. Public policy debate often becomes bogged down in economics or subverted by political expediency. Lost in the intricacies of most contemporary policy analysis (or the tedium) is the fact that any policy or program affects real people. Because the guiding social value for the churches is love for others, they should be proactive in ensuring that the value dimension remains central to public policy debate.

When it comes to aging policy, Christians need to make sure not only that "things are done right" but that "the right things are done." Perhaps this is what Christians have to contribute in this arena—that is, not specialized technical competence to propose specific policy or to make detailed economic analyses of various proposals, but zeal that any policy proposed meet the needs of *all* members of society in a way that accords with values identified as Christian (or that at least is in harmony with Christian values).

235

THE "NAIVETÉ" OF CHRISTIAN CONTRIBUTIONS TO PUBLIC POLICY

A comment needs to be made here about a disparaging remark often heard when Christians venture into the "real world" of public policy—namely, the charge that their point of view is "hopelessly naive," "politically unrealistic," or "extremely idealistic." My current response to such comments, I must admit, is colored rather deeply by what God is doing in the world right now. These words are being written in the fall of 1991 during the breakup of the Soviet Union, an event of incredible significance that could not possibly have been foreseen even a short time ago. Therefore, when anyone says to me that a Christian vision for aging policy is "impossible," "unrealistic," or the like, I cannot resist saying, "Look at what has happened in eastern Europe and especially in the Soviet Union recently and tell me again that anything is impossible! Even the Israelis and Arabs are finally getting together to begin conversations toward a possible resolution of the Middle East problem, and North and South Korea have signed a non-aggression treaty."

Too often we seem to forget the basic lesson of Christianity—that with God all things are possible—a lesson vividly demonstrated to the first Christians in the resurrection of Jesus but perhaps buried today beneath Easter-sermon familiarity and chocolate-bunny secularism. Columnist Meg Greenfield uses another biblical allusion to express this same sense of near-wonder at world events. Describing what she calls the "Jericho factor," she says,

> Just look around you at all the institutions deemed impregnable and invulnerable, not to mention eternal, that have come crashing down in recent days and years. The past couple of decades have been the decades of surprises; every ironclad assumption seemed to crash; . . . every structure thought to be beyond the reach of criticism and external pressure, most recently including the whole Soviet communist enterprise, was proved otherwise.[38]

As recently as 1988, Daniel Callahan dismissed a reduction in the defense budget as a way to make available more resources for other needs by pointing out that "in 1980 the United States elected a President whose plank was to increase defense expenditures and to lower spending on domestic welfare programs." He concluded, "There is no reason to believe that, in 1988 or shortly thereafter, the American people are prepared for any significant decrease in defense expenditures."[39] Yet on September 27, 1991 (three short years later), that president's vice president, now elected chief executive himself on a very similar platform, called for a reduction in the nation's nuclear arsenal that would have been unimaginable even months earlier. If these things can happen with such amazing rapidity in the "hard-nosed" world of international geopolitics, in a relationship in which "zero-sum" has been the operative attitude for almost 75 years, with no explicit planning or even input on the parts of many of those most affected, I have trouble accepting that *any* policy proposal in the area of aging can be considered "unrealistic" or "naive."

The feasibility and desirability of suggestions growing out of Christian values need to be debated (as do those stemming from *any* set of values), and other proposals need to be made and evaluated. Whatever the merits of any particular analyses and ideas, the discussion of these issues must continue, and Christians must remember that they have something distinctive to add to the discussion that should not be withheld out of fear of being labeled naive or idealistic. Christians sometimes are called beyond the practical, the political, and the worldly to an ideal that the world desperately needs to hear again and again whenever human want and suffering are at issue.

A FINAL WORD

This last discussion suggests a final word. As we have seen, one of the strengths of value congruence analysis is that during its application it encourages the constant reexamination of values deemed important for policy debate in order to determine if necessary ones have been omitted. A fitting conclusion to this chapter and to this book, then, is to acknowledge that as I have lived over the past year in constant awareness of the demographic realities presented earlier, and as I have struggled to make sense of our current aging policy and of various critiques of it, I have come to realize that one very significant Christian value was not addressed in chapter 5, a value that has great relevance for any genuinely Christian consideration of every issue addressed in this book. This value is *hope*. Theologian Jürgen Moltmann's excellent essay, "Hope and Planning," presents the matter well.

The relationship between hope and planning (and what should "public policy" be but planning?), according to Moltmann, is a simple one: Both "represent the future in different ways." Both are based on dissatisfaction with the current state of affairs, and though without planning hope has no realistic goals to seek, without hope there is no motivation for planning. Both hope and planning "find, in new possibilities, ways leading towards another future. Both are, then, based on the idea that the reality of human life is that history in which the existing and the possible can be fused with one another, in which the possible is realized and the new can be made possible."[40] It is hope that "sees the advent of the future and reaches out for it in open expectation," forsaking the old and the inadequate. And the future, for "the Israelite and the Christian spirit," lies in "the advent of that new thing which God has promised."[41] For the Christian specifically, hope originates in "the belief that the *novum* of salvation and of freedom for an unredeemed world has appeared in and through Christ. Therefore, hope directs itself toward the corresponding new creation of all things." It is through the resurrection of Christ and the hope that it arouses that "the future of God exerts an influence in the present."[42]

The resurrection of Christ, then, is the foundation for Christian hope. But before the resurrection was the cross, which "reveals what is truly evil in the world, . . . the unredeemed condition of the world and its sinking into nothingness." [43] Thus

Christian hope is not an unrealistic refusal to accept the negativities of life but a realization that even those negativities, even a whole world "groaning in labor pains" (Rom. 8:22), cannot prevail against the power of God. In Christ's resurrection,

> Hope is always kindled anew. In him, the future of righteousness and the passing of evil can be hoped for; in him the future of life and the passing of death can be hoped for; in him, the coming of freedom and the passing of humiliation can be hoped for; in him, the future of men's true humanity and the passing of inhumanity can be hoped for.[44]

The apostle Paul knew a great deal about Christian hope, writing to the Christians at Corinth, "If for this life only we have hoped in Christ, we are of all people most to be pitied" (1 Cor. 15:19). Paul of course referred specifically to hope in the resurrection of Jesus Christ, but Christians know that precisely because that hope was justified, God's promises, however unrealistic they may seem in light of the "existing and the possible," can be believed. As Moltmann puts it, "Hope recognizes the power and also the faithfulness of God in this story of the resurrection of the crucified one."[45] Hard-headed realism is essential to live in the world and to function in the public policy arena, but if *God* has promised a "new thing," how can Christians not hope (and therefore plan and work) for it?

LIGHT FROM A NEW SOURCE: THE RISE IN "MINORITY RELIGIONS"

THE IMPORTANCE OF "MINORITY RELIGIONS" FOR PUBLIC POLICY

An eighteen-year-old Chinese-American in Miami, the first of her family to be born in the United States, writes in a college term paper, "Why, I asked myself, do my grandparents have to be so different?" Why, indeed? One important reason is likely their religious background, so different from the dominant tradition of this country, based as it is on Judaism and Christianity. Yet the vast majority of those who make policy for the elderly and provide service to them know little about religions that are rapidly gaining in importance as this country's population, in addition to growing older, shows signs of increasing religious heterogeneity, largely as a result of immigration from the Middle East, India, and other parts of Asia.

For example, if current trends persist, Islam will soon become the second largest faith in the United States, surpassing Judaism. Furthermore, according to the 1990 Census, this country now has over 600,000 Asians and Native Americans over the age of 65, a large majority of them Asians. This number had almost doubled since 1980[1] and suggests that Hinduism, Buddhism, and native Chinese religions continue to grow in numbers of adherents as well. Little wonder that well known bioethicist H. Tristram Englehardt, Jr., has noted, "In the future it will no longer be plausible to speak of the Judeo-Christian heritage providing a taken-for-granted basis for American life, for we will have an increasingly important representation of Islamic, Hindu, and Buddhist believers."[2]

Although at first this issue may not appear to be very significant from a public policy perspective, sound policy must take into consideration the needs of *all* members of the "public," even if all such needs cannot be met. There is no question that up to this time, the value assumptions underlying aging policy have been based upon Judaism and Christianity. However, with the rise in the number of adherents of other religions—persons who are members of our society and to whom public policy must be sensitive—responsible aging policy will need to consider the values of those faith traditions as well.

To do this, policymakers—not to mention gerontologists, social workers, geriatricians, and others who serve the elderly—must become acquainted with the basic values of religions outside the dominant traditions of this culture, especially those of Hinduism, Buddhism, and Islam. Such individuals would do well to recall the old Bantu proverb that wisely asserts, "The person who never leaves home thinks mother is the only cook," a more figurative way of making the same point made by Max Mueller, the "founding father" of comparative religions, in his assertion, "Who knows one religion knows none." A lack of knowledge of minority religions can lead to a failure of understanding the perspectives on aging—and thus the needs and the desires concerning programs dealing with the elderly—of a growing number of the residents of this country.

Some might question such emphasis upon the importance of these religions, especially in a book that offers an explicitly *Christian* consideration of the ethical implications of public policy on aging. Several things can be said in response. First, Paul's statement in 1 Corinthians 9:22, "I have become all things to all people, that I might by all means save some," is instructive, suggesting that even from a strictly evangelistic point of view, interaction with those whose beliefs differ from one's own is not only legitimate but virtually essential (earlier, in v. 20, Paul states explicitly, for example, that he "became as a Jew," a religion of which his language indicates he no longer considered himself a part). Peter's vision at Joppa in Acts 10, in which he is vividly shown that he "should not call anyone profane or unclean" (v. 28), strongly supports this interpretation.

Second, at the very least, familiarity with others' religions is important in order to know why they believe, act, and feel as they do. If one wants to establish meaningful conversation with followers of other religions on any topic, and certainly to develop public policies and programs that will meet their legitimate needs as members of the larger community, one must be willing to attempt to understand their values. As I have said, religion is almost always implicated in that venture to some extent.

Finally, although Christianity cannot be harmonized with these other religions in terms of basic theological matters, on issues concerning aging and the proper treatment of the elderly more commonality exists than one might expect. Furthermore, cultures based on these religions still exhibit some attitudes and practices in this area that are more in line with the actual teachings of historic Christianity than are those of our society, teachings that have largely been lost in the rush to accept the values of "Americanism" described in chapter 6. Application of the classic Christian virtue of humility may allow us to learn something from these religions that *will* be of value as we strive to address the significant problems facing the aging United States over the next five decades. Toward this end, this appendix is offered as an introduction to the major beliefs and values of some of these "minority" religions that bear on matters of aging.

It is impossible even to summarize all the teachings of these religions relevant to our topic. Instead, therefore, just a couple of themes common to them will be highlighted, themes that are of special importance in understanding and serving elders from these traditions—namely, *filial piety* and *attitudes toward aging and death*. First, though, because of the lingering lack of familiarity with these religions, a brief summary of each will help to set the stage.

A BRIEF OVERVIEW OF IMPORTANT MINORITY RELIGIONS IN THE UNITED STATES

Hinduism

Unlike most religions, which can point to a specific person or at least event as their source, Hinduism has no such clear-cut beginning. Rather, the religion known today as Hinduism arose from a merging of the indigenous religion of the Indian subcontinent with that brought in by a wave of conquerors, the Aryans, who gradually overran India during the period 2000-1500 B.C.E. These people produced a body of ritual hymns (the Vedas) concerned with such things as the origin of the universe, the nature of the gods, and proper human behavior in relationship to the gods. Later, philosophical reflections on the Vedas arose (the Upanishads) that argued for the existence of one Supreme Reality, a World Soul called Brahman (or Paramatman) that underlies and is the source of all there is (Brahman has been called, flippantly perhaps but descriptively, the "cosmic isness"). All that exists is Brahman, and Brahman is all that really exists. Liberation from the endless cycle of birth-death-rebirth that characterizes all earthly existence (*samsara,* reincarnation or the transmigration of souls) is achieved simply by recognizing the identity of one's true soul (Atman) with Brahman. Because this path was rather difficult for ordinary folk to pursue, between about 400 B.C.E. and 200 C.E. so-called devotional or sectarian Hinduism arose. This more popular form of Hinduism offered release through devotion to various deities (best represented by its most familiar text, the *Bhagavad-Gita* or "Lord's Song"). Of the 650 million Hindus worldwide, well over 90 percent live in India, though there is a growing American Hindu community, especially in professions like medicine and various service industries.

Buddhism

Buddhism, a sixth-century B.C.E. Hindu offshoot, arose out of the personal quest of one man, Siddhartha Gautama of the Shakyas, for answers to the "big questions" of life that all thoughtful human beings wrestle with at some point in their lives. Indulged and sheltered as a child, in his twenties Siddhartha was exposed to the "Four Sights"—an old man, a sick person, a corpse, and a meditating monk—thus learning that life really consists of growing old, getting sick, and dying, but a way of escape exists. After several years of seeking, during which he tried and rejected both the current Hindu teaching and rigorous asceticism (self-denial), through meditation Siddhartha finally perceived the true nature of reality and the way of release, emerging as the Buddha (the "enlightened" or "awakened" one). The answer he found is known as the Four Noble Truths: (1) life is dislocated, off its true center, and therefore characterized by constant suffering; (2) the cause of this suffering is selfish craving; (3) the way of escape from suffering is to overcome such craving; and (4) the way to overcome desire is the Eightfold Path, a systematic remaking of the entire personality. The goal is escape from desire and thus from the seemingly endless cycle of reincarnation into a peaceful, deathless, unchanging state called *nirvana,* which the Buddha steadfastly refused to describe. Indeed, Buddhism has been called the religion that teaches "the death that ends death." Perhaps the Buddha's most distinctive doctrine is *anatta* or "no-self," the conviction that "I" (along with *every*thing that is contingent or transitory [*anicca*]) do not fully exist. In short, in the Buddhist universe there is no being, only becoming. Soon after the Buddha's death, Buddhism split into two main branches: Theravada (the "way of the elders"), a monk- and meditation-centered religion; and Mahayana (the "big raft"), the more popular missionary branch that stresses devotion and concern for the suffering of others as well as for one's own liberation. Today there are over 300 million Buddhists worldwide, with about 350,000 in North America, mostly immigrants from Korea, Vietnam, Japan, China, Thailand, Cambodia, and Sri Lanka.

Confucianism

Native Chinese religions are important to this inquiry because they have become part of a complex religiocultural blend with Buddhism in China and Vietnam, and with Buddhism and Shinto in Japan and Korea. Confucianism rather than Taoism will be the focus here because it is the source of a central component of the Eastern attitude toward aging and the elderly (though Taoism is important because of a current that runs through it that suggests the attainability of physical longevity, perhaps even immortality). Confucianism begins with a Chinese contemporary of the Buddha, a sage we call Confucius, whose teachings are recorded primarily in a volume called the *Analects* and were popularized and spread two centuries later by a disciple named Mencius. Confucius believed himself to be passing on the best of the ancient Chinese traditions as taught and lived by the great wise men of the past, sages who were not reclusive monks but men of affairs who had forged their wisdom from their experience in order to foster public order. Confucianism is thus not so much a religion in the traditional Western understanding as it is a highly rationalistic ethical system, based on the family and kinship structures of imperial China. It became the official ideology of the state around 220 B.C.E. and remained so until the rise of the Republic in 1911. Even in modern China, the key Confucian values of loyalty, social responsibility, and conformity are still stressed, and the "five constant virtues" as defined by Confucius—benevolence, righteousness, propriety, wisdom, and fidelity—continue to be foundational in modern Chinese culture. Confucianism teaches also that "the universe is orderly rather than chaotic and that there is supposed to be harmony within and among 'the five cardinal relationships' ":[3] father/son, older/younger brother, husband/wife, elder/younger member of society in general, and ruler/subject. Note that these relationships are *not* symmetrical (i.e., between equals). For Confucius the ideal society is feudal and consists in finding one's place in the hierarchy and doing the duties associated with it. As we shall see shortly, the heart of the Confucian ethic—the concept of *filial piety*—is of great interest to us.

Islam

Islam is the youngest Semitic religion, sharing most of its basic theology with Judaism and Christianity and accepting the Bible as originally authentic revelations from God. Muslims point to Muhammad as the "seal of the prophets," through whom Islam entered the world in its full and final form during the early decades of the seventh century C.E. in Arabia. Islam is noteworthy for its absolute insistence on the oneness, grandeur, and mercy of God (Allah), and for its stress on the necessity for religion to serve as the basis for any decent society (i.e., religion and society, faith and politics, are inseparable in Islam). The Quran, Islam's holy book transmitted through Muhammad, is considered by many Muslims to be the eternal, unchanging word of God, serving the function not only of the Bible in Judaism and Christianity but also of Christ for Christians. The teaching of Islam centers on the Five Pillars: (1) the creed ("There is no god but God, and Muhammad is God's Messenger"); (2) prayer five times a day; (3) alms for the poor; (4) daytime fasting during the month of Ramadan; and (5) the pilgrimage to Mecca. Shortly after the Prophet's death, Islam split into two main factions, basically over the question of succession: the Sunnis (today's majority party, with 85 percent of Muslims worldwide), who favored election of the Caliph ("Successor") by the community; and the Shiites (about 14 percent), who favored blood succession. Today Islam is the world's fastest-growing religion, with over a billion adherents worldwide, concentrated primarily in the Middle East but dominating Indonesia and increasing rapidly elsewhere, especially in Africa, the nations of the former U.S.S.R., and, as noted, the U.S., where today there are some six million Muslims.

TWO TEACHINGS OF SPECIAL IMPORTANCE
FOR AGING POLICY

Filial Piety

With this background, it is time to ask what these religions teach specifically about aging that might be useful for policymakers to keep in mind in light of the increasing number of their adherents in this country. At the heart of virtually all the minority religions of interest in this regard lies a much greater expectation of filial piety than has been the norm among the majority religions of our culture (though the notion is not absent from the original teaching of Judaism and Christianity, as we saw in chapter 5). This basic concept profoundly influences attitudes toward dependence/independence, long-term care arrangements, financial relationships, and much more.

Confucianism is the primary source of the concept for Chinese religion, which has ultimately "flavored" the entire Eastern perspective. Confucius himself asks, "Filial piety and fraternal love—are they not the root of virtue, especially the former?" Generally, filial piety required three things of children with regard to their elderly parents. First, children owed parents *absolute obedience,* with disobedience or even a show of disrespect "one of the most heinous offenses known in classical Chinese society,"[4] at times being considered a capital offense. The *Hsiao King,* the Confucian book of filial piety, affirms that "there are 3,000 offenses against which the five punishments are directed; there is none of them greater than to be unfilial."[5]

Second, *devotion* to parents of an almost religious nature was expected because the children owe their lives to their parents (cf. Western notions of *God* as Creator). As people aged, a compounding effect occurred also: Because grandparents were the originators of the parents (to whom the devotion just mentioned was owed), the grandparents took on the heightened aura of "superparents." Furthermore, the parents and grandparents were the nearest ancestors, and ancestors were to be revered. This devotion included maintenance of burial sites and family shrines and performance of the proper rituals, extending filial piety even beyond the death of the parents.

Finally, children were obligated to provide *material support* to their parents in their old age, and this obligation even became part of the laws of Confucian-influenced countries. For example, the powerful Meiji regime in Japan (est. 1868) incorporated in its civil code the provision that *priority* must be given to parents as long as they live, even over one's own children, a law rescinded only by the Constitution of 1948 (the generations are now "*mutually* responsible").

An old story dramatically illustrates the depth to which this notion of filial piety permeated the Chinese consciousness and the seriousness with which such obligations were taken:

> A poor man named Kuo and his wife had a serious problem. Kuo's aged mother was sick in bed and required medicine and food, which he could ill afford. After intense conversation with his wife, Kuo decided the only solution to the problem was to "get rid" of their 3-year-old only son in order to free up some of their limited resources. Their reasoning was that he had only one mother but they could always have another child. So Kuo went outside and began to dig a pit in which to bury the child. Shortly after he began to dig, however, he struck gold. It seems that the gods were so moved by Kuo's spirit of filial piety that they rewarded him by letting him keep his son.[6]

Clearly in Chinese culture obligations to one's elderly parents took precedence over those toward one's own offspring.

Generalizing from this basis *within* the family, Confucius extended the concept *beyond* the bounds of the home: "A youth, when at home, should be filial, and, abroad, respectful to his elders" (*Analects* I:6). Confucian society as a whole was structured to ensure that the younger members paid proper deference to the older. So central was the notion of filial piety that the *Hsiao King* declares, "Filial piety is the way of Heaven, the principle of Earth, and the practical duty of man."[7] As appealing as such a system may sound to those concerned about the treatment accorded many of the elderly in our society, it should be remembered that in any society gaps often exist between the ideal and the real, and Confucianism sometimes led to tyranny by the elderly that resulted in both psychological and physical oppression of the younger members of the family.

It is not only native Chinese religion, however, that stresses this obligation; the responsibility of children to care for their elderly parents is also an important feature of Hinduism, Buddhism, and Islam. For example, among Buddhist lay people the proper way of life is set forth in *Sangala Sutta,* a discourse given to a wise man named Sangala. Relationships and duties among family members are explicitly stated, one of which is that children should look after their elderly parents. Indeed, the Buddha refers to the parents as *Brahma,* "a word which denotes the highest and the most sacred in Indian thought."[8]

After parents, reverence is prescribed for teachers and elders, whether relatives or not. If one lacks parents, other elderly persons should be sought because an essential ingredient in the good life is to have people to revere and respect. "The tradition of paying respects to elders is a source of spiritual strength."[9] Beyond respect, the elderly Buddhist should be able to expect all the blessings of old age, "such as honor, love, obedience and troops of friends." Doing good deeds influences one's future rebirths in a positive direction, and showing respect to parents and other elders is "one of the best deeds of merit."[10] In fact, the Buddha himself said, "He who wishes to serve and attend on the Buddha, / Such a one should serve and attend on the sick and the aged."[11]

Sura 17 of the Quran, Islam's holy book, contains Allah's decree that children are to be kind to parents, not speak to them contemptuously, and are to address them in honor and humility: "Thy Lord has decreed . . . to be good to parents, whether one or both of them attains old age with thee; say not to them 'Fie,' neither chide them, but speak unto them words respectful, and lower to them the wing of humbleness out of mercy." The passage concludes, "Lord! bestow on them your mercy even as they tenderly brought me up when I was little" (17:23-24). What makes this statement especially noteworthy is that the sequence begins, "Set not up with God another god, or thou wilt sit

249

condemned and forsaken. Thy Lord has decreed you shall not serve any but Him, and to be good to parents. . . ." Given the extreme emphasis in the Quran on the radical oneness of God, the juxtaposition of the command to honor elderly parents with the command to serve God alone greatly heightens the significance of the former (cf. the same connection between "fear of God" and honor toward the elderly in rabbinic interpretations of the Fifth Commandment and in Lev. 19:32). Such honor is not optional for Muslims, any more than is belief in the oneness of Allah! Citing this and other passages in the Quran, H. R. Moody concludes that "filial piety or respect for parents in their old age is of utmost importance. Except perhaps for Confucianism, no religion is as insistent as Islam on the importance of filial respect."[12]

Furthermore, growing out of its belief in the oneness of God, who is also creator of all that exists, Islam lays great stress on the commonality of human experience—including aging—and on the unity of all believers in the one true God. Thus individuals cannot be differentiated based on apparent outward changes. Hakim Mohammed Said therefore concludes, "In an Islamic society an old person has as much right to safety of life and property as a young man has. . . . Morally there can be no greater ungratefulness than that a man should neglect and despise an old person whose heir he is."[13] Indeed, Muslim economics is based on the notion of collective responsibility, with those who are able obligated to help those less able (formalized, in fact, in one of the Five Pillars of Islam, the *zakat* or "poor due"). Thus, although parents retain the place of first importance, "in an Islamic society, every old and disabled person deserves the same respect, compassion, and solicitude that the parents do because Islam stands guarantor to the security of life."[14]

Conflicts with American Culture

In a society like the contemporary United States, it is not hard to imagine the problems elderly people from traditions such as the ones just described experience as the younger generations embody and express the prevailing cultural values. Most of the younger family members have grown up with or adopted American values such as independence as the mark of success, personal worth judged by achievement rather than mere existence, and expectations of governmental support for the elderly. Thus they are not particularly disposed to render with great enthusiasm many of the traditional obligations of filial piety, setting the stage for considerable conflict, disappointment, and stress. For example, among Chinese families in the United States, when family issues are discussed, the younger members tend to concentrate on marital relationships whereas the older members express much more concern about relationships with descendants.[15]

This kind of discrepancy in basic values suggests one particularly dangerous stereotype that persists—namely, that families in these traditions *will* provide all the care their older members need, often leading to a serious lack of public programs and services in areas with large minority populations. It also should be noted that professional and institutional aid is a relatively new concept to older Asians particularly, who are accustomed to receiving such help from family and friends. So even when assistance is available, it may not be greeted with the enthusiasm and appreciation that the service providers would like.

In fairness, a word should be said about the problems such expectations by the elderly cause for the younger people as well. The concept of "sandwich generation" was described in chapter 2, but for the middle generation from religious/cultural traditions like those described above, the pressure is especially intense. Often reared in the mother country, frequently leaving their homes less than totally voluntarily, and forced to adapt to "the American way" as quickly as possible in order to survive and support their families, these people not only have to adjust to a new culture themselves; they also must try to live up to the values and the expectations that their parents hold concerning the parents' care, while at the same time rearing their children and instilling in them some mix of their own traditions and American attitudes toward the elderly.

As the Chinese student I mentioned at the beginning of this appendix described her grandmother's visits, "It is not she who cooks for us but my mother who cooks primarily for her. My mother is at my grandmother's every beck and call, transforming *my mother* into *her servant.* Consequently, my view of the aged was completely skewed." When her parents announced that they would never subject her or her siblings to the same kind of burden, she "felt a strange pang of guilt, a strong sense of filial duty, and an intense feeling of respect for them; nevertheless, I could not comprehend the emotional turmoil within me." After reflection, she discovered the source of her dilemma: "My personal internal conflict is one of choosing between the Chinese tradition of respect and familial care for the elderly (as in the case of my maternal grandmother) and the American tradition of independence and self-support (the plan my parents propose to follow)." Policymakers and service providers therefore should be aware that adult children from these traditions may have special problems and needs not experienced by those from the dominant religions.

Old Age and Death

Having explored some minority religions' teachings that exert great influence on attitudes toward the elderly, a brief consideration is in order of what these religions have to say about aging itself and its inevitable result, death. Islam, as is its wont in so many areas, is completely straightforward in recognizing the realities of growing old. The Quran, for instance, calls old age "the vilest state of life, that after knowing somewhat, they may know nothing" (16:70, repeated in 22:5), and in the aptly titled sura "Afternoon," we read, "Verily, by the Afternoon, Man is in the way of loss; except for those who counsel one another to patience and to the Truth" (103). In sura 30, we are told, "God is He that created you out of weakness, then he appointed after weakness strength, then after strength He appointed weakness and grey hairs" (30:50). Furthermore, "to whomsoever we give long life, we turn back in the process of creation" (36:68); that is, an old person becomes like a child once again, both physically dependent and mentally incapable. No sugar-coating of old age here, no rhapsodizing about the "golden years"!

Yet old age is seen as an important time also: Just as reflection on the beginning of life forces one to acknowledge one's dependence then, so at the end one is reminded of the fundamental human condition, complete dependence upon Allah and his unending mercy (cf. Quran 22:5ff.). It is this recognition that is in fact the very meaning of the word *Islam* (cf. Hebrew *shalom*): that perfect peace that comes from acknowledging one's dependence upon Allah and submitting one's will totally to God. Thus in addition to frank recognition of the losses of aging, Islam also offers old age as a reminder (*dhikr*) of the most important lesson a person can learn.

Apart from its emphasis on the oneness of Allah and human dependence upon God, Islam stresses perhaps most the doctrine of the hereafter. For the Muslim, life *after* death is as real and tangible as life in the "here and now." Indeed, the two are merely parts of a continuum, with death the passage between them. As we just saw, the Quran speaks frequently of human evolution from a lump of clay through strength back to weakness, concluding, "Then after that you shall surely die, then on the Day of Resurrection you shall surely be raised up" (23:15). For the person who believes and does good deeds, death is not to be feared: "Prosperous are the believers. . . . Those are the inheritors who shall inherit Paradise therein dwelling forever" (23:1, 10). For the faithful Muslim, then, death does not end a person's life. It merely opens the door to the next and by far most glorious stage in human evolution, Paradise, frequently and graphically described throughout the Quran.

Before this final step can be taken, however, the soul enters an intermediary stage known as *barzakh* or "chastisement in the grave." Although not Quranic in origin, this foretaste of things to come is well attested in the Hadith (traditions about the sayings and the deeds of Muhammad) and seems to have been accepted by Islam in order to bring some urgency into the notion of judgment. After all, who knows when the final Day of Judgment is to be? In the state of *barzakh* one begins to reap the

253

fruits of one's earthly life; the windows of heaven and hell are opened to the dead so that, as a familiar Hadith puts it, "Judgment begins immediately upon death."[16]

Moving farther east, death has been a central concern of Hinduism from its start. Indeed, "interpreting the experience of death was a principal motive of the Upanishadic literature."[17] Underlying the attitude toward aging and death in Hinduism (and what follows applies also to Buddhism, with minor changes in terminology and detail) is the fundamental notion of *samsara,* the cycle of birth-death-rebirth that continues until one achieves release (*moksha*). It is important to realize that in this scheme death is seen as the opposite not of life but rather of birth, and unless one has gained enlightenment, one will be reborn in another body according to the law of *karma,* or universal moral cause and effect. What is to be feared, then, is not old age but rather a premature or untimely death. This sad fate prevents one both from reaching the stage of life in which enlightenment is most likely to be achieved and from paying the accumulated debt of karma, which then must carry over into one's next incarnation, causing it to be worse than it otherwise might have been. In fact, traditional Hinduism has seen the last two of the four stages of life—explicitly limited to what we might call "retirement" age and beyond—as precisely that time in which one can finally devote one's total energy and concentration to attaining spiritual enlightenment. In this role, the older people serve as models for younger members of society and are to be served as far as their personal needs are concerned so that they can pursue their quest without distraction.

Still, as we saw earlier with Islam, the Hindu attitude toward the process of aging also recognized and even stressed the negative side as well. Although the Vedic literature saw aging as a natural and inevitable aspect of human existence, a significant evolution took place (probably under Buddhist influence). By the end of the first millennium c.e., for example, the important metaphysical commentary *Yogavasistha* could say that "old age, which preys on the flesh of the human body, takes as much delight in devouring its youthful blossom as a cat does in feeding upon a mouse."[18] Other equally vivid descriptions of the various losses brought upon the human being by old age abound.

Thus both Islam and Hinduism (as well as Buddhism) take a realistic approach to aging, not disguising the losses that all human beings experience as they age, a process that culminates in the greatest earthly loss, that of death. On the other hand, these traditions teach that the elderly are worthy of special respect and honor because of their age, at least partially mitigating the pain of the losses. Perhaps our culture could take a lesson from this attitude, instead of trying to pretend that the losses do not occur or can be avoided, put off, or at least hidden. Unlike the view of these more traditional cultures, our attitude precludes the possibility of offering any enhancement of personal prestige and worth in their place.

CONCLUSION

In conclusion, if the aging policy of this country is to serve all the members of the society, and if its purpose is genuinely to help the elderly (and their families), we must understand the crucial role that religious beliefs play in attitudes toward aging. Where those beliefs differ from our own, we must gain some familiarity with them. Local communities of believers are usually quite willing to share their beliefs and practices with genuinely interested outsiders, and they may have specific resources of value. Of course, really getting to know elders (and their children and grandchildren) from these traditions remains the best way to ascertain and address the particular needs of individuals and families. Those responsible for making public policy on aging in this country (as well as anyone else who wants to be well informed about what is important to *all* those whom such policy will affect) should make the effort to become acquainted with the increasing number of Americans from minority religious traditions.

NOTES

PREFACE

1. Harry R. Moody, *Abundance of Life: Human Development for an Aging Society* (New York: Columbia University Press, 1988), p. 138.

INTRODUCTION

1. A. A. Milne, *The World of Pooh* (New York: E. P. Dutton & Company, 1957), p. 7. For directing my attention to this quotation, I am indebted to Michael G. Dolence, "Evaluation Criteria for an Enrollment Management Program," *Planning for Higher Education* 18 (1989-90): 1.
2. Quoted in Laurence J. Peter, ed., *Peter's Quotations: Ideas for Our Time* (New York: Bantam Books, 1977), p. 228.
3. It will become apparent later that I have serious reservations about the widespread use of this arbitrary age to determine much of what happens to people who are more different from one another at the age of 65 and beyond than perhaps at any earlier time in their lives. Nonetheless, the age of 65 is so firmly ingrained in our system—including being the standard on which virtually all of the statistics concerning "the elderly" are based—that it is impossible to deviate from it in general use without creating burdens that far outweigh any benefits.
4. Phillip Longman, *Born to Pay: The New Politics of Aging* (Boston: Houghton Mifflin, 1987), p. 32.
5. Janet Otwell and Janet Costello, *Ninety for the '90s: A Final Report* (Springfield: Illinois Department on Aging, 1990), p. 2.

6. Carroll Estes, *The Aging Enterprise: A Critical Examination of Social Policies and Services for the Aged* (San Francisco: Jossey-Bass, 1979), p. 1.
7. Ken Dychtwald and Joe Flower, *Age Wave: The Challenges and Opportunities of an Aging America* (New York: Bantam Books, 1990), p. xix.
8. Theodore R. Marmor, Jerry L. Mashaw, and Philip L. Harvey, *America's Misunderstood Welfare State: Persistent Myths, Enduring Realities* (New York: Basic Books, 1990), p. 215.
9. Quoted in Peter, ed., *Peter's Quotations*, p. 223.
10. Elias S. Cohen, "Gerontology: Past, Present and Future," *Aging Today* 12 (April/May 1991): 3.
11. Longman, *Born to Pay*, p. 34.
12. Marmor et al., *America's Misunderstood Welfare State*, p. 238.
13. A very useful resource, because of its currency and broad focus, is *Theology and Public Policy*, the journal of the Churches' Center for Theology and Public Policy (4500 Massachusetts Avenue, NW, Washington, DC 20016-5690), one of the sponsors of the series in which this book appears. Among many helpful articles on this topic in various issues of the journal since its inception in fall 1989, particularly informative is one by Roy Enquist titled "A Paraclete in the Public Square: Toward a Theology of Advocacy" (*Theology and Public Policy* 2 [Fall 1990]: 17-33). Enquist not only offers a reasonable normative proposal but provides a very helpful summary of four major understandings of political advocacy held by Christians in the United States.
14. I speak in this chapter of the role of the *churches* because I am writing from a Christian perspective in a series co-sponsored by a Christian publisher and a Christian research center. Later, distinctive Christian beliefs will become important for much of what I have to say. For the purposes of this chapter, "religious institutions" can be substituted appropriately for "churches" and "religious persons" for "Christians."
15. Marmor et al., *America's Misunderstood Welfare State*, p. 239.
16. Daniel Callahan, "Can Old Age Be Given a Public Meaning?," *Second Opinion* 15 (November 1990): 21. He continues, "This can be especially important in efforts to understand suffering, human mortality, the life cycle, and the passing of the generations. We need all the help we can get on those, the most troubling of the problems old age must encounter."
17. James A. Nash, "Narrowing the Ethics-Action Gap," *Theology and Public Policy* 3 (Fall 1991): 5. Perhaps if Christians begin to despair of resolving the problems raised by the aging of America, they should remember that it was not too much more than a century ago that abolishing slavery was considered "politically impossible."
18. Duncan B. Forrester, *Beliefs, Values and Policies: Conviction Politics in a Secular Age* (New York: Oxford University Press, 1989), p. 61.
19. "Hope and Planning," in Jürgen Moltmann, *Hope and Planning*, trans. Margaret Clarkson (New York: Harper & Row, 1971), pp. 195, 194. On p. 181, Moltmann says that the "otherness" of the uncertain future in contrast to the known present lies in its ability to generate something "new." "This 'newness,' which the otherness of the future determines, lies on the border between what is possible and what is impossible. The new is

there when the impossible becomes possible, when the unthinkable is thought, when the undiscovered is found and discovered." It is hard not to think of Is. 65:17-25, 2 Cor. 5:16-21, and Rev. 21:1-4 here.

20. Robert Bellah, quoted in "The Good Society," an interview in *Ethics & Policy* (Fall 1991): 5.

21. This statement appears especially appropriate with regard to the elderly. According to Harold Koenig, a researcher at Duke University, involvement in churches and synagogues is the most common form of voluntary activity among the elderly in the U.S. Indeed, membership of older people in religious organizations exceeds that in all other voluntary social groups combined. Half of all persons 65 and older attend a religious service of some kind at least weekly. And in one study, when asked whether religious beliefs help them to cope with sickness and to keep going in rough times, an amazing 90 percent of respondents 60 and older responded affirmatively ("Religion and Mental Health," a speech delivered at the Forum on Religion and Aging Special Program, American Society on Aging annual meeting, March 1990).

22. Daniel Callahan, discussing the prospect and importance of forging a "public meaning" for old age, asserts, "Some important, widely shared traditions can be drawn upon, and the fact that many do not share them, or even reject them, is not alone a reason to put them aside. They are the *only* resources we have, and if some object to their public use, the burden of finding alternative approaches and traditions should fall upon them." Among the traditions he identifies is "the religious tradition embodied in the precept that children should honor their parents and take responsibility for their welfare in old age if necessary" ("Can Old Age Be Given a Public Meaning?" pp. 19-20). Historian W. Andrew Achenbaum supports the point when he says, "We can attempt to change our values and reform our programs, but there are limits to our ability to create incentives or to manipulate ideas in ways that have no basis in historical traditions or in current reality" (*Shades of Gray: Old Age, American Values, and Federal Policies Since 1920* [Boston: Little, Brown and Company, 1983], p. 176).

23. Bellah, "The Good Society," p. 5.

24. Robert N. Bellah, Richard Madsen, William M. Sullivan, Ann Swidler, and Steven M. Tipton, *The Good Society* (New York: Alfred A. Knopf, 1991), p. 179. They continue, "Indeed, the 'free exercise' clause of the First Amendment to the Constitution guarantees the right of religious bodies to public expression, just as much as the 'no establishment' clause ensures that none will gain any favored governmental status" (pp. 179-80).

25. Forrester, *Beliefs, Values and Policies*, p. vii.

26. Hessel Bouma III, Douglas Diekema, Edward Langerak, Theodore Rottman, and Allen Verhey, *Christian Faith, Health, and Medical Practice* (Grand Rapids: Wm. B. Eerdmans Publishing Company, 1989), pp. 2-3.

27. Paul Tillich, *The Spiritual Situation in Our Technical Society*, ed. J. Mark Thomas (Macon, Ga.: Mercer University Press, 1988), p. 20, quoted in J. Mark Thomas, "The Quest for Economic Justice," in J. Mark Thomas and Vernon Visick, eds., *God and Capitalism: A Prophetic Critique of Market Economy* (Madison, Wis.: A-R Editions, 1991), p. 2.

28. Harry R. Moody sounds much the same note of hope, and interestingly alludes to a number of the themes of this book, at the end of his excellent volume, *Abundance of Life: Human Development for an Aging Society* ([New York: Columbia University Press, 1988], p. 265): "Is the new abundance of life now produced by gains in longevity to be seen as a problem or an opportunity? Are younger and older generations simply interest groups, or are all generations bound in obligations toward a common good? To insist that the future remains open is to insist that human beings have in their power the capacity to act, on whatever scale, and to move toward an abundance of life shared by all generations."

1. THE DILEMMA: THE NUMBERS GAME

1. Theodore Marmor, Jerry Mashaw, and Philip Harvey, *America's Misunderstood Welfare State: Persistent Myths, Enduring Realities* (New York: Basic Books, 1990), pp. 216, 218.
2. Ibid., p. 219.
3. The statistics in this section come from several sources: *A Profile of Older Americans: 1990,* a pamphlet distributed by the American Association of Retired Persons (AARP), researched and compiled by Donald G. Fowles of the Administration on Aging, U.S. Department of Health and Human Services; Ken Dychtwald and Joe Flower, *Age Wave: The Challenges and Opportunities of an Aging America* (New York: Bantam Books, 1990), chapter 1; Jerry Gerber, Janet Wolff, Walter Klores, and Gene Brown, *Lifetrends: The Future of Baby Boomers and Other Aging Americans* (New York: Macmillan, 1989), primarily chapter 1; and "Good and Bad News from 1990 Census," *Aging Today* 12 (April/May 1991): 1-2. Helpful historical data can be found in David H. Fischer, *Growing Old in America*, expanded edition (New York: Oxford University Press, 1978), especially the Appendix.
4. James H. Schulz, Allan Borowski, and William H. Crown, *Economics of Population Aging: The "Graying" of Australia, Japan, and the United States* (New York: Auburn House, 1991), p. 9.
5. Although the focus of this book is the United States, it is worthy of note that worldwide, of all the human beings who have ever reached the age of 65, *one-half* to *two-thirds* are alive today.
6. One graphic example with particular relevance to public policy is the wide variation in rates of institutionalization among different cohorts of the elderly. According to the AARP's *Profile of Older Americans: 1990* (p. 4), although a relatively small portion of all those 65 and older lived in nursing homes in 1985 (5 percent, or 1.3 million), the percentage increased significantly with age: From a low of 1 percent for those 65-74, the number rises to 6 percent for those 75-84 and to 22 percent for those 85 and older.
7. *Median* and *mean* need to be distinguished in order to avoid confusion in understanding some of the statistics used in this book. *Median* refers to the

value above which half of all observations in the sample will occur and below which the other half will occur (in our case, half of the population will be older than the median age and half younger). *Mean* is the technical term for the more familiar *average*, that is, the value obtained when all values in the sample are added and then divided by the total number of observations in the sample. The mean therefore is affected more by changes at the high or low end of the scale.

8. Barbara Rieman Herzog, *Aging and Income: Programs and Prospects for the Elderly,* special publication no. 4 sponsored by the Gerontological Society (New York: Human Sciences Press, 1978), p. 11.
9. Marc Levinson, "Retire or Bust," *Newsweek* (November 25, 1991): 50.
10. Schultz et al., *Economics of Population Aging,* pp. 69-70.
11. In fact, concern about the projected imbalance in the middle decades of the next century between workers and those dependent upon them for their support has led some commentators to recommend relaxation of immigration quotas now as a way to improve the "dependency ratio." The assumption is that immigrants will continue their pattern of higher fertility, thus producing more workers to support the large numbers of baby-boom retirees. For obvious reasons, this recommendation has an unsavory flavor to it. Indeed, the whole "dependency ratio" argument that causes such alarm, though not without merit on the surface, is more ambiguous than critics of current aging policy suggest when they use only the elderly dependency ratio instead of the total dependency ratio (that of *all* persons in "nonproducing" groups to workers). The issue is too complex to evaluate here, but after exhaustive study of the matter, James Schulz et al. assert unequivocally, "Adjusting dependency ratios for the relative private expenditures of all population age groups, we found that an important conclusion remains unchanged: total dependency ratios will be lower when members of the baby boom retire than they were when the baby boomers were children in the 1950s and 1960s" because of the projected decrease in the number of children (*Economics of Population Aging,* p. 338). This conclusion is echoed by a number of other authorities. Less quantitatively based but possessing perhaps more emotional appeal is the question asked by Jerry Gerber and his coauthors, "Why is the ratio of taxpaying workers to retirees so often brought up, while we never ask how many workers it takes to support the building of an aircraft carrier?" (*Lifetrends,* p. 137).

2. THE DILEMMA: BEYOND THE NUMBERS GAME

1. Donna Cohen and Carl Eisdorfer, *The Loss of Self: A Family Resource for the Care of Alzheimer's Disease and Related Disorders* (New York: W. W. Norton, 1986), p. 11.
2. Ken Dychtwald and Joe Flower, *Age Wave: The Challenges and Opportunities of an Aging America* (New York: Bantam Books, 1990), p. 13, bold type in original.

261

3. Ibid., p. 17.
4. The data in this paragraph come primarily from Beth B. Hess, "Growing Old in America in the 1990s," in Beth B. Hess and Elizabeth W. Markson, eds., *Growing Old in America*, 4th ed. (New Brunswick, N.J.: Transaction Publishers, 1991), pp. 6-8, 10-11, 281.
5. Marilyn Moon, "Public Policies: Are They Gender-Neutral?," *Generations* 14 (Summer 1990): 59-60.
6. These data come from Beth B. Hess, "Gender & Aging: The Demographic Parameters," *Generations* 14 (Summer 1990): 13; and AARP, *A Profile of Older Americans: 1990,* researched and compiled by Donald G. Fowles of the Administration on Aging, U.S. Department of Health and Human Services, pp. 3-4.
7. Hess, "Growing Old in America in the 1990s," p. 8. Cynics and feminists might observe, as has been the case with abortion, that were men as directly affected by the issue as women are, public policy would quickly take a considerably different and more sympathetic turn.
8. Stephen Crystal, *America's Old Age Crisis: Public Policy and the Two Worlds of Aging* (New York: Basic Books, 1982), p. 26.
9. Paul Ryscavage (Senior Labor Economist with the Census Bureau's Housing and Household Economics Statistics Division), "Aging in the 1990 Census: What Will We Learn?," symposium at the annual meeting of the American Society on Aging, New Orleans, Louisiana, March 18, 1991. See note 12 for specific data to support Ryscavage's first point.
10. For example, in 1987 54.3 percent of the poor elderly had accumulated home equity, which averaged $20,502. Among the near-poor (those with incomes between the official poverty line and 150 percent of it), the corresponding figures were 59.6 percent and $26,415. For all others, 79.9 percent had home equity that averaged $40,143. It should be noted that for the elderly who live alone, all of these figures were lower by amounts that ranged from 5 percent to over 10 percent. See Judith D. Kasper, *Aging Alone: Profiles and Projections,* a report of the Commonwealth Fund Commission on Elderly People Living Alone (1988), p. 42.
11. Moon, "Public Policies: Are They Gender-Neutral?," p. 60.
12. Richard J. Margolis (*Risking Old Age in America* [Boulder, Colo.: Westview Press, 1990], p. 7), for example, observes that *Forbes* magazine used as the cutoff for inclusion on its annual list of America's 400 richest people a net worth of $93 million in 1982; in 1987 the figure had risen to $225 million. The number of billionaires rose from 14 to 49 between just 1985 and 1987. Even more tellingly, Theodore R. Marmor et al. (*America's Misunderstood Welfare State: Persistent Myths, Enduring Realities* [New York: Basic Books, 1990], pp. 8-9) point out that a 10.8 percent decline in average real income occurred between 1973 and 1987 for the poorest 20 percent of Americans living in families, with almost all the decrease actually taking place after 1979; during the same time, the average real income of the wealthiest 20 percent rose 24.1 percent (revised figures since Marmor wrote place this number closer to 30), a net increase in the income gap of 34.9 percent. The increase in inequality was even greater for families with children. And it is not just the poor who have suffered: Senator Bill Bradley, Democrat from New Jersey ("We yearn for straight talk about race, Mr. President," *Miami*

Herald, July 28, 1991), has pointed out that in 1977 the average middle-income American family earned $31,000, the same amount it earned in 1990 after a thirteen-year period of high inflation; over the same period the income of the richest 1 percent of families climbed from $280,000 to $549,000. Bradley follows these numbers with a question: "How could the majority of voters have supported governments whose primary achievement was to make the rich richer?" The basic point is that there *are* some older people living very comfortably, but it is not because they are receiving ever larger public benefits. They are part of the one group in our country that has gained from a general redistribution of wealth in recent years: the wealthy, *regardless* of their age! For example, the richest 5 percent of Americans—the 3.3 million families with incomes over $102,000—will have seen their after-tax income, after inflation, grow almost 60 percent over the fifteen-year period ending in 1992, according to 1990 calculations of the Congressional Budget Office based on Census Bureau data. The top 20 percent (including this 5 percent) show the roughly 30 percent increase in income mentioned above, and the next 20 percent have a barely noticeable rise. The bottom three quintiles all decline, with progressively greater decreases the poorer each group already is. See Karen Pennar, "The Rich Are Richer—And America May Be The Poorer," *Business Week* (November 18, 1991): 85.

13. Margolis (*Risking Old Age in America,* pp. 11-13) and Marmor et al., (*America's Misunderstood Welfare State,* pp. 249-250, n. 9) give further details about the federal poverty line and the method used to calculate it. See Margolis especially (p. 13) for discussion of the nutritional needs of older people.

14. The inadequacy of this assumption and of the consequent calculation is clearly shown by a 1984 study by the National Consumer Law Project (cited by Margolis, *Risking Old Age in America,* pp. 82-83). Focusing on households whose total income was from Supplemental Security Income, the study found that home heating costs, not food, constitute the poor's major expense: During the coldest three months, almost one-third of the maximum SSI benefit went to home heating in forty states; in nine others, over one-half; and in Maine, almost three-quarters.

15. Louis W. Sullivan, "Annual Update of the HHS Poverty Guidelines," *Federal Register* 57 (February 14, 1992): 5456.

16. Advocates Senior Alert Process (A.S.A.P.), *Update* 6 (November 1990): 8. Gerontologists Robert N. Butler, Myrna I. Lewis, and Trey Sunderland say of the elderly poverty figures based on the official poverty line, "In our opinion this is a gross underestimation of poverty. We believe 25% of older persons are poor by more realistic standards" (*Aging and Mental Health: Positive Psychosocial and Biomedical Approaches,* 4th ed. [New York: Macmillan, 1991], p. 16).

17. The 1989 figures used in this paragraph come from the AARP pamphlet, *A Profile of Older Americans: 1990,* pp. 10-11. More recent Census Bureau data show that in 1990 the poverty rate for those 65 and older rose to 12.2 percent, or 3,658,000 persons. See Advocates Senior Alert Process (A.S.A.P.), *Update* 8 (February-March 1992): 9.

18. Stephen Crystal, *America's Old Age Crisis* (New York: Basic Books, 1982), p. 9.
19. Robert H. Binstock, "The Elderly in America: Their Economic Resources, Income Status, and Costs," in William P. Browne and Laura Katz Olson, *Aging and Public Policy: The Politics of Growing Old in America* (Westport, Conn.: Greenwood Press, 1983), p. 32.
20. Statistics in this section come from David Fischer, *Growing Old in America,* expanded edition (New York: Oxford University Press, 1978), pp. 142-46, 279; Gerber et al., *Lifetrends: The Future of Baby Boomers and Other Aging Americans* (New York: Macmillan, 1989), pp. 74-79; and Schulz et al., *Economics of Population Aging: The "Graying" of Australia, Japan, and the United States* (New York: Auburn House, 1991), pp. 12-15.
21. Cynthia Taeuber (Chief of the U.S. Census Bureau's Age and Sex Statistics Branch), "Aging in the 1990 Census: What Will We Learn?," symposium at the annual meeting of the American Society on Aging, New Orleans, March 18, 1991.
22. National Council on the Aging, "The Aging Revolution," *Perspective on Aging* (May/June 1991): 4.
23. Elias S. Cohen, "Gerontology: Past, Present and Future," *Aging Today* 12 (April/May 1991): 3.
24. Fischer, *Growing Old in America,* pp. 145, 279.
25. Spencer Rich, "Study Says Women Provide Most Home Care for Elderly," *Washington Post,* August 4, 1986.
26. William Oriol, "In a Turbulent Economy, The U.S. Work Force Is Aging," *Perspective on Aging* (March/April 1991): 7.
27. Maximiliane Szinovacz, "Women and Retirement," in Hess and Markson, eds., *Growing Old in America,* pp. 294-95.
28. Elaine Brody, " 'Women in the Middle' and Family Help to Older People," *Gerontologist* 21 (1981): 474.
29. Robyn I. Stone and Peter Kemper, "Spouses and Children of Disabled Elders: How Large a Constituency for Long-term Care Reform?" *Milbank Quarterly* 67 (1989): 499. The other data in this section also come from this helpful article.
30. According to a study by sociologist Peter Uhlenberg of the University of North Carolina at Chapel Hill (reported by Bernard Bauer, "Divorced Dads Often Lose Touch with Kids," *Miami Herald,* August 20, 1991), whereas 90 percent of married men over 50 had weekly contact with their adult children, only half of the study's 261 divorced fathers of the same age did. Even more significant, a third of the divorced men had lost contact completely with at least one of their children. After observing that "adult children are the principal source of caregiving to older people [we must assume that he actually said or at least meant 'after spouses']," Uhlenberg concluded that older divorced fathers "are not only lacking a spouse, they're also lacking children who will come in and provide support."
31. For an interesting treatment of this issue, see Jeffrey P. Rosenfeld, "To Heir Is Human: Updated," in Hess and Markson, eds., *Growing Old in America,* pp. 531-38.
32. AARP, *Profile of Older Americans,* p. 3.

33. Elbert Cole, "Congregation Response to Aging," a symposium at the annual meeting of the National Council on the Aging, Miami Beach, May 1991.
34. "Grandparents and Crack Babies," *San Francisco Bay Guardian*, March 14, 1990, quoted in *The Aging Connection* (April/May 1990): 4.
35. Joyce T. Berry, "Caring for the Nation's Aging Poor," closing general session of the annual meeting of the American Society on Aging, San Diego, March 17, 1992.
36. Trudy Lieberman, "The Crisis in Health Insurance, Part 2: Health Insurance for All?," *Consumer Reports* 55 (September 1990): 608.
37. According to Census Bureau data reported by R. A. Zaldivar ("Bleak Recession Figures Stir Call for Poverty Relief," *Miami Herald*, September 27, 1991), the number of uninsured rose to 34.7 million in 1990 from 33.4 million in 1989, an increase of 1.3 million. Some estimates place the number of those underinsured at an additional 50 million, for a total of over one-third of all Americans without adequate health insurance.
38. National Committee to Preserve Social Security and Medicare, Policy and Research Department, *Issue Brief: Universal Access to Health Care*, Washington, D.C.: 1991.
39. Tom Wicker, "Code Blue on Insurance," *Miami Herald*, July 24, 1991. In 1989, 45 percent of the net profits of those businesses went for health care. Many observers cite such figures among the reasons for the increasing inability of American business to compete in the international market-place. For example, it is estimated that employee health-care costs increase the price of a typical American-made car by $1086.
40. Most of the data in this and the next two paragraphs come from the AARP pamphlet, *A Profile of Older Americans: 1990,* pp. 12-14, with supplementary information from Elizabeth W. Markson, "Physiological Changes, Illness, and Health Care Use in Later life," in Hess and Markson, *Growing Old in America*, pp. 181-83.
41. "Empty Pocketbooks," *The Aging Connection* (April/May 1990): 12, citing the 1988 report of the U.S. House Select Committee on Aging, *Emptying the Elderly's Pocketbooks: Growing Impact of Rising Health Care Costs.*
42. James S. House, Ronald C. Kessler, A. Regula Herzog, Richard P. Mero, Ann M. Kinney, and Martha J. Breslow, "Age, Socioeconomic Status, and Health," *Milbank Quarterly* 68 (1990): 401-2.
43. Hess, "Gender & Aging," pp. 14-15.
44. Stone and Kemper, "Spouses and Children of Disabled Elders," pp. 485, 502. On p. 485, they assert that whatever suggestions are made concerning financing and delivery of long-term care for the elderly, "the family is, and will continue to be, a critical component of the long-term care system." The statistics in the text, along with many others of considerable interest but beyond the scope of this discussion, come from pp. 490-93. The authors arrived at their numbers through a sophisticated method of statistical analysis and projection, based on the 1984 National Long-Term Care Survey. Their assertion that LTC is a problem of all ages receives further support from the fact that somewhere between three and four million more people *under* the age of 65 need such care (Edward F. Howard,

"Long-Term Care: On the Comeback Trail?," *Generations* 15 [Summer/ Fall 1991]: 31).

45. Trudy Lieberman, "An Empty Promise to the Elderly?," *Consumer Reports* 56 (June 1991): 429.

46. Karen C. Holden and Timothy M. Smeeding, "The Poor, the Rich, and the Insecure Elderly Caught in Between," *Milbank Quarterly* 68 (1990): 191.

47. Richard G. Rogers, Andrei Rogers, and Alain Belanger, "Active Life among the Elderly in the United States: Multistate Life-table Estimates and Population Projections," *Milbank Quarterly* 67 (1989): 375.

48. Holden and Smeeding, "The Poor, the Rich, and the Insecure Elderly Caught in Between," pp. 201, 214.

49. Lieberman, "An Empty Promise to the Elderly?" p. 425.

50. Ibid., p. 434.

51. Indeed, the *Consumer Reports* article (p. 435) cites the projection of the prestigious Brookings Institution that in 30 years such policies will be affordable to only around one-quarter of *all* elderly people, an estimate that does not take into account the added cost of the improvements that virtually all commentators say these policies must have, such as mandatory inflation and nonforfeiture protection. Not surprisingly, the article's ultimate conclusion is that "Congress should . . . enact a national, publicly financed program to pay for long-term care for all Americans."

52. Karen Davis, Paula Grant, and Diane Rowland, "Alone and Poor," *Generations* 14 (Summer 1990): 45.

53. Holden and Smeeding, "The Poor, the Rich, and the Insecure Elderly Caught in Between," p. 199.

54. Stone and Kemper, "Spouses and Children of Disabled Elders," p. 497.

55. Hess, "Gender and Aging," p. 15.

56. Rhonda J. V. Montgomery and Mary McGlinn Datwyler, "Women & Men in the Caregiving Role," *Generations* 14 (Summer 1990): 38.

3. CURRENT RESPONSES: PROGRAMS AND POLICIES

1. Stephen Crystal, *America's Old Age Crisis: Public Policy and the Two Worlds of Aging* (New York: Basic Books, 1982), p. 20. Stanley J. Brody corroborates this view somewhat more substantively ("Strategic Planning: The Catastrophic Approach," *The Gerontologist* 27 [1987]: 131): "It is held by many that there has been no common underlying goal of public policy: That it has been an exercise in improvisation and expediency, in disjointed incrementalism or muddling through to some ill-defined or even non-defined end."

2. Robert Binstock, "Aging, Politics, and Public Policy," in Beth B. Hess and Elizabeth W. Markson, eds., *Growing Old in America*, 4th ed. (New Brunswick, N.J.: Transaction Publishers, 1991), pp. 325-26. Most commentators see growth of this magnitude as hardly possible.

3. Theodore R. Marmor, Jerry L. Mashaw, and Philip L. Harvey, *America's*

Misunderstood Welfare State: Persistent Myths, Enduring Realities (New York: Basic Books, 1990), pp. 32-33.

4. And such books abound. Two of the better recent ones are Merton C. Bernstein and Joan Brodshang Bernstein, *Social Security: The System That Works* (New York: Basic Books, 1988), and Marmor et al., *America's Misunderstood Welfare State.* A less sympathetic treatment is found in Michael Boskin, *Too Many Promises: The Uncertain Future of Social Security* (Homewood, Ill.: Dow Jones-Irwin, 1986). Not surprisingly, virtually all of the books that deal with the "crisis" of the aging of America also address, in one way or another, the role Social Security plays.

5. Quoted in Jerry Gerber, Janet Wolff, Walter Klores, and Gene Brown, *Lifetrends: The Future of Baby Boomers and Other Aging Americans* (New York: Macmillan, 1989), p. 103.

6. An interesting exercise might be to conduct an informal poll of family, friends, and co-workers, asking simply what *FICA* stands for or for a fuller description of Social Security. In such surveys of undergraduate honors students at the University of Miami, I have found that about 10 percent can identify FICA and a like number can give a somewhat adequate summary of the basic elements of the Social Security program. Members of the Institute of Retired Professionals auditing the classes do considerably better!

7. Brody, "Strategic Planning," p. 132.

8. For example, Theodore Marmor et al. (*America's Misunderstood Welfare State*, p. 30) observe that the various criticisms of Social Security today "often proceed from assumptions about purpose that make sense within one ideological framework but not others." As a result, the critics confuse purpose with method or result, as if they criticized an airline's performance, efficiency, type of equipment, and chances of staying in business because it flies turboprops to Portland when *they* want to go by jet to Seattle.

9. W. Andrew Achenbaum, *Shades of Gray: Old Age, American Values, and Federal Policies Since 1920* (Boston: Little, Brown and Company, 1983), p. 43.

10. James H. Schulz, Allan Borowski, and William H. Crown, *Economics of Population Aging: The "Graying" of Australia, Japan, and the United States* (New York: Auburn House, 1991), p. 178.

11. Brody, "Strategic Planning," p. 132.

12. Schulz et al., *Economics of Population Aging*, p. 178.

13. Ibid., p. 179.

14. Richard J. Margolis, *Risking Old Age in America* (Boulder: Westview Press, 1990), p. 22.

15. "Seniors Feel Double Financial Pinch," *Miami Herald*, October 18, 1991.

16. Brody, "Strategic Planning," p. 133.

17. Margolis, *Risking Old Age in America*, p. 29.

18. U.S. Department of Health and Human Services, Social Security Administration, *Your Social Security Taxes . . . What They're Paying for and Where the Money Goes*, Pub. No. 05-10010 (1991), p. 10.

19. Judith Kasper, *Aging Alone: Profiles and Projections*, a Report of the

Commonwealth Fund Commission on Elderly People Living Alone (1988), p. 40.

20. The data in this paragraph come from U.S. Department of Health and Human Services, Social Security Administration, *Social Security's Pledge to Beneficiaries, Taxpayers, and Future Workers*, Pub. No. 05-10073 (1989), p. 4, and from U.S. Department of Health and Human Services, Social Security Administration, *Survivors*, Pub. No. 05-10084 (1991), p. 3.

21. U.S. Department of Health and Human Services, Social Security Administration, *Retirement*, Pub. No. 05-10035 (1991), pp. 8-9.

22. Michael Boskin, *Too Many Promises*, p. 181. Boskin's figures come from Social Security Administration documents and contain projections for payroll tax rates for employer and employee in 2030: Optimistic assumptions yield a rate of 9 percent each, intermediate assumptions 14 percent, and pessimistic assumptions 24 percent (assuming no accumulation of surpluses from earlier years, a major assumption that reflects a political issue currently hotly debated).

23. Social Security Administration, *Your Social Security Taxes*, p. 8. In a May 1991 speech to the National Council on the Aging convention, Social Security Commissioner Gwendolyn King, citing the 1991 annual report of the Social Security Trustees, asserted that sufficient funds would accumulate without any tax increase to pay benefits for the next 50 years. Assuming these funds are allowed to accumulate and are not used to resolve problems closer at hand, critics of Social Security might grant the point; their question, though, is what happens in year *51*!

24. If merely discovering the size of one's potential retirement benefit is the goal, the Social Security Administration will be happy to provide a "personal earnings and benefit estimate." If more specific information is desired concerning the actual method of calculation, the publication, *How Your Retirement Benefit Is Figured* (U.S. Department of Health and Human Services, Social Security Administration, Pub. No. 05-10070 [1991]), is relatively comprehensible.

25. Social Security Administration, *Retirement*, p. 5.

26. Social Security Administration, *How Your Retirement Benefit Is Figured*, p. 2.

27. U.S. Department of Health and Human Services, Social Security Administration, *Disability*, Pub. No. 05-10029 (1991), p. 4.

28. U.S. Department of Health and Human Services, Social Security Administration, *SSI: Supplemental Security Income*, Pub. No. 05-11000 (1991), pp. 3-5.

29. Marilyn Moon, "Public Policies: Are They Gender-Neutral?," *Generations* 14 (Summer 1990): 61.

30. Boskin, *Too Many Promises*, pp. 13-14. On p. 85, Boskin points out that a 65 year old retiring in 1970 had paid 32 percent of the benefits he or she could expect to receive.

31. Ibid., p. 14.

32. Ibid., p. 8.

33. Ken Dychtwald and Joe Flower, *Age Wave: The Challenges and Opportunities of an Aging America* (New York: Bantam Books, 1990), p. 74.

34. Quoted in Margolis, *Risking Old Age in America*, p. 23.

35. Ibid.

36. Fay Lomax Cook, "Congress and the Public: Convergent and Divergent Opinions on Social Security," in *Social Security and the Budget,* ed. Henry J. Aaron (Lanham, Md.: University Press of America, 1990), pp. 79-107, cited in Marmor et al., *America's Misunderstood Welfare State,* pp. 47-48, 133-34.
37. Cited in "Notebook," *Second Opinion* 17 (July 1991): 131.
38. It has been observed that Medicare operates in a completely opposite fashion from virtually all other insurance policies or theories. In other schemes (such as automobile or private "major medical" insurance), the insured pays a relatively small deductible and the insurance pays for the larger balance. Medicare also has a deductible, but the longer one is institutionalized, payments also go down as costs mount, until finally the patient becomes completely responsible for all costs. (I am indebted to Steven G. Ullmann for this analysis.)
39. Margolis, *Risking Old Age in America,* p. 59.
40. In an address to a conference on health care ethics in Tampa on December 4, 1991, Florida State Senator Jeanne Malchon suggested that the common name "health-care delivery system" is a gross misnomer on all counts. First, the thrust is not health care but "sickness treatment." Next, nothing is delivered; sick people must go out and get it. And finally, by no means can what we have be called a "system." On a related matter, Malchon made the point that one of the greatest failings of our current approach is its lack of emphasis on primary/preventive care. She illustrated the point by saying that we do not provide treatment for a poor child with a sore throat that can become a strep throat that can lead to rheumatic fever and ultimately to end-stage renal disease. Her fitting judgment was that such an approach is "totally irrational by any standard."
41. Kasper, *Aging Alone: Profiles and Projections,* p. 44.
42. "Study: Poor Miss Out on Medicaid," *Miami Herald,* June 18, 1991; "Time, Cost Cited in Health Gap: Some Don't Get Aid for Poor," *Miami Herald,* July 25, 1991.
43. Donna Cohen and Carl Eisdorfer, *Loss of Self: A Family Resource for the Cure of Alzheimer's Disease and Related Disorders* (New York: W. W. Norton, 1986), p. 311. Because Medicaid varies from state to state, in New York families pay as much as 90 percent.
44. Trudy Lieberman, "An Empty Promise to the Elderly?," *Consumer Reports* 56 (June 1991): 435.
45. Noralou P. Roos, Evelyn Shapiro, and Robert Tate, "Does a Small Minority of Elderly Account for a Majority of Health Care Expenditures?: A Sixteen-Year Perspective," *Milbank Quarterly* 67 (1989): 367.
46. Brody, "Strategic Planning," p. 135.
47. Advocates Senior Alert Process (A.S.A.P.), *Update* 6 (November 1990): 2.
48. Most of the descriptive information in this section comes from A.S.A.P., *Special Report: Congress Poised to Renew Older Americans Act* (March 1990): 1-5. It is worthy to note that as of March 1992, the reauthorization of the Act referred to in this report was still pending in Congress, delayed by a late amendment that would totally eliminate the Social Security retirement test described earlier. This action would cost $28 billion in tax revenues over five years, which Congress would have to make up through program

cuts or tax increases. Some elder advocates charge that the Act is being "held hostage" until after the 1992 election because Congress is reluctant either to reject the amendment, and thus risk offending the largely upper-income elderly who would benefit most from a repeal, or to adopt it and have to devise a way to pay for it that is also sure to anger some constituencies. See A.S.A.P., "Older Americans Act Reauthorization Still Up in the Air," *Update* 8 (February-March 1992): 6.

4. CURRENT RESPONSES: ORGANIZATIONS RELATED TO THE ELDERLY

1. Henry J. Pratt, "National Interest Groups Among the Elderly: Consolidation and Constraint," in William P. Browne and Laura Katz Olson, eds., *Aging and Public Policy: The Politics of Growing Old in America* (Westport, Conn.: Greenwood Press, 1983), p. 145.
2. Several of these organizations have recognized the importance of religious concerns for the elderly. For example, the American Society on Aging ("the largest professional association in the field of aging") has created a special interest group known as the Forum on Religion, Spirituality, and Aging (FRSA) to promote "programs, policies, and educational opportunities which empower the experience and expression of religion and spirituality in later life." In addition to the regular ASA publications, members of FRSA receive a quarterly newsletter, "Aging and Spirituality," that conveys information of particular interest to the religious community. Further information may be obtained by writing ASA at 833 Market Street, Suite 512, San Francisco, Calif. 94103 (telephone 415-882-2810).
3. The information in this paragraph comes from Jerry Gerber, Janet Wolff, Walter Klores, and Gene Brown, *Lifetrends: The Future of Baby Boomers and Other Aging Americans* (New York: Macmillan, 1989), pp. 134-36; Ken Dychtwald and Joe Flower, *Age Wave: The Challenges and Opportunities of an Aging America* (New York: Bantam Books, 1990), pp. 55-56; and Christine Day, *What Older Americans Think: Interest Groups and Aging Policy* (Princeton: Princeton University Press, 1990), pp. 25-26.
4. It is interesting to note that in 1983 the membership age was lowered to 50; today 40 percent of AARP's members are *under* 65 (Day, *What Older Americans Think*, p. 25).
5. See Pratt, "National Interest Groups Among the Elderly," pp. 164-78, for discussion of some reasons for this.
6. Robert H. Binstock, "Aging, Politics, and Public Policy," in Beth B. Hess and Elizabeth W. Markson, eds., *Growing Old in America*, 4th ed. (New Brunswick, N.J.: Transaction Publishers, 1991), pp. 332-33.
7. Gerber et al., *Lifetrends*, p. 139.
8. Robert Hudson and Judith Gonyea, "A Perspective on Women in Politics: Political Mobilization & Older Women," *Generations* 14 (Summer 1990): 69.

9. Binstock, "Aging, Politics, and Public Policy," pp. 333-34.
10. The data on voting patterns through 1986 come from Dychtwald and Flower, *Age Wave,* p. 60. The figures for 1988 are from "In the News: A Reminder to Candidates," *Perspectives on Aging* 21 (January/February 1992): 2.
11. Day, *What Older Americans Think,* p. 37.
12. Harold Fey, "Politics and the Elderly: Toward a Sharing of Resources," *The Christian Century* (December 14, 1988): 1153, 1154.
13. Dychtwald and Flower, *Age Wave,* p. 78, bold type in original. On pp. 63-64, they declare, "As a result of the rapid increase in the power and clout of America's older citizens, a battle is brewing that threatens to divide the nation and set generation against generation for decades to come. These intergenerational conflicts . . . more than anything else . . . will be about the distribution of our nation's resources."
14. Phillip Longman, *Born to Pay: The New Politics of Aging* (Boston: Houghton Mifflin, 1987), p. 2.
15. Jill Quadagno, "Generational Equity and the Politics of the Welfare State," in Hess and Markson, *Growing Old in America,* p. 342.
16. These statistics, and there are many more equally discouraging ones that could be cited, are truly deplorable, and even more so in light of the fact pointed out in chapter 2 about the widening disparity between the rich and the poor of all generations: At the same time that one out of five of our nation's children lives in poverty, all children between the ages of 4 and 12 spend $6.1 billion a year (Jean Marabella, "For Kids, Zillions of Opinions," *Miami Herald,* August 1, 1991.) It is unlikely that much of that expenditure comes from those "ones" out of five.
17. Samuel H. Preston, "Children and the Elderly in the U.S.," *Scientific American* 251 (December 1984): 49.
18. A more negative and therefore more frightening concern often colors this discussion also. This fear is well illustrated by the comment of Martha Musgrove in a May 31, 1988, *Miami Herald* column entitled "Florida's Children at the Back of the Budget Line": After cataloguing the Florida legislature's failure to provide needed funds for vitually every program aimed at children and youth, Musgrove concludes, "Children who are neglected, abused, angry, and ignorant grow up and all too frequently become a bigger, more threatening burden. Florida's prisons are full of them." It should be noted, not incidentally, that most experts predict that the age distribution of the population of the United States in the first quarter of the next century will approximate Florida's current demographic profile.
19. Preston, "Children and the Elderly in the U.S.," p. 49.
20. "The Morning After," *The Atlantic Monthly* (October 1987): 43-69. Peterson subsequently developed his ideas in a book written with Neil Howe, entitled *On Borrowed Time: How the Growth in Entitlement Spending Threatens America's Future* (San Francisco: ICS Press, 1988).
21. Peterson, "The Morning After," p. 60.
22. Ibid., p. 68.

23. Ibid., pp. 68-69. Elsewhere (p. 44), he says of these benefits, "or, to put it bluntly, welfare for the middle class and up."
24. In *Abundance of Life* ([New York: Columbia University Press, 1988], p. 109), Harry R. Moody raises an interesting point concerning this possible combination of "private" providers of old-age security: "A critical question is whether the marketplace element and the voluntarist element can effectively coexist, since they are based on diametrically opposite views of human nature: selfishness versus altruism." A strong advocate of privatization is Peter Ferrara, who makes his case in, among other works, *Social Security Reform: The Family Plan* (Washington, D.C.: Heritage Foundation, 1982). For a concise critique of privatization by someone sympathetic to its philosophical assumptions, see Michael J. Boskin, *Too Many Promises: The Uncertain Future of Social Security* (Homewood, Ill.: Dow Jones-Irwin, 1986), pp. 100-4.
25. For example, in a typical year, about one-third of Medicare expenditures are incurred by fewer than 3 percent of those 65 and older, and around 10 percent are responsible for almost three-fourths of all Medicare costs. A frequently cited statistic on this issue is that almost a third of the Medicare budget is expended on patients in the last year of life, an obviously "wasteful" expenditure in the opinion of a number of critics. This complaint, however, contains a serious flaw, well illustrated by a question used on an intelligence test for elementary school children: "The last car of a train is most likely to be involved in an accident. If we get rid of the last car of all trains, will we greatly reduce the accident rate?" The problem is that in many cases we do not know what is going to be "the last year" of a person's life and thus it is impossible to eliminate "the last car of the train of life." This does not mean, however, that all expenditures for terminally ill patients are therefore justified.
26. Daniel Callahan, *Setting Limits: Medical Goals in an Aging Society* (New York: Simon & Schuster, 1987), p. 66. Subsequently, Callahan explored these issues further in another book that actually reads as if it should have come before *Setting Limits*. The second book is *What Kind of Life? The Limits of Medical Progress* (New York: Simon & Schuster, 1990).
27. Callahan, *Setting Limits*, pp. 137-38.
28. Binstock, "Aging, Politics, and Public Policy," p. 328.
29. Quoted in Gerber et al., *Lifetrends*, p. 148. The material that follows in the text is from a speech at the annual meeting of the American Society on Aging in New Orleans in March 1991.

5. VALUES: THE THEOLOGICAL/ETHICAL DIMENSION

1. Theodore R. Marmor, Jerry L. Mashaw, and Philip Harvey, *America's Misunderstood Welfare State: Persistent Myths, Enduring Realities* (New York: Basic Books, 1990), p. 31.
2. Norman Daniels, *Am I My Parents' Keeper? An Essay on Justice Between the Young and the Old* (New York: Oxford University Press, 1988), p. 59.

3. On p. 68, Daniels says, "A natural place to seek principles of justice for regulating health-care institutions is by examining different general theories of justice." Again, although such resources may and should be utilized by Christians for guidance, the "natural" place for *believers* to turn is the resources of their own theological/ethical tradition. Indeed, as Bradley J. Longfield suggests more generally, "Clearly, if the mainstream churches are to resolve their identity crisis, they will have to do so on the basis of a biblical and creedal faith that is distinct from the values and norms of the surrounding culture" (*The Presbyterian Controversy: Fundamentalists, Modernists, & Moderates* [New York: Oxford University Press, 1991], n.p., excerpted in Duke Divinity School, *Divinity News & Notes* 7 [Spring 1991]: 10). Audrey R. Chapman agrees that the churches "lack a theological distinctiveness and coherence that would confer the incentive and ability to apply theological and biblical traditions to contemporary political issues" ("Theology and Public Policy: Closing the Gap," *Theology and Public Policy* 3 [Fall, 1991]: 43).
4. For some of the material that follows, I draw on my earlier book, *Full of Years: Aging and the Elderly in the Bible and Today* (Nashville: Abingdon Press, 1987), chapters 2-6.
5. Søren Kierkegaard, *Works of Love*, trans. David F. Swenson and Lillian M. Swenson (Princeton: Princeton University Press, 1946), p. 19, quoted in Paul Ramsey, *Basic Christian Ethics* (New York: Charles Scribner's Sons, 1950), p. 93.
6. Ramsey, *Basic Christian Ethics*, p. 93. On p. 246, Ramsey makes another comment, again following Kierkegaard, that also applies to our topic: "instead of talking about how the object of love ought to be in order to be worthy of love, Christian ethics talks about how love ought to be in order to be love."
7. Interestingly, in vv. 4-5, Yahweh asserts, "There will, however, be no one in need among you, . . . if only you will obey the LORD your God, by diligently observing this entire commandment that I command you today." That is, true obedience to God's command to share with those in need would eliminate poverty, a telling reminder to Christians today. Also, it is sometimes pointed out that this command to share applies only to fellow Israelites, an assessment of the passage that appears accurate. The conclusion often drawn from this interpretation, however—that one's obligation toward the needy today is similarly limited, perhaps only to fellow believers—is countered completely for contemporary Christians by Jesus' teaching in the parable of the good Samaritan (see discussion above).
8. Gerrit G. de Kruijf, "The Christian in the Crowded Public Square: The Hidden Tension Between Prophecy and Democracy," *The Annual of the Society of Christian Ethics* (1991): 38.
9. Hessel Bouma III, Douglas Diekema, Edward Langerak, Theodore Rottman, and Allen Verhey, *Christian Faith, Health, and Medical Practice* (Grand Rapids: William B. Eerdmans, 1989), p. 22.
10. For a more detailed discussion of this important topic, see Sapp, *Full of Years*, chapters 2 and 3.
11. See Sapp, *Full of Years*, pp. 81-92, for further consideration of the commandment and its importance for religious gerontology.

273

12. Rolf Knierim, "Age and Aging in the Old Testament," in William M. Clements, ed., *Ministry with the Aging: Designs, Challenges, Foundations* (New York: Harper & Row, 1981), p. 29.
13. Norman Gottwald, "From Tribal Existence to Empire: The Socio-Historical Context for the Rise of the Hebrew Prophets," in J. Mark Thomas and Vernon Visick, eds., *God and Capitalism: A Prophetic Critique of Market Economy* (Madison, Wis.: A-R Editions, 1991), pp. 15, 16. On p. 26, Gottwald further specifies the standard that a communitarian model sets for a society, and especially for its political economy: "Does that mode of production, and the power relations governing it, build up the whole community, providing it basic services and creating opportunities to realize the life possibilities of the greatest number of people?"
14. Ibid., p. 19.
15. H. Wheeler Robinson's *Corporate Personality in Ancient Israel* ([Philadelphia: Fortress Press, 1964]) remains instructive on this point. *Ancestors* and *descendants* in the text do not refer solely to a person's blood relatives but to all members of the community who precede and follow that person.
16. Quoted in Tim Nickens, "Journey Home Underscores Chiles' Vision," *Miami Herald*, July 28, 1991, emphasis added.
17. Bouma et al., *Christian Faith, Health, and Medical Practice*, p. 22.
18. " 'Blitz building': Habitat trademark," *NCOA Networks*, June 28, 1991. Fuller's last remark seems increasingly to be the crux of the matter, whatever the issue. In a November 1, 1991, editorial entitled "The New War on Poverty," the *Miami Herald* concludes, after listing some of the "technical" steps necessary, "The most important ingredient, however, is civic will."
19. I do not mean to suggest here that a minimum level of material well-being is not an essential element of a decent life and a goal that Christians should strongly advocate for everyone. My concern is rather with our society's emphasis that one's very value as a human being is dependent on what one has and what one consumes—that is, on one's material possessions.
20. Greg Arling, "The Elderly Widow and Her Family, Neighbors and Friends," *Journal of Marriage and the Family* 38 (1976): n.p., quoted in Jerry Gerber, Janet Wolff, Walter Klores, and Gene Brown, *Lifetrends: The Future of Baby Boomers and Other Aging Americans* (New York: Macmillan, 1989), p. 152.
21. Gerber et al., *Lifetrends*, p. 152.
22. Peter Berger, Brigitte Berger, and Hansfired Kellner, *The Homeless Mind: Modernization and Consciousness* (New York: Random House, 1974), p. 185, quoted in Harry R. Moody, *Abundance of Life: Human Development Policies for an Aging Society* (New York: Columbia University Press, 1988), p. 27.
23. The Harrington quotation is from *The Immortalist: An Approach to the Engineering of Man's Divinity* (New York: Random House, 1969), p. 3; the Hendin quotation is from *Death as a Fact of Life* (New York: Warner Books, 1973), p. 85. Both are quoted in William E. Phipps, *Death: Confronting the Reality* (Atlanta: John Knox Press, 1987), pp. 8 and 85, respectively.
24. Daniel Callahan, *Setting Limits: Medical Goals in an Aging Society* (New York: Simon & Schuster, 1987), p. 32.

25. Daniel Callahan, *What Kind of Life? The Limits of Medical Progress* (New York: Simon & Schuster, 1990), pp. 63, 65.
26. Thomas Cole, "The Specter of Old Age: History, Politics, and Culture in an Aging America," in Beth B. Hess and Elizabeth W. Markson, eds., *Growing Old in America*, 4th ed. (New Brunswick, N.J.: Transaction Publishers, 1991), p. 34.
27. For a fuller discussion of the Old Testament's view of death, see Lloyd Bailey, *Biblical Perspectives on Death*, Biblical Theology Series, no. 5 (Philadelphia: Fortress Press, 1979), pp. 23-74.
28. Janice Castro, "Condition: Critical," *Time* (November 25, 1991): 38.
29. Ken Dychtwald and Joe Flower, *Age Wave: The Challenges and Opportunities of an Aging America* (New York: Bantam Books, 1990), p. 20.
30. John Arras and Robert Hunt, "Introduction: Ethical Theory in the Medical Context," in John Arras and Nancy Rhoden, eds., *Ethical Issues in Modern Medicine*, 3rd ed. (Mountain View, Calif.: Mayfield Publishing Company), p. 2 (italics in original).
31. Amitai Etzioni, "Spare the Old, Save the Young," *The Nation* (June 11, 1988): 818-822, reprinted in Thomas A. Mappes and Jane S. Zembaty, eds., *Biomedical Ethics*, 3rd ed. (New York: McGraw-Hill, 1991), p. 594.
32. In *Am I My Parents' Keeper?* (p. 116), Norman Daniels states bluntly that, considering the greatly enhanced health of people under 75, "our current policies seem archaic."
33. Robert Morris and Scott A. Bass, "A New Class in America: A Revisionist View of Retirement," in Hess and Markson, *Growing Old in America*, p. 93. It must be admitted that the Reformed notion of temporal success as a sign of election, embedded in the values of this country by the Puritans and used as the central focus of Max Weber's landmark *Protestant Ethic and the Spirit of Capitalism*, probably contributes to this struggle. If success in one's work is a mark of being among the elect, loss of that work may call into question a person's sense of self-worth and confidence in an assured future. I am not claiming that most contemporary Americans are as self-consciously theological in their understanding of life as this comment might suggest, but the basic concept remains alive in our secular mythos.
34. *The Wisdom of Martin Luther*, compiled by N. Alfred Balmer (St. Louis: Concordia Publishing House, 1973), pp. 52-53.
35. Joe Holland, *Creative Communion: Toward a Spirituality of Work* (New York: Paulist Press, 1989), p. 36. The entire book rewards reading.
36. Daniels, *Am I My Parents' Keeper?*, p. 116.
37. Morris and Bass, "A New Class in America," p. 98.
38. Etzioni, "Spare the Old, Save the Young," p. 594.
39. Morris and Bass, "A New Class in America," p. 101.
40. For data on this issue, see Michael J. Boskin, *Too Many Promises: The Uncertain Future of Social Security* (Homewood, Ill.: Dow Jones-Irwin, 1986), pp. 57-59. After presenting several tables that show retirement rates varying widely depending on the physical demands and danger of different occupations, Boskin wisely concludes, "This evidence should make us wary of national retirement policies that fail to allow substantial options for those who, for a variety of reasons, may wish to, or have to, retire at different ages" (pp. 58-59).

275

41. In *Basic Christian Ethics* (p. 337), Paul Ramsey draws another important and relevant conclusion from the biblical assertion of the self-interested character of human nature. He avers that the time will never come when legislators can cease to try "to arrange it that every one who favors a measure shall run the risk of being the one disfavored by its terms." He then concludes, "Right is secured and sin checked only if no one has an interest in making the conditions more burdensome than he himself is willing to bear." This last sentence should serve as a pointed warning for all policymakers whose assets make them highly unlikely ever to be in the situations of many of those for whom they are making policy (and, perhaps, also as a warning to comfortably situated Christian ethicists who purport to speak for those less well off!).
42. Quoted in Laurence J. Peter, ed., *Peter's Quotations: Ideas for Our Time* (New York: Bantam Books, 1977), p. 219.
43. Marmor et al., *America's Misunderstood Welfare State*, p. 165.
44. Ibid.
45. Garrett Hardin, "The Tragedy of the Commons," *Science* 162 (1968): 1247.
46. Ibid.
47. Marmor et al., *America's Misunderstood Welfare State*, p. 158.

6. VALUES: UNDERSTANDING THE POSITIONS

1. AGE's position seems to suggest that "ageism" is a thing of the past. That this is not so was brought home to me subtly yet significantly by a recent radio news report of a light plane crash. The reporter said, "The *elderly* pilot of a plane that crashed yesterday said today that pilot error was to blame" (italics mine). I am sure few people thought about the implications of the use of that identifier, but it is hard to imagine a reporter's ever saying, "The *African-American* pilot . . . ," "the *Jewish* pilot . . . ," or even "the *female* pilot. . . . " Similarly, the comic strip "B.C." offers a definition of *fossil beds*: "Where old people sleep" (January 17, 1992). Again, few groups in our country could be so freely identified with a negative term.
2. The view of the elderly espoused by proponents of generational equity gains some support from a bumper sticker commonly seen in retirement areas: "I'm not retired—I'm busy spending my kids' inheritance."
3. Janet Otwell and Janet Costello, *Ninety for the '90s: A Final Report* (Springfield, Ill.: Illinois Department on Aging, 1990), p. 39.
4. Robert B. Hudson and Eric R. Kingson, "Inclusive and Fair: The Case for Universality in Social Programs," *Generations* 15 (Summer/Fall 1991): 53. They point out that means-tested cash benefits (like SSI) further reduced the poverty rate to 12.9 percent.
5. Ibid.
6. Ibid., pp. 53-54.
7. Robert H. Binstock, "Aging, Politics, and Public Policy," in Beth B. Hess

and Elizabeth W. Markson, eds., *Growing Old in America,* 4th ed. (New Brunswick, N.J.: Transaction Publishers, 1991), p. 328.

8. Many of these have been cited already. The following present the various positions from a number of perspectives in a relatively accessible fashion (for more complete information, see the bibliography): Phillip Longman, *Born To Pay: The New Politics of Aging in America*; Peter Peterson and Neil Howe, *On Borrowed Time: How the Growth in Entitlement Spending Threatens America's Future*; Michael J. Boskin, *Too Many Promises: The Uncertain Future of Social Security*; Richard Margolis, *Risking Old Age in America*; Theodore Marmor et al., *America's Misunderstood Welfare State: Persistent Myths, Enduring Realities*; and Robert H. Binstock and Stephen G. Post, eds., *Too Old for Health Care? Controversies in Medicine, Law, Economics, and Ethics.*

9. For further information on the cultural use of metaphor, see George Lakoff and Mark Johnson, *Metaphors We Live By* (Chicago: University of Chicago Press, 1980). The authors contend that metaphors often influence greatly (and subconsciously) the ways we think, experience the world, and act.

10. Duncan Luce and Howard Raiffa, *Games and Decisions: Introduction and Critical Survey* (New York: John Wiley & Sons, 1957), p. 10.

11. Quoted on the cover of Anatol Rapoport, *Two-Person Game Theory: The Essential Ideas* (Ann Arbor: University of Michigan Press, 1966).

12. Luce and Raiffa, *Games and Decisions,* p. 13.

13. Ibid., p. 85.

14. Rapoport, *Two-Person Game Theory,* p. 130.

15. Ibid., p. 36.

16. Luce and Raiffa, *Games and Decisions,* p. 5.

17. Rapoport, *Two-Person Game Theory,* p. 194.

18. Ibid., p. 19.

19. Ibid., p. 24.

20. Ibid., p. 36.

21. Luce and Raiffa, *Games and Decisions,* p. 22.

22. Rapoport, *Two-Person Game Theory,* p. 36.

23. Robert Reich, *Tales of a New America* (New York: Times Books, 1987), p. 237. Note the similarity to some of the descriptions above of the zero-sum game in the language Reich uses to describe the "prevailing myths" of our culture.

24. Rapoport, *Two-Person Game Theory,* p. 94.

25. Larry Churchill, *Rationing Health Care in America: Perceptions and Principles of Justice* (Notre Dame, Ind.: University of Notre Dame Press, 1987), p. 135.

26. Andrei Simic, "Aging, World View, and Intergenerational Relations in America and Yugoslavia," in Jay Sokolovsky, ed., *The Cultural Context of Aging: Worldwide Perspectives* (New York: Bergin & Garvey, 1990), p. 92.

27. Ibid., p. 93.

28. Ibid., p. 94.

29. Ibid.

30. Ibid., p. 95.

31. Robert N. Bellah, Richard Madsen, William M. Sullivan, Ann Swidler, and Steven M. Tipton, *Habits of the Heart: Individualism and Commitment in American Life* (Berkeley: University of California Press, 1985), p. 285.

32. A clear example of this attitude is today's professional athlete. For example, on January 6, 1992, forsaking the Kansas City Royals with whom he had played for five years, Danny Tartabull signed a contract with the New York Yankees that will pay him $5.1 million for each of the next five seasons, making him the major leagues' fifth-most-highly-paid baseball player at that time (on March 2, Ryne Sandberg signed with the Chicago Cubs for $7.1 million a year for four years). Dave Anderson of the *New York Times* writes that experts agree that Tartabull possesses one undeniable attribute: "His quest for glory. He wants to be the 'big guy' on the team. . . . He wants the burden of restoring the Yankees' glory." With the Royals, however, he was "not a dependable *team*mate," caring more about his batting average than the team's success, and "he didn't mix with his teammates" ("Tartabull Brings Headlines, Headaches," *Miami Herald,* January 7, 1992, emphasis added). Not surprisingly, Tartabull "drives a red Ferrari. He owns more than 50 Italian suits and about 65 pairs of reptile-skin shoes" (Dan LeBatard, "Yankees Make Tartabull 5th Richest Player," *Miami Herald,* January 7, 1992). "Success" here seems to be interpreted in fundamentally *self*-directed terms.

33. Bellah et al., *Habits of the Heart,* p. 285.

34. Ibid., p. viii.

35. Luce and Raiffa, *Games and Decisions,* p. 6.

36. Marmor et al., *America's Misunderstood Welfare State,* p. 216 (emphasis added).

37. Recall the information presented in chapter 3 about the attitudes of younger people toward the elderly, especially with regard to expenditures such as Social Security and Medicare. Ken Dychtwald and Joe Flower offer this overall summary (*Age Wave: The Challenges and Opportunities of an Aging America* [New York: Bantam Books, 1990], p. 85): "Every national study that has been conducted on this theme reports that in general, young and old have great respect and affection for each other and want to do whatever is fair to assure health and financial security for all generations."

38. Marmor et al., *America's Misunderstood Welfare State,* p. 219.

39. Ibid., p. 222.

40. Further consideration of this common root is instructive. Both words trace their derivation to the Latin *communis,* meaning "shared by all or many," which in turn comes from the prefix *com* ("with") and the root *munus* ("obligatory service" or "duty"). Thus the original meaning of *community* seems to have been a group that shares, and in particular one that shares duties and services. "Communication" means literally to "make common," with the same sense of sharing such obligations. Obviously communication is essential to the formation and maintenance of community.

41. Rapoport, *Two-Person Game Theory,* p. 127.

42. Ibid., p. 125. One of the basic goals of the participants in a two-person zero-sum game is to maximize their "security levels," defined as the lowest payoff one can expect from any particular strategy in the game.

43. Ibid., p. 157.

44. William Temple, *Christianity and Social Order* (New York: Seabury Press, 1977), p. 61. Another twentieth-century British Christian, C. S. Lewis, uses the same travel metaphor but applies it at a different point in the journey. Lewis points out that progress means getting nearer where you want to be, and if you have taken a wrong turn somewhere, continuing to hurry down that same road can hardly be called progress. In fact, the person who recognizes the wrong turn most quickly, turns around, and gets back to the right road first is really the most progressive (*Mere Christianity* [New York: Macmillan, 1952], p. 36). We are in that position with regard to the issue before us, and what we need to do is admit we are rushing down the wrong road, turn around, and try to get back to some of the basic values—justice, mercy, community, and concern for others even if it means sacrifice on our part—that are necessary if the needs of all are to be met equitably and adequately.
45. Marmor et al., *America's Misunderstood Welfare State*, p. 239.
46. Daniel Callahan, "Meeting Needs and Rationing Care," *Law, Medicine, and Health Care* 16 (Winter 1988): 261-66, reprinted in Thomas A. Mappes and Jane S. Zembaty, eds., *Biomedical Ethics*, 3rd ed. (New York: McGraw-Hill, 1991), pp. 575-81. Although Callahan is referring specifically to the health-care system, his analysis applies equally well to all aspects of public policy concerning the elderly.
47. Pursuit of this alternative is what Callahan is about in his two important books mentioned earlier, *Setting Limits* and *What Kind of Life?* The widespread and often unthinking criticism directed at Callahan, especially for the first book, well illustrates his point about the disturbing nature of inquiry at this level. Indeed, in a review essay entitled "Allocating Health Resources" (*Hastings Center Report* 18 [April/May 1988]: 14), Callahan says, "Yet as some of us have discovered, to suggest that age itself be used as a standard for the rationing or limiting of care is an invitation to opprobrium."
48. Callahan, "Allocating Health Resources," an expanded version of the article by the same title cited in the previous note (*Hastings Center Report* 18 [April/May 1988]: 14-20), in John D. Arras and Nancy Rhoden, eds., *Ethical Issues in Modern Medicine*, 3rd ed. (Mountain View, Calif.: Mayfield Publishing Company, 1989), p. 524. In their important book, *Habits of the Heart*, Robert Bellah et al. make the same point. They assert that "the way a free society meets its problems depends not only on its economic and administrative resources but on its political imagination." They then claim that "we have never before faced a situation that called our deepest assumptions so radically into question. Our problems are not just political. They are moral and have to do with the meaning of life" (p. 271).
49. Rapoport, *Two-Person Game Theory*, p. 214. On the preceding page, Rapoport makes it even clearer that game theory does not hold the answer: "Genuinely rational conflict resolution demands an inquiry into the genesis of conflict," and, he goes on, "this is precisely what game theory," despite its sophisticated methods, "completely ignores." Game theory begins only after the utilities are given and "never questions the rationality of the goals pursued by the contending parties."

279

50. Actually, this statement might be open to question, as some people today claim that the churches (at least the "mainline Protestant churches") have by and large lost this traditional function in the rush to accommodate themselves to prevailing changes in social mores. An interesting case study of the validity of this claim is *Keeping Body and Soul Together: Sexuality, Spirituality and Social Justice,* a report of the Special Committee on Human Sexuality of the Presbyterian Church (USA). The report, considered by many to be nothing more than the sanctioning with theological jargon of all that has been wrong with sexual morality since the 1960s, generated tremendous controversy before being resoundingly rejected by the denomination's 203rd General Assembly in June 1991. Thus it appears that, at least in the PCUSA, the jury is still out on the church's stance on value instruction and revision.

51. Reich, *Tales of a New America,* pp. 237-38. On p. 50, he expresses the perspective we must strive to instill in all Americans, young and old: "To a greater extent and for subtler reasons than either modern conservatism or modern liberalism appreciate, life on this planet has become less a set of contests in which one party can be victorious, and more an intricate set of relationships which either succeed or fail—we win or we lose together."

7. SHEDDING LIGHT: A "VALUE CONGRUENCE ANALYSIS"

1. James A. Nash, *Theology and Public Policy* 3 (Fall 1991): 4-5.
2. Ibid., p. 5.
3. I use the term *strategy* throughout this chapter in a loosely technical sense to mean a particular way of addressing an issue that has been identified as needing a public policy response. Thus the word can be understood as roughly synonymous with "policies and/or programs."
4. The value congruence analysis proposed here grows out of a planning methodology used by Michael G. Dolence, strategic planning administrator at California State University, Los Angeles, during a "strategic enrollment planning and management" seminar at the annual meeting of the Society of College and University Planners in Denver on July 23, 1989. According to a personal communication, Dolence's approach and terminology were inspired by a futures-research methodology called "cross-impact analysis," "a method for revising estimated probabilities of future events in terms of estimated interactions among those events" (Norman C. Dalkey, "An Elementary Cross-Impact Analysis," in Harold A. Linstone and Murray Turoff, eds., *The Delphi Method: Techniques and Applications* [Reading, Mass.: Addison-Wesley, 1975], p. 327). Dolence's application was not to public policy but to the use of key performance indicators for enrollment management in higher education, and he has not yet developed his methodology using a formal model and terminology such as I propose here.

5. The model's flexibility allows for the use of any set of values identified as relevant and important. For example, a four-fold test that has been suggested for evaluating programs for the elderly would provide a good starting point for a secular group. These values are *affordability, availability, accessibility,* and *appropriateness,* all four of which need to be present for a successful and effective program. A program or service that costs too much is not going to survive indefinitely, especially in today's cost-conscious climate, and therefore it will do little good. If a program is not available to the people who need what it offers, those it is supposed to serve will not benefit. Similarly, the program may be available, but if those for whom it is intended cannot achieve access to it, they gain nothing (one thinks of SSI or the 1989 provision for Medicaid to pay Medicare premiums). Finally, a program may meet the first three criteria but not be appropriate for its target population, thus rendering it unappealing and ineffective at best and offensive and degrading at worst.

6. If time allows, an even better approach is for the strategy (column) ratings to be assigned during one session and then put aside. Then, during a second session, value (row) ratings are made without reference to the first set of ratings (note that this method calls for *new,* independent ratings across rows rather than the comparison of existing ratings described in the methodology in the text). Finally, at a third session, the two sets of ratings are compared and discrepancies resolved.

7. In technical terms, a method such as I am proposing in this chapter is called "iterative," suggesting that the process must go through a number of "iterations" or repetitions before satisfactory completion. As should be apparent by now, this notion is especially descriptive of a proper use of value congruence analysis.

8. This particular value has caused me a great deal of difficulty. I found myself tending toward a radically theological understanding of it as *God*'s justice, which looked suspiciously like "mercy/adequacy" when applied to the needy members of society (see chapter 8)! I had to remind myself constantly that in fairness to those who propose privatization, justice/equity in this context should be interpreted as a fair return on investment (or on "contributions" to Social Security).

8. SHEDDING LIGHT: FURTHER THOUGHTS ON
THE CHURCHES AND PUBLIC POLICY

1. Robert Reich, *Tales of a New America* (New York: Times Books, 1987), pp. xi-xii. Concerning our interests more specifically, Jonathan Rauch has observed, "Economically the burden [of aging populations] is probably manageable. The important question is whether it is politically manageable" ("Kids as Capital," *The Atlantic Monthly* [August 1989]: 57, quoted in James H. Schulz, Allan Borowski, and William H. Crown, *Economics of Population Aging: The "Graying" of Australia, Japan, and the United States* [New York: Auburn House, 1991], p. 3).

2. Reich, *Tales of a New America,* p. 6 (emphasis added).
3. One could almost imagine that Social Security grew out of a process very similar to the value congruence analysis suggested in this book, employed by a group consisting of some who stressed the importance of adequacy and others who argued for the importance of equity. Whatever the actual mechanism of deliberation, it is clear that the formulators of the program identified the major values relevant to the policy they were developing and then tried to incorporate them into their program, which bears many of the marks of one that might have been suggested by the use of the model (and even the values) I have proposed.
4. Theodore R. Marmor, Jerry L. Mashaw, and Philip L. Harvey, *America's Misunderstood Welfare State: Persistent Myths, Enduring Realities* (New York: Basic Books, 1990), p. 30.
5. Indeed, this notion is generally credited with giving Social Security its immense popularity throughout its history (and still today, as surveys reported earlier clearly show): Because of the common misperception that OASI payments are a "return on investment" and therefore one's due, connotations of "welfare" so antithetical to the American spirit have been avoided. Today, however, this notion may be coming back to haunt the system as younger people are voicing concern about whether they are going to "get theirs" when the time comes.
6. Paul Ramsey, *Basic Christian Ethics* (New York: Charles Scribner's Sons, 1950), p. 243.
7. Ibid., p. 10.
8. In this context it is hard not to think of the closing words of Portia's famous speech in *The Merchant of Venice* (Act iv, scene 1):

> And earthly power doth then show likest God's
> When mercy seasons justice. Therefore, . . .
> Though justice be thy plea, consider this,
> That in the course of justice, none of us
> Should see salvation: we do pray for mercy;
> And that same prayer doth teach us all to render
> The deeds of mercy.

9. Ramsey, *Basic Christian Ethics,* p. 17.
10. Norman Gottwald, "From Tribal Existence to Empire: The Socio-Historical Context for the Rise of the Hebrew Prophets," in J. Mark Thomas and Vernon Visick, eds., *God and Capitalism: A Prophetic Critique of Market Economy* (Madison, Wis.: A-R Editions, 1991), p. 27. Gottwald's conclusion on the same page expresses the perspective of this book well: "So, we are left with the logically perplexing but morally empowering paradox that the Bible is both grossly irrelevant in direct application to current economic problems and incredibly relevant in vision and principle for grasping opportunities and obligations to make the whole earth and its bounty serve the welfare of the whole human family."
11. A brief consideration of the words being discussed is instructive. The secular principle is *adequacy,* a minimalist term if ever there were one.

282

Adequacy is better than nothing, and it is right to insist on at least this much for everybody. But any one who genuinely cares for his or her fellow human beings must want more for them than this. *Mercy* represents so much more. It is a word that implies by its very meaning that one gives more than is the other's due, in fact, gives exactly the opposite of what is due (or, conversely, does not demand from another what is due to oneself). Similarly, *equity* represents a positive step in human relationships, suggesting basic fairness, treatment of likes in a like manner; and again, the improvement in the human condition achieved through a serious commitment to the principle of equity is not to be dismissed lightly. *Justice*, on the other hand, once more goes far beyond equity, meaning also treatment of likes in an *un*like manner if necessary to promote genuine equality and community. The secular virtues owe much to their theological analogues, which surpass them in depth and richness, and their meaning could be enhanced by recalling the religious roots from which they came.

12. This conclusion is supported, as is the entire discussion above, by the specific values of concern for the needy and, with regard to aging policy, respect for the elderly articulated in chapter 5.

13. Vernon L. Greene, "Generational Equity: A View from Middle Age," *Aging Today* (August/September 1991): 3.

14. Vernon L. Greene, "Human Capitalism and Intergenerational Justice," *The Gerontologist* 29 (1989): 724. This argument might be applied especially to medical care and some of the proposals to ration such care based on age (recall Daniel Callahan's proposals discussed in chapter 4). The taxes and other contributions of today's elderly made possible the explosive advance of medicine in recent decades. One could raise serious questions about the *equity* of denying them access to the very care they made possible (as I have indicated, however, this is no brief for unlimited care for the elderly).

15. Norman Daniels, *Am I My Parents' Keeper? An Essay on Justice Between the Young and the Old* (New York: Oxford University Press, 1988), p. 137. James Schulz and his coauthors undertake a lengthy and detailed examination of many of the claims made by AGE, including especially the concern about increasing "dependency ratios"—that is, that by the time the baby boomers retire there will be many too few workers to support them. Their conclusion is straightforward (and printed in italics in their book): "Thus the debate over how best to run an economic system is not primarily an aging discussion. In fact, the aging of populations may have little to do with the outcome" (*Economics of Population Aging*, p. 341).

16. Eric Kingson, Barbara Hirshorn, and John Cornman, *Ties That Bind: The Interdependence of Generations* (Washington, D.C.: Seven Locks Press, 1986), p. 13, quoted in Schulz et al., *Economics of Population Aging*, p. 23. In "Human Capitalism and Intergenerational Justice," Vernon L. Greene similarly notes "the large measure of hypocrisy and cynical political opportunism in framing the question as one of 'intergenerational justice.' " He acknowledges that the efforts and the motives of advocates of generational equity may not be "intrinsically wrong," but "concern for poor kids, future generations, and intergenerational justice has little to do with it" (p. 723).

17. Norman Daniels, *Am I My Parents' Keeper?*, p. 138.
18. Richard J. Margolis points out that AGE is right in claiming that the "American dream *has* lost some of its luster" and that "an enormous transfer of wealth and income" has taken place, "thanks mainly to simultaneous federal cuts in high-income taxes and low-income benefits." The transfer has not been from the young to the old, however: "The lion's share of that transfer has flowed between classes rather than generations." In support of his claim he cites some of the same figures reported in chapter 2 of this book concerning the declining size of the middle class, the increasing disparity between rich and poor, and the rise in the number of the extremely wealthy (*Risking Old Age in America* [Boulder, Colo.: Westview Press, 1990], p. 7).
19. Gary M. Nelson, "Fair Public-Cost View Must Include Direct, Indirect Spending," *The Aging Connection* 10 (October/November 1989): 10. Fernando Torres-Gil, immediate past president of the American Society on Aging, puts the entire situation into helpful perspective when he observes, "It looks as if we have so many programs and benefits for the elderly because we have so few for everyone else" (" 'Targeting' Is a Four-Letter Word: The Coming of Backdoor Rationing," a symposium at the annual meeting of the American Society on Aging, San Diego, March 16, 1992).
20. Beth B. Hess, "Gender & Aging: The Demographic Parameters," *Generations* 14 (Summer 1990): 15. Hess further observes that the well-intentioned effort to use inclusive language also glosses over the heterogeneity of the elderly. She says that "authors often refer to a genderless, classless, raceless 'older person,' thus obscuring the full effect of structured inequality."
21. Mark Twain, *Wit and Wisecracks*, selected by Doris Bernadete (Mount Vernon, N.Y.: Peter Pauper Press, 1961), p. 26.
22. Stephen Crystal, *America's Old Age Crisis: Old Age, American Values, and Federal Policies Since 1920* (Boston: Little, Brown and Company, 1983), p. 157.
23. For example, a recent Gallup poll found that 89 percent of those surveyed believed the American health-care system "needs fundamental change." This is an extremely high proportion of positive responses for *any* question on this kind of poll, and it is hard to imagine that such feelings will not be translated into action. Indeed, George Bush, who consistently opposed a national health plan during the early years of his administration, began in late 1991 to explore possible options in this direction and in early 1992 offered the outline of his plan.
24. William Foege, former director of the Centers for Disease Control, points out that the 25-year increase in life expectancy at birth achieved this century means only six extra years of life for a middle-aged person because most of the 25 years resulted from improvements in infant and child mortality. He observes that "all of twentieth-century science and medicine can give me only six additional years of life at this age," but research shows that "simple things" like eating properly, exercising, and not smoking can extend the life of a person his age 11 years. Thus, he concludes, "I am twice as powerful as all of twentieth-century science and medicine in

determining my own health destiny" ("The Vision of the Possible: What the Churches Can Do," *Second Opinion* 13 [March 1990]: 39).

25. The problem is well illustrated by the conclusion to Robert J. Samuelson's column in *Newsweek*, "Pampering the Elderly (II)" ([November 26, 1990]: 58), prompted by "a lot of angry mail" he received in response to "Pampering the Elderly" ([October 29, 1990]: 61). In the first column he presented the basic AGE argument that the federal government has become a "gigantic machine for taxing workers to support retirees" because the "elderly are considered a group that deserves to be pampered and whose political power requires them to be pampered." Noting the tone of his mail after that column, Samuelson rightly asserts, "What we most need is the ability to discuss openly the implications of an aging society. We can't foresee every new problem, and we will need to adapt as we go along. It's important that anyone who suggests policy changes not be automatically dismissed as a vindictive, lying senior-hater."

26. Along these lines, an older woman who is very active in community affairs, including politics, told me, "Older people have a responsibility to show young people that the elderly still can make worthwhile contributions to society. That will not only help the elderly get better treatment from the young but also will help young people deal with getting old better."

27. Meredith Minkler, "Guest Editorial: We Need to Advocate for This Nation's Children," *The Aging Connection* (June/July 1988): 3.

28. For a fuller treatment of this important issue, see Stephen Sapp, *Full of Years: Aging and the Elderly in the Bible and Today* (Nashville: Abingdon Press, 1987), pp. 150-52.

29. The values reflected here bear some resemblance to the recommendations of several people for the elderly today. For example, in 1984 Colorado Governor Richard Lamm created quite a stir when he was quoted as having said that the elderly have a "duty to die and get out of the way" so that younger people can have a greater share of society's limited resources. Lamm was technically misquoted: He directed his remarks at excessive life-extending technology and included everyone, regardless of age, in his admonition. Still, because the situation he referred to is most closely associated with older persons, the reaction to his remarks was not completely unfair. Subsequent remarks and writing by Lamm support this interpretation.

30. A useful article in this regard is Audrey R. Chapman, "Theology and Public Policy: Closing the Gap," *Theology and Public Policy* 3 (Fall 1991): 39-45. This journal regularly publishes provocative and helpful articles relating to this matter.

31. See Sapp, *Full of Years*, pp. 188-92, for further consideration of some of these matters.

32. I am well aware that it is popular today to assail those who advocate "family values" as "really supporting . . . the old-fashioned white middle-class setup, where [men] get to be the unquestionable boss, . . . stuck in the whitest part of the 1950s and miss[ing] the days when all of the non-white males knew their places, African-Americans knew where to sit, and women of all colors knew that their men were more important than they were" (Ellen Snortland, " 'Traditional Family Values' Is Code for 'Dad is the

285

Boss,' " *Miami Herald,* May 31, 1992). When such advocacy is a calculated political effort to blame the victims of social neglect and to exonerate those who might improve the conditions that result from this neglect, it should be condemned. Obviously, I cannot enter into a detailed discussion of this matter here. My intention is certainly not to place blame or imply causation, but I urge that we not "throw the baby out with the bath water." Based on analyses in this book (see especially pp. 59-67 and 166-68) and elsewhere, as well as personal experience, I maintain that efforts to foster healthy families—acknowledging that evolution in traditional models of the family is necessary—can have only a positive influence on American society, especially as our country continues to age.

33. For a brief examination of the impact of Alzheimer's disease on the family, see Stephen Sapp, *When Alzheimer's Disease Strikes* (Ft. Lauderdale, Fla.: Desert Ministries, 1990).

34. Hess, "Gender & Aging," p. 12 (emphasis added).

35. W. Andrew Achenbaum, *Shades of Gray: Old Age, American Values, and Federal Policies Since 1920* (Boston: Little, Brown and Company, 1983), p. 176.

36. Harry R. Moody, *Abundance of Life: Human Development Policies for an Aging Society* (New York: Columbia University Press, 1988), p. 262.

37. Samuelson, "Pampering the Elderly (II)": 58. The next figures come from Phillip Longman, *Born to Pay: The New Politics of Aging in America* (Boston: Houghton Mifflin, 1987), p. 99, quoting Carolyn K. Davis, former administrator of the Health Care Financing Administration.

38. Meg Greenfield, "The Dropout Democrats," *Newsweek* (September 16, 1991): 72.

39. Daniel Callahan, "Meeting Needs and Rationing Care," *Law, Medicine, and Health Care* 16 (Winter 1988): 261-66, reprinted in Thomas A. Mappes and Jane S. Zembaty, eds., *Biomedical Ethics,* 3rd ed. (New York: McGraw-Hill, 1991), p. 577.

40. In Jürgen Moltmann, *Hope and Planning,* trans. Margaret Clarkson (New York: Harper & Row, 1971), p. 178.

41. Ibid., p. 182.

42. Ibid., p. 183.

43. Ibid., p. 194.

44. Ibid., pp. 194-95.

45. Ibid., p. 183.

APPENDIX

1. Cynthia Taeuber (Chief of the U.S. Census Bureau's Age and Sex Statistics Branch), "Aging in the 1990 Census: What Will We Learn?," symposium at the annual meeting of the American Society on Aging, New Orleans, Louisiana, March 18, 1991. Conservative estimates place the number of Hindus and Buddhists worldwide at around one billion, with an equal

number of Muslims. Whatever the number of followers of these religions in the United States, their importance throughout the rapidly shrinking world makes it incumbent upon U.S. policymakers to be familiar with at least the basics of these faiths.

2. H. Tristram Englehardt, Jr., "Fashioning an Ethic for Life and Death in a Post-Modern Society," *Hastings Center Report* 19 (January/February 1989), Special Supplement, "Mercy, Murder, and Morality:" 8. Corroboration of the point being made in this paragraph comes from an article by Ari L. Goldman, "Islamic Group Seeks Equal Time for Ramadan" (*Miami Herald*, January 3, 1992). In letters to David Rockefeller, former chairman of Chase Manhattan Bank, and John F. Kelly, postmaster of New York, Dr. Mohammed T. Mehdi, secretary general of the National Council on Islamic Affairs, noted the prevalence of Christmas trees and Hanukkah menorahs in stores, banks, and post offices during the holiday season and urged that "the banks and post offices should honor Islam as they honor Christianity and Judaism" by displaying the crescent and five-pointed star of Islam during the holy season of Ramadan. "Celebrating Islam and recognizing it as an integral part of the American society is a tribute to the ever-expanding America," Mehdi asserted. "I trust that banks and the post office will not wish to discriminate against Islam."

It should be noted, however, that from a *historical* perspective, the heritage of Judaism and Christianity remains the source of the fundamental worldview and value-orientation of this country, as well as of the dominant thought pattern behind the documents on which our governmental system is founded. Because of this fact, values growing out of the Jewish-Christian tradition remain central to any ethical consideration of public policy on aging, as is argued elsewhere in this book.

3. Ada Elizabeth Sher, *Aging in Post-Mao China: The Politics of Veneration* (Boulder, Colo.: Westview Press, 1984), p. 19.

4. Donald O. Cowgill, *Aging Around the World* (Belmont, Calif.: Wadsworth Publishing Company, 1986), p. 43.

5. Ibid., p. 67.

6. Adapted from Marguerite Kermis, *Mental Health in Later Life: The Adaptive Process* (Monterey, Calif./Boston: Jones and Bartlett, 1986), p. 326.

7. Cowgill, *Aging Around the World*, p. 67.

8. Daw Khin Myo Chit, "Add Life to Years the Buddhist Way," in William M. Clements, ed., *Religion, Aging and Health: A Global Perspective* (New York: Haworth Press, 1989), p. 42.

9. Ibid., p. 43.

10. Ibid., p. 44.

11. Ibid., p. 58.

12. H. R. Moody, "The Islamic Vision of Aging & Death," *Generations* 14 (Fall 1990): 15.

13. Hakim Mohammed Said, "Islam and the Health of the Elderly," in Clements, *Religion, Aging and Health*, pp. 28, 30.

14. Ibid., p. 31.

15. Jennie Keith, Christine L. Fry, and Charlotte Ikels, "Community as Context for Successful Aging," in Jay Sokolovsky, ed., *The Cultural Context of Aging: Worldwide Perspectives* (New York: Bergin & Garvey, 1990), p. 257.

16. Quoted in Fazlur Rahman, *Health and Medicine in the Islamic Tradition: Change and Identity* (New York: Crossroad, 1987), p. 127.
17. Prakash N. Desai, *Health and Medicine in the Hindu Tradition: Continuity and Cohesion* (New York: Crossroad, 1989), p. 31.
18. Shrinivas Tilak, *Religion and Aging in the Indian Tradition* (Albany: SUNY Press, 1989), p. 79.

SELECTED BIBLIOGRAPHY

BOOKS

Achenbaum, W. Andrew. *Shades of Gray: Old Age, American Values, and Federal Policies Since 1920*. Boston: Little, Brown and Company, 1983.

Arras, John, and Rhoden, Nancy, eds. *Ethical Issues in Modern Medicine*, 3rd ed. Mountain View, Calif.: Mayfield Publishing Company, 1989.

Bailey, Lloyd. *Biblical Perspectives on Death*. Biblical Theology Series, no. 5. Philadelphia: Fortress Press, 1979.

Bellah, Robert N.; Madsen, Richard; Sullivan, William M.; Swidler, Ann; and Tipton, Steven M. *The Good Society*. New York: Alfred A. Knopf, 1991.

————. *Habits of the Heart: Individualism and Commitment in American Life*. Berkeley: University of California Press, 1985.

Bernstein, Merton C., and Bernstein, Joan Brodshang. *Social Security: The System That Works*. New York: Basic Books, 1988.

Binstock, Robert H., and Post, Stephen G., eds. *Too Old for Health Care? Controversies in Medicine, Law, Economics, and Ethics*. Baltimore: Johns Hopkins University Press, 1991.

Boskin, Michael. *Too Many Promises: The Uncertain Future of Social Security*. Homewood, Ill.: Dow Jones-Irwin, 1986.

Bouma, Hessel III; Diekema, Douglas; Langerak, Edward; Rottman, Theodore; and Verhey, Allen. *Christian Faith, Health, and Medical Practice*. Grand Rapids: William B. Eerdmans, 1989.

Browne, William P., and Olson, Laura Katz, eds. *Aging and Public Policy: The Politics of Growing Old in America*. Westport, Conn.: Greenwood Press, 1983.

Butler, Robert N. *Why Survive? Being Old in America*. New York: Harper & Row, 1975.

Butler, Robert N.; Lewis, Myrna I.; and Sunderland, Trey. *Aging and Mental Health: Positive Psychosocial and Biomedical Approaches*, 4th ed. New York: Macmillan, 1991.

Callahan, Daniel. *What Kind of Life? The Limits of Medical Progress*. New York: Simon & Schuster, 1990.

———. *Setting Limits: Medical Goals in an Aging Society*. New York: Simon & Schuster, 1987.

Churchill, Larry. *Rationing Health Care in America: Perceptions and Principles of Justice*. Notre Dame, Ind.: University of Notre Dame Press, 1987.

Clements, William M., ed. *Ministry with the Aging: Designs, Challenges, Foundations*. New York: Harper & Row, 1981.

———, ed. *Religion, Aging and Health: A Global Perspective*. New York: Haworth Press, 1989.

Cohen, Donna, and Eisdorfer, Carl. *The Loss of Self: A Family Resource for the Care of Alzheimer's Disease and Related Disorders*. New York: W. W. Norton, 1986.

Cowgill, Donald O. *Aging Around the World*. Belmont, Calif.: Wadsworth, 1986.

Crystal, Stephen. *America's Old Age Crisis: Public Policy and the Two Worlds of Aging*. New York: Basic Books, 1982.

Daniels, Norman. *Am I My Parents' Keeper? An Essay on Justice Between the Young and the Old*. New York: Oxford University Press, 1988.

Day, Christine. *What Older Americans Think: Interest Groups and Aging Policy*. Princeton: Princeton University Press, 1990.

Dychtwald, Ken, and Flower, Joe. *Age Wave: The Challenges and Opportunities of an Aging America*. New York: Bantam Books, 1990.

Estes, Carroll. *The Aging Enterprise: A Critical Examination of Social Policies and Services for the Aged*. San Francisco: Jossey-Bass, 1979.

Ferrara, Peter. *Social Security Reform: The Family Plan*. Washington, D.C.: Heritage Foundation, 1982.

Fischer, David H. *Growing Old in America*, expanded ed. New York: Oxford University Press, 1978.

Forrester, Duncan B. *Beliefs, Values and Policies: Conviction Politics in a Secular Age*. New York: Oxford University Press, 1989.

Gerber, Jerry; Wolff, Janet; Klores, Walter; and Brown, Gene. *Lifetrends: The Future of Baby Boomers and Other Aging Americans*. New York: Macmillan, 1989.

Herzog, Barbara Rieman. *Aging and Income: Programs and Prospects for the Elderly*, special pub. no. 4 sponsored by the Gerontological Society. New York: Human Sciences Press, 1978.

Hess, Beth B., and Markson, Elizabeth W., eds. *Growing Old in America*, 4th ed. New Brunswick, N.J.: Transaction Publishers, 1991.

Holland, Joe. *Creative Communion: Toward a Spirituality of Work*. New York: Paulist Press, 1989.

Kasper, Judith D. *Aging Alone: Profiles and Projections*. Report of the Commonwealth Fund Commission on Elderly People Living Alone, 1988.

Kermis, Marguerite. *Mental Health in Later Life: The Adaptive Process*. Monterey, Calif./Boston: Jones and Bartlett, 1986.

Lakoff, George, and Johnson, Mark. *Metaphors We Live By*. Chicago: University of Chicago Press, 1980.

Lewis, C. S. *Mere Christianity*. New York: Macmillan, 1952.

Linstone, Harold A., and Turoff, Murray, eds. *The Delphi Method: Techniques and Applications*. Reading, Mass.: Addison-Wesley, 1975.

Longman, Phillip. *Born to Pay: The New Politics of Aging*. Boston: Houghton Mifflin, 1987.

Luce, R. Duncan, and Raiffa, Howard. *Games and Decisions: Introduction and Critical Survey.* New York: John Wiley, 1957.

Luther, Martin. *The Wisdom of Martin Luther.* Compiled by N. Alfred Balmer. St. Louis: Concordia Publishing House, 1973.

McCollough, Thomas E. *The Moral Imagination and Public Life: Raising the Ethical Question.* Chatham, N.J.: Chatham House Publishers, 1991.

Mappes, Thomas A., and Zembaty, Jane S., eds. *Biomedical Ethics,* 3rd ed. New York: McGraw-Hill, 1991.

Margolis, Richard J. *Risking Old Age in America.* Boulder, Colo.: Westview Press, 1990.

Marmor, Theodore R.; Mashaw, Jerry L.; and Harvey, Philip L. *America's Misunderstood Welfare State: Persistent Myths, Enduring Realities.* New York: Basic Books, 1990.

Milne, A. A. *The World of Pooh.* New York: E. P. Dutton & Company, 1957.

Moltmann, Jürgen. *Hope and Planning.* Trans. Margaret Clarkson. New York: Harper & Row, 1971.

Moody, Harry R. *Abundance of Life: Human Development Policies for an Aging Society.* New York: Columbia University Press, 1988.

Otwell, Janet, and Costello, Janet. *Ninety for the '90s: A Final Report.* Springfield, Ill.: Illinois Department on Aging, 1990.

Peter, Laurence J., ed. *Peter's Quotations: Ideas for Our Time.* New York: Bantam Books, 1977.

Peterson, Peter G., and Howe, Neil. *On Borrowed Time: How the Growth in Entitlement Spending Threatens America's Future.* San Francisco: ICS Press, 1988.

Phipps, William E. *Death: Confronting the Reality.* Atlanta: John Knox Press, 1987.

Rahman, Fazlur. *Health and Medicine in the Islamic Tradition: Change and Identity.* New York: Crossroad, 1987.

Ramsey, Paul. *Basic Christian Ethics.* New York: Charles Scribner's Sons, 1950.

Rapoport, Anatol. *Two-Person Game Theory: The Essential Ideas.* Ann Arbor: University of Michigan Press, 1966.

Reich, Robert. *Tales of a New America.* New York: Times Books, 1987.

Sapp, Stephen. *When Alzheimer's Disease Strikes.* Ft. Lauderdale, Fla.: Desert Ministries, 1990.

———. *Full of Years: Aging and the Elderly in the Bible and Today.* Nashville: Abingdon Press, 1987.

Schulz, James H.; Borowski, Allan; and Crown, William H. *Economics of Population Aging: The "Graying" of Australia, Japan, and the United States.* New York: Auburn House, 1991.

Sher, Ada Elizabeth. *Aging in Post-Mao China: The Politics of Veneration.* Boulder, Colo.: Westview Press, 1984.

Sokolovsky, Jay, ed. *The Cultural Context of Aging: Worldwide Perspectives.* New York: Bergin & Garvey, 1990.

Temple, William. *Christianity and Social Order.* New York: Seabury Press, 1977.

Thomas, J. Mark, and Visick, Vernon, eds. *God and Capitalism: A Prophetic Critique of Market Economy.* Madison, Wis.: A-R Editions, 1991.

Tilak, Shrinivas. *Religion and Aging in the Indian Tradition.* Albany: SUNY Press, 1989.

291

Twain, Mark. *Wit and Wisecracks*. Selected by Doris Bernadete. Mount Vernon, NY: Peter Pauper Press, 1961.

U.S. Department of Health and Human Services, Health Care Financing Administration. *1991 Guide to Health Insurance for People with Medicare*. Pub. no. HCFA-02110. Washington: Government Printing Office, 1991.

U.S. Department of Health and Human Services, Social Security Administration. *Disability*. Pub. no. 05-10029 (1991).

———. *How Your Retirement Benefit Is Figured*. Pub. no. 05-10070 (1991).

———. *Retirement*. Pub. no. 05-10035 (1991).

———. *SSI: Supplemental Security Income*. Pub. no. 05-11000 (1991).

———. *Survivors*. Pub. no. 05-10084 (1991).

———. *Your Social Security Taxes . . . What They're Paying For And Where The Money Goes*. Pub. no. 05-10010 (1991).

———. *Social Security's Pledge to Beneficiaries, Taxpayers, and Future Workers*. Pub. no. 05-10073 (1989).

ARTICLES

Bellah, Robert. "The Good Society" (interview). *Ethics & Policy* (Fall 1991): 5.

Brody, Elaine. " 'Women in the Middle' and Family Help to Older People." *Gerontologist* 21 (1981): 471-80.

Brody, Stanley J. "Strategic Planning: The Catastrophic Approach." *Gerontologist* 27 (1987): 131-38.

Callahan, Daniel. "Can Old Age Be Given a Public Meaning?" *Second Opinion* 15 (November 1990): 12-23.

———. "Allocating Health Resources." *Hastings Center Report* 18 (April/May 1988): 14-20.

Castro, Janice. "Condition: Critical." *Time* (November 25, 1991): 34-42.

Chapman, Audrey R. "Theology and Public Policy: Closing the Gap." *Theology and Public Policy* 3 (Fall 1991): 39-45.

Cohen, Elias S. "Gerontology: Past, Present and Future." *Aging Today* (April/May 1991): 3.

Davis, Karen; Grant, Paula; and Rowland, Diane. "Alone and Poor." *Generations* 14 (Summer 1990): 43-47.

Dolence, Michael G. "Evaluation Criteria for an Enrollment Management Program." *Planning for Higher Education* 18 (1989-90): 1.

Englehardt, H. Tristram, Jr. "Fashioning an Ethic for Life and Death in a Post-Modern Society." *Hastings Center Report* 19 (January/February 1989), Special Supplement, "Mercy, Murder, and Morality: Perspectives on Euthanasia": 7-9.

Enquist, Roy. "A Paraclete in the Public Square: Toward a Theology of Advocacy." *Theology and Public Policy* 2 (Fall 1990): 17-33.

Fey, Harold E. "Politics and the Elderly: Toward a Sharing of Resources." *The Christian Century* (December 14, 1988): 1153-55.

Foege, William. "The Vision of the Possible: What the Churches Can Do." *Second Opinion* 13 (March 1990): 36-42.

Greene, Vernon L. "Generational Equity: A View from Middle Age." *Aging Today* (August/September 1991): 3.

———. "Human Capitalism and Intergenerational Justice." *The Gerontologist* 29 (1989): 723-24.

Greenfield, Meg. "The Dropout Democrats." *Newsweek* (September 16, 1991): 72.

Hardin, Garrett. "The Tragedy of the Commons." *Science* 162 (1968): 1243-48.

Hess, Beth B. "Gender & Aging: The Demographic Parameters." *Generations* 14 (Summer 1990): 12-15.

Holden, Karen C., and Smeeding, Timothy M. "The Poor, the Rich, and the Insecure Elderly Caught in Between." *Milbank Quarterly* 68 (1990): 191-219.

House, James S.; Kessler, Ronald C.; Herzog, A. Regula; Mero, Richard P.; Kinney, Ann M., and Breslow, Martha J. "Age, Socioeconomic Status, and Health." *Milbank Quarterly* 68 (1990): 383-411.

Howard, Edward F. "Long-Term Care: On the Comeback Trail?" *Generations* 15 (Summer/Fall 1991): 31-34.

Hudson, Robert B., and Gonyea, Judith. "A Perspective on Women in Politics: Political Mobilization & Older Women." *Generations* 14 (Summer 1990): 69.

———, and Kingson, Eric R. "Inclusive and Fair: The Case for Universality in Social Programs." *Generations* 15 (Summer/Fall 1991): 51-56.

Kruijf, Gerrit G. de. "The Christian in the Crowded Public Square: The Hidden Tension Between Prophecy and Democracy." *The Annual of the Society of Christian Ethics* (1991): 21-42.

Lieberman, Trudy. "An Empty Promise to the Elderly?" *Consumer Reports* 56 (June 1991): 425-42.

———. "The Crisis in Health Insurance, Part 2: Health Insurance for All?" *Consumer Reports* 55 (September 1990): 608-17.

Minkler, Meredith. "Guest Editorial: We Need to Advocate for This Nation's Children." *The Aging Connection* (June/July 1988): 3.

Montgomery, Rhonda J. V., and Datwyler, Mary McGlinn. "Women & Men in the Caregiving Role." *Generations* 14 (Summer 1990): 34-38.

Moody, H. R. "The Islamic Vision of Aging & Death." *Generations* 14 (Fall 1990): 15-18.

Moon, Marilyn. "Public Policies: Are They Gender-Neutral?" *Generations* 14 (Summer 1990): 59-63.

Nash, James A. "Narrowing the Ethics-Action Gap." *Theology and Public Policy* 3 (Fall 1991): 4-5.

Nelson, Gary M. "Fair Public-Cost View Must Include Direct, Indirect Spending." *The Aging Connection* (October/November 1989): 10.

Pennar, Karen. "The Rich Are Richer—And America May Be The Poorer." *Business Week* (November 18, 1991): 85, 88.

Peterson, Peter. "The Morning After." *Atlantic Monthly* (October 1987): 43-69.

Preston, Samuel H. "Children and the Elderly in the U.S." *Scientific American* 251 (December 1984): 44-49.

293

Rogers, Richard G.; Rogers, Andrei; and Belanger, Alain. "Active Life among the Elderly in the United States: Multistate Life-table Estimates and Population Projections." *Milbank Quarterly* 67 (1989): 370-411.

Roos, Noralou P.; Shapiro, Evelyn; and Tate, Robert. "Does a Small Minority of Elderly Account for a Majority of Health Care Expenditures?: A Sixteen-Year Perspective." *Milbank Quarterly* 67 (1989): 347-69.

Samuelson, Robert J. "Pampering the Elderly (II)." *Newsweek* (November 26, 1990): 58.

———. "Pampering the Elderly." *Newsweek* (October 29, 1990): 61.

Sapp, Stephen. "Ethical Issues in Intergenerational Equity." *Journal of Religious Gerontology* 7 (1991): 1-15.

Stone, Robyn I., and Kemper, Peter. "Spouses and Children of Disabled Elders: How Large a Constituency for Long-Term Care Reform?" *Milbank Quarterly* 67 (1989): 485-506.

Torres-Gil, Fernando. "Aging for the Twenty-first Century: Process, Politics, & Policy." *Generations* 12 (Summer 1988): 5-9.

adequacy (see also *equity*). The principle that all persons should be assured an adequate standard of living, especially in their later years; one of the twin pillars on which Social Security was founded.

Baby Boomers. Name given to the roughly 75 million children born in the United States between 1946 and 1964, the result of a marked rise in childbearing by American women following World War II.

cohort. A group of people who share a particular demographic characteristic, in this case, all persons born during a specified period of time.

equity (see also *adequacy*). The principle that a relationship should exist between what a worker pays into the system and what he or she gets back, so that he or she receives a fair (or equitable) return relative to what others have contributed; one of the two basic values underlying Social Security.

fertility. Measured in various ways, the rate of production of new members of a society and thus, along with mortality and immigration, a major factor in population growth and aging.

FICA. Federal Income Contributions Act, the act that authorizes payroll deductions for Social Security (currently set at 15.3 percent, divided equally between employee and employer).

filial piety. A central tenet of Confucianism and other Eastern religions that demands that offspring render to their parents obedience, devotion, and material support throughout the lifetime of the parents (and even afterward).

generational equity. A phrase associated with the view that the elderly receive a disproportionate share of society's resources at the expense of other age groups, especially children, and that a more equitable distribution should be sought through mechanisms like means testing of benefits and privatization of Social Security.

gray power. A term used to suggest that because of their numbers, organization, and high rate of voting, the elderly are able to exercise considerable control over the political process in the United States.

long-term care. Non-curative care of elderly and other chronically disabled persons, including services such as adult day-care, in-home assistance of various kinds, and care in residential facilities like adult congregate living facilities and intermediate and skilled nursing facilities.

means testing. The allocation of public benefits on the basis of need, most often through a computation of income or a combination of income and assets.

Medicaid. The joint federal-state means-tested program designed to provide health care to low-income persons of all ages.

Medicare. Officially called "Hospital Insurance," the part of Social Security that provides persons over 65 with (1) basic hospital coverage (Part A) financed through payroll deductions, deductibles, and copayments; and (2) optional outpatient coverage (Part B), for which a separate premium is charged.

morbidity. The proportion of ill persons in a given population, important in discussions of aging policy because in technologically advanced societies increased life expectancy—though producing more favorable mortality rates—leads to increased morbidity and need for long-term care.

mortality. The rate of death in a particular population, typically higher in less developed countries (especially among infants and children) and lower in more advanced societies (not only among younger persons but also among older people, as advanced medical technology allows considerable extension of lives that would otherwise end); a major factor in the age distribution of populations.

privatization. A proposed revision of retirement policy that calls for shifting primary involvement in providing for old age to the private sector and limiting public responsibility to those deemed truly needy.

sandwich generation. Those individuals who have significant personal care responsibilities for both children and older persons and thus find themselves "in the middle" of a very stressful situation.

Social Security. The major public program in the United States for the support of older persons, actually composed of several parts: Old Age and Survivors Insurance (OASI), Disability Insurance (DI), and Hospital Insurance (HI).

Supplemental Security Income (SSI). The means-tested federal program—administered by the Social Security Administration but funded out of general revenues rather than payroll taxes—that provides the needy elderly, blind, and disabled a basic level of income by supplementing whatever they receive from other sources.

utility. In game theory, whatever a decision-maker in the game prefers as his or her "payoff" for winning and therefore seeks to maximize.

value congruence analysis. A seven-step process that examines a situation calling for a policy response, identifies relevant values important to the individual or group performing the analysis, and determines whether existing or proposed policies and programs embody those values.

zero-sum game. A game in which the participants compete directly for a limited payoff, so that a win for one necessarily means an equal loss for the other; suggested as a metaphor in this book for the attitude that underlies the generational equity movement—namely, that the same finite pool of resources is available to younger and older generations, and if one generation gains something, the other must necessarily lose it.

INDEX

Adequacy, 81-82, 83-85, 89, 91, 96, 136-38, 157, 160, 202-4, 207, 216, 217, 219, 282n11. *See also* Mercy

Administration on Aging (AoA), 104-5

American Association of Retired Persons (AARP), 108, 109-12, 157, 202

American Society on Aging, 51, 73, 109, 159, 223, 226, 270n2

Americans for Generational Equity (AGE), 156, 202, 208, 210-11, 212, 285n25; description of, 16, 115-20; valid claims of, 215-21. *See also* Generational equity

Area Agency on Aging (AAA), 105-6

Baby boom, 37, 39, 42, 43, 46-47, 57, 65, 76, 85, 89, 98, 117, 121, 147, 202

Bellah, Robert, 23-24, 25, 169, 279n48

Berry, Joyce T. (U.S. Commissioner on Aging), 51, 67, 73, 159

Binstock, Robert H., 56, 112, 120, 277n8

Boskin, Michael J., 94, 267n4, 272n24, 275n40, 277n8

Bouma, Hessel III, 27, 134

Brody, Stanley J., 80-81, 83-84, 103, 266n1

Buddhism, 138; brief description of, 244-45; filial piety in, 249; number of adherents in North America, 244

Callahan, Daniel, 22, 120, 142, 174-75, 217, 237, 279n47

Children: decreased number of, 37, 60; impact of American childrearing practices on, 166-68; increased responsibilities of elderly to care for,

297

DEMCO